INTO GOD'S PRESENCE

McMaster New Testament Studies

The McMaster New Testament Studies series, edited by Richard N. Longenecker, is designed to address particular themes in the New Testament that
are of concern to Christians today. Written in a style easily accessible to
ministers, students, and laypeople by contributors who are proven experts
in their fields of study, the volumes in this series reflect the best of current
biblical scholarship while also speaking directly to the pastoral needs of
people in the church today.

Into God's Presence

Prayer in the New Testament

Edited by

Richard N. Longenecker

WILLIAM B. EERDMANS PUBLISHING COMPANY
GRAND RAPIDS, MICHIGAN / CAMBRIDGE, U.K.

© 2001 Wm. B. Eerdmans Publishing Co.

All rights reserved

Wm. B. Eerdmans Publishing Co.
255 Jefferson Ave. S.E., Grand Rapids, Michigan 49503 /
P.O. Box 163, Cambridge CB3 9PU U.K.

Printed in the United States of America

06 05 04 03 02 01   7 6 5 4 3 2 1

Library of Congress Cataloging-in-Publication Data

Into God's presence : prayer in the New Testament /
edited by Richard N. Longenecker.
p.   cm.
Includes bibliographical references and indexes.
ISBN 0-8028-4883-4 (pbk. : alk. paper)
1. Bible.   N.T. — Prayers — History and criticism.
I. Longenecker, Richard N.

BS2545.P67 I58 2001
248.3'2'09015 — dc21
2001040311

www.eerdmans.com

Contents

CONTENTS

II. JESUS AND THE GOSPELS

III. ACTS THROUGH THE APOCALYPSE

Contributors

David E. Aune, B.A., M.A., M.A., Ph.D. (Chicago). Professor of New Testament and Christian origins, Department of Theology, University of Notre Dame, Notre Dame, Indiana

Richard Bauckham, B.A., M.A., Ph.D. (Cambridge). Professor of New Testament Studies and Bishop Wardlaw professor, St. Mary's College, University of St. Andrews, St. Andrews, Scotland

Stephen Farris, B.A., D.Min., Th.M., Ph.D. (Cambridge). Professor of Preaching and Worship, Knox College, University of Toronto, Toronto, Ontario

Asher Finkel, Ph.D. (Tübingen). Professor and Chair, Department of Jewish and Christian Studies, Seton Hall University, South Orange, New Jersey

Joel B. Green, B.S., M.Th., Ph.D. (Aberdeen). Dean of the School of Theology and Professor of New Testament Interpretation, Asbury Theological Seminary, Wilmore, Kentucky

Andrew T. Lincoln, B.A., M.A., M.Div., Ph.D. (Cambridge). Portland Professor of New Testament, Cheltenham and Gloucester College, Cheltenham, England

Richard N. Longenecker, B.A., M.A., Ph.D. (Edinburgh), D.D. (Wycliffe). Distinguished Professor of New Testament, Bethel Seminary, St. Paul,

Minnesota; formerly distinguished professor of New Testament, McMaster Divinity College, McMaster University, Hamilton, Ontario.

I. Howard Marshall, B.A., M.A., B.D., Ph.D. (Aberdeen), D.D. (Asbury). Honorary Research Professor of New Testament, King's College, University of Aberdeen, Aberdeen, Scotland

J. Ramsey Michaels, B.A., B.D., Th.M., Th.D. (Harvard). Professor Emeritus of Religious Studies, Southwest Missouri State University, Springfield, Missouri

Eileen M. Schuller, B.A., M.A., Ph.D. (Harvard). Professor and Chair, Department of Religious Studies, McMaster University, Hamilton, Ontario

Christopher R. Seitz, A.B., M.T.S., S.T.M., M.A., M.Phil., Ph.D. (Yale). Professor of Old Testament and Theological Studies, St. Mary's College, University of St. Andrews, St. Andrews, Scotland

N. T. Wright, M.A., D.Phil., D.D. (Oxford), Hon. D.D. (Aberdeen). Canon, Westminster Abbey, London, England

Preface

THIS IS THE fifth volume in the McMaster New Testament Studies series, sponsored by McMaster Divinity College, Hamilton, Ontario, Canada. The series is designed to address particular themes in the New Testament that are (or should be) of crucial concern to Christians today. The contributors are selected because of their proven expertise in the areas assigned and their known ability to write intelligibly for readers who are not necessarily academics. Each article included in these symposium volumes, therefore, will evidence first-class biblical scholarship, but will also be written in a manner capable of capturing the interest of intelligent lay people, theological students, and ministers. In purpose, the articles will be both scholarly and pastoral. In format, they will be styled to reflect the best of contemporary, constructive scholarship, but in a way that is able to be understood by and speaks to the needs of alert and intelligent people in the church today.

This fifth volume in the MNTS series focuses on prayer in the New Testament. It is a topic that has been treated extensively in the commentaries, systematic theologies, and devotional writings of the Christian church. Nonetheless, we believe it deserves a better treatment than usually received in either the scholarly or the popular press. So we have prepared this fifth MNTS volume with the hope that a more responsible exegetical treatment of prayer in the New Testament will prove to be of help to many earnest Christians who seek to think and live in a more Christian fashion, and thereby have a positive impact on the church at large.

Our heartfelt thanks are expressed to the faculty, administration, and

PREFACE

boards of McMaster Divinity College for their encouragement and support of the entire project. Likewise, we express our deep appreciation to the family of Herbert Henry Bingham, B.A., B.Th., D.D., a noted Canadian Baptist minister and administrator of the previous generation, which generously funded the fifth annual "H. H. Bingham Colloquium in New Testament" at McMaster Divinity College, held during June 21-22, 1999. It was at that colloquium that the authors of the present volume presented their papers and received criticism from one another, from the editor, and from others in attendance, before then reworking and polishing their papers, as necessary, prior to final editing and the normal publication process. Most heartily, however, we thank those who have written articles for this volume, for they have taken time out of busy academic schedules to write in a more popular fashion — in many cases, distilling from their academic publications material of pertinence for the Christian church generally. And we thank Bill Eerdmans and the Wm. B. Eerdmans Publishing Company for their continued support and expertise in publishing this series.

THE EDITOR

Introduction

PRAYER IS THE LIFEBLOOD of religion, the indispensable factor in every form of piety and faith. It lies at the heart of all religious experience. It expresses, in essence, a person's deepest convictions about God, this world, human life, and all human relationships. And it reflects the vitality of a person's central convictions and controlling spirituality.

One cannot know the religion of Israel without a lively appreciation of the psalms and prayers included within the Old Testament or Jewish Scriptures. One cannot understand Greco-Roman religions without some knowledge of the place and function of prayer within them. One cannot feel the heartbeat of Judaism without coming into contact with Jewish attitudes toward prayer and developments of liturgy during the period of Second Temple Judaism — as these were included within the extant sectarian writings of the day, were codified by the rabbis in the Talmud, and have continued to be expressed down through the centuries in traditional Orthodox forms and more latterly in Reform and Conservative fashion. One cannot claim to understand the New Testament without grasping the importance and function of prayer in the life and ministry of Jesus, in his teachings, and among his earliest followers — appreciating both old and new features in their prayers, and feeling the vitality of their new relationship with God in their praying. And one cannot experience new life "in Christ" as a Christian without entering into personal relationship with God through Christ in prayer.

Prayer, however, has not always been a matter of major concern among Christians — whether among scholars, clergy, or laity. It was virtually ignored by the framers of the church's creeds, whose focus was on issues having to do with christology, soteriology, and ecclesiology. It has often been treated in a perfunctory manner by biblical commentators and systematic theologians, who — while recognizing its presence in the materials dealt with — often seem to lack interest or enthusiasm for the topic, and so have frequently treated it in a rather superficial or routine manner. All-too-often, in fact, prayer has been considered somewhat illegitimate for scholarly study, since it is "too personal" to be an apt subject for critical or historical scrutiny, somewhat irrelevant to the church's mission and proclamation, since it is "too otherworldly" to be helpful in addressing the larger issues of social, political, or economic reform, and even somewhat unnecessary for evangelism, since it is "too quietistic" for the organization and activism necessary for outreach.

Nonetheless, prayer is more fundamental than any of our histories about or philosophies of religion, more basic than any of our social, political, or economic theories, and more elemental than any of our evangelistic endeavors, biblical commentaries, or systematic theologies. It is the cry wrung from the human heart, the aspiration of the human soul, the confidence of the human spirit that brings us into the presence of the Holy One. It originates in the life of every person long before any clear definition or adequate understanding of God is articulated, and certainly long before any social, political, or economic theory takes form. As a phenomenon of human life, prayer seems to be a basic feature in the experience of every person. As a phenomenon of religion, it is central to every religion and to every form of spiritual experience.

But while prayer is universal, it must not be treated merely in generic fashion. As human beings we are not to be viewed — apart from our philosophical constructs and certain oversimplified ideologies — simply as people in the abstract. We are all specific individuals who stand within a concrete, specific religious tradition. So while prayer is a datum of religious experience generally, it is also a task for theological understanding. And that means, for the Christian, an understanding of prayer as it is portrayed in the life, ministry, and teaching of Jesus and as it is presented in the writings of his canonical followers — giving attention always to its basis in the revelation of God in the Old Testament, its parallels with and differences from Jewish and Greco-Roman prayers of the day, and its developments as seen within the New Testament itself.

What follows in this book, therefore, are twelve articles written by twelve first-rate biblical scholars that attempt to understand prayer in the New Testament — all the while profiting from various studies of prayer in the Bible and certain cognate religious writings that have already been published and seeking to use the tools of contemporary biblical scholarship in a responsible manner. The articles build on the scholarly expertise of their respective authors. But they are presented in a manner intended to be understood by intelligent lay people, theological students, and ministers. Each article has a "Selected Bibliography" of no more than sixteen entries for further study, with many of the works cited being foundational for that article itself. All of the articles, however, are devoid of discussion-type footnotes, which either interact with competing positions or bring in subsidiary materials. Even documentary-type footnotes, set in abbreviated form in parentheses within the text, were included only when felt to be absolutely necessary.

Unabashedly, the authors of this volume have reflected their own confessional perspectives, taken certain critical stances, and used a variety of interpretive methods in their respective treatments. The only criterion they have followed is that of greatest compatibility with the material being studied. It is expected that their academic expertise will be evident in what they write. More than that, however, it is hoped that through their efforts the subject of prayer in the New Testament will be better presented than is usually the case. And what is prayed for is that by such a truer and abler presentation, Christians will be instructed and challenged to live more genuine lives as Jesus' followers and the Christian church will be benefited in carrying out the tasks of its God-given mission.

THE EDITOR

PART I

The Setting

CHAPTER 1

Prayer in the Old Testament
or Hebrew Bible

CHRISTOPHER R. SEITZ

As I SURVEY THE TOPIC of the present volume and note the titles of the articles in it, I do so with a mixture of envy, liminality, and contentment. Envy, in that most of the other titles seem so much less global than my own — in some cases, possessing truly enviable restriction. Liminality, in that I am manifestly dealing with what could be called the "background" of the main topic of the book — occupying a sort of anteroom or foyer that one must pass through in order to get into the house itself. But also contentment, for an opening chapter on "Prayer in the Old Testament or Hebrew Bible" demands something of a wide-angle lens treatment — and that sort of approach is what I believe is needed in the discipline today.

The prevailing tendency in biblical studies is to divide things up and put them into separate bins, thereby creating an ecology where historical differentiation is seen as a goal unto itself and axiomatic of good biblical scholarship. Frequently missing from such a division of labor, however, is an ecology where synthesis and interconnections are prized as goods that must guide the discipline of exegesis and inform our interpretation of the biblical witness, tasks that should not just be left to what an onlooker may or may not be able to provide.

My particular assignment invites either integration or yet one more effort at a new taxonomy. I have settled for the former. Furthermore, because such integration must attend to the maximal limits of the Old Testament canon, it becomes immediately clear that this sort of approach must face the question of integration within the larger scope of the Christian Scriptures as well. For to speak of "integration" and "comprehensiveness" carries with it an obligation to be clear regarding the nature of the literature under scrutiny and the basic assumptions of interpretation — that is, whether for Christians, or for Jews, or for the merely curious (including biblical historians from various tribes with their representative sachems or chieftains).

Any treatment of prayer in the Old Testament that is sensitive to its canonical shape and full scope, therefore, invites reflection from the very start on how such prayer functions in relation to prayer in the New Testament and as a datum of the Christian faith. Or, to change the architectural metaphor, prayer in the New Testament must be seen as a fleshing out of a scaffolding that has already been fully raised and is intact in the Scriptures of Israel.

At the moment that Jesus uses the first person plural "*Our* Father" in response to a question about how to pray (cf. Matt. 6:9), the shoe should drop! For understood from the context of the Scriptures of Israel, Jesus is enclosing believers into a relationship that he has with the Father, whose name is "the name above every name." And that name is sounded forth and responded to in prayer, in all its rich variety, in one place only — that is, within the Scriptures of Israel.

It is for the most central theological reason, then, in accordance with the theological logic that governs both testaments of Christian Scripture, that any treatment of prayer must begin with prayer in the Old Testament. This is no anteroom, but the very place where the logic of God's unfolding plan with humanity — including the intimate speech with God that is called prayer — is set forth. The New Testament does not re-calibrate these bearings. Rather, it operates within them, setting them out in an eschatological display of firstfruits that is more familiarly referred to as "The Gospel."

1. A Word about Procedure

In what follows, I will look at numerous examples of prayer and praying in the Old Testament — from Enosh to Job, to Moses, to David, to Hezekiah, to Jonah, to the sailors who throw him overboard, to Sennacherib, and finally to the man called the "suffering servant." I am not going to attempt to deal with all of this material in detail. Rather, I will sketch out matters in broad brush and try to give a comprehensive picture of prayer in the Old Testament. So I will be moving at a fast clip and assume when I mention one line of Scripture that the entire story will rise up in all of its rich detail within the reader's imagination.

But I am not giving such a sweeping treatment for its own sake. What I want to do is to say something about how prayer points to a theological truth about God. What I want to do is to set forth how the canon of Christian Scripture, in its older, first part, presents prayer for a reader it has already anticipated. In other words, the examples of prayer in the Old Testament are not just lying around like seams of ore in the ground, raw and in need of refining (if, in fact, they are to be used at all). Prayer — like prophecy, law, creation, worship, or wisdom — is presented in the Old Testament in such a way as to give the reader clues as to its abiding significance. To study the Old Testament, therefore, is not like visiting a museum (however much the historicism in vogue since the late nineteenth century has encouraged such a view). Rather, to open the Old Testament is to encounter the living God!

Often in trying to comprehend the role of the reader in the interpretation of Scripture, scholars of late have spoken about a "hermeneutics of suspicion" or a "hermeneutics of trust." Such language signals that the Bible is provocative literature, which makes claims on its readers — that the Bible is not to be taken as simply inert sherds dug up from the past to be scrutinized as one would study fossils. But neither suspicion nor trust is an option on offer for our choosing if we are to understand the character of the narrative's sacred disclosure and appreciate our privilege in being able to glimpse beyond the veil at all. In effect, to overstate the Bible's historical character is all-too-often to understate its theological dimension from the start.

2. Prayer and the Name of God (YHWH)

Our discussion of prayer is based on one major assumption: that prayer turns on an intimate knowledge of the named God of Israel, who revealed who he is to a particular people at the Red Sea and at Mt. Sinai — and who, on these terms and this ground, is accessible in prayer. Prayer in the Old Testament is not special content, particular technique, or the quality of a person's spirituality. Rather, it is talk with the living God! And to talk with the living God is, for Israel, to know God's name.

By convention, I will in what follows refer to this personal name of God (YHWH) as "the Lord." I am, however, mindful of the inadequacy of this convention for expressing what the divine name expressed in Israel — however much we may be told that the convention is traceable to a reverential move designed to protect God's name against misuse (which, in turn, reveals how much the name was the virtual "real presence" of the person of the Holy One of Israel; cf. Exod. 34:6-7). Indeed, the existence of this convention makes it extremely difficult to emphasize how much prayer in the Old Testament is tied to the personal dimension of God as this is carried in God's name, for the modern and late-modern use of the name Yahweh can recapture none of this personal dimension. It may, in fact, even produce the opposite effect — not to mention the manifold problems for Christian theology that such a neologism introduces, whether of modalism or of an unacceptable confusion about relations among the persons of the Godhead in an "immanent trinity."

It should not be forgotten, as well, that alongside this reverential convention was also a conspiring factor from another quarter, which is presupposed and carried over into the New Testament — that is, the emergence of the sacred name of Jesus and the implications of the sanctity of Jesus' name for Christian belief and worship. For God gave his "name above all names," as the early Christian confession contained in Phil. 2:6-11 has it, to the One he exalted to his right hand (v. 9).

In the Old Testament, it is God's personal name and the disclosure of his name to Israel that, in the very first instance, makes prayer possible. Prayer is fundamentally about God's holy, named self being made accessible to humans by God and on his own sovereign terms. However we are meant to understand the character of this disclosure before Israel's experiences at the Red Sea and Mt. Sinai, Gen. 4:26 insists that prayer is, at bottom line, a "calling on the name of the Lord." Underlying this third-person use of "the Lord" is a first-person clarification in the form of a solemn self-introduction made in Exodus 3 and Exodus 6, which is capable of being paraphrased as: "I am the Lord, who will be as I will be in the events that I bring about" — as expressed in God's deliverance of his people at the Sea, before Pharaoh and all creation, and his revelation of the Torah at Sinai. Prayer is only possible on the strength of these disclosures.

Yet prayer also can imply a general access to God, which is what we mean when we speak of "prayer" in its own inherently general sense. How can this be so? How can God be accessible to those he discloses himself to, and only them, and yet also be accessible and meaningful in general terms?

Our treatment of prayer, therefore, will be in two main parts. The first will reflect on prayer within and outside of the covenant. It will consider the theological significance of this "inside and outside" reality of prayer. Part two will look at prayer within the covenant relationship in the strict sense. The emphasis in this second part will fall on the "one and the many" as essential to prayer's intercessory logic.

Though many Old Testament figures will be treated in passing, I will in the final section focus on three pray-ers: Moses, David, and the man called "the suffering servant." Just as there is a complex relationship between generic and specific prayers in the Old Testament or Hebrew Bible, so, too, there is within Israel a complex relationship between the prayers of the one and the prayers of the many. This relationship between the one and the many is taken up bodily in the New Testament. It represents the governing type or figure with which earliest Christian confessions were keen to correlate the actions and identity of Jesus, the Christ. The New Testament refers to this figural correlation using the expression "in accordance with (or, 'in fulfillment of') the Scriptures" (cf. 1 Cor. 15:3). The theological truth conveyed by such language is as follows: who Jesus was and is — that is, the New Testament's adaptation of the divine name, "I am who I will be," which is fitted for the logic of its incarnational presentation — is known in relationship to the God who revealed himself to Israel and through Israel to the world, both in blessing and in curse.

Therefore, if prayer is to be understood rightly, it must be situated within the reality of God's disclosure of himself, which is the central revelatory truth at the heart of the Old Testament. And here, even though expressed in dialectical relationship to Israel's Torah, is to be found the explanation for Paul's phraseology in referring to the Scriptures as "the oracles of God" (i.e., the One Named and Holy God), which oracles had been entrusted to the Jews (Rom. 3:2).

3. Prayer and Christian Scripture, Old and New

Two facts about prayer in the New Testament are basic: that Jesus prayed and that Jesus taught his disciples to pray. One might conclude from this that Christian prayer involves an understanding of (1) the manner of Jesus' praying, (2) the content of his prayer, and (3) how these features have been passed to the church, whose self-understanding is to be governed (at least in some measure) by (4) depictions of the followers of Jesus at prayer in the New Testament and (5) teachings of the New Testament writers on the subject of prayer. All of this would justify a study of prayer that focuses primarily on the New Testament witness.

At the same time, however, Christians need always to be aware that prayer did not begin with Jesus. All sorts of people have prayed, to all sorts of gods, and from time immemorial. Prayer, in fact, could well be as universal an instinct as eating or sleeping. And in that witness called the Scriptures of Israel, prayer begins very early with Enosh in that lapidary statement of Gen. 4:26: "Now at that time men began to call upon the name of the LORD."

This Enosh was distinctly a pre-Abraham, pre-Israelite son of Adam. His name literally means "humanity" — that is, the genus of human beings broadly considered. Prayer emerges, therefore, together with the offerings of Cain and Abel, as soon as the flaming sword is set down East of Eden. It does not only first occur at that time when God chooses a special people who will be the means of blessing to all the nations — a people who will come to see that they have direct-dial service, and not just a party line, into God's presence (and will pay a higher surcharge for it too).

Still, it is noteworthy — even if, ironically, often underappreciated by many Gentile interpreters — that the Scriptures of Israel tell us things about prayer that are not exclusively tied to Israel. Indeed, it will be a thesis of the first main section to follow that what is true about prayer, as these Scriptures relate it, only comes to full realization as one grasps the universality of prayer as a human instinct.

Because prayer takes place both within and outside of God's covenant relationship with his people, it has the capacity to show us something about God's double-edged life with Israel — that is, his love and commitment on the one hand, and his jealousy on the other. And, by figural extension, it expresses also something about his relations with both the Christian church and Judaism. Seen from Israel's own unique perspective, as the canon reveals this, this means that prayer can become a means of imitating those outside that covenant relationship, and so result in idolatrous and vain pleadings. Such "praying" drives God to silence or to withdrawal, as in the Book of Isaiah. Or, prayer can bring about a more quotidian demonstration of God's judgment, as when pagan sailors pray to Israel's LORD and not to their own gods, whilst Jonah, God's prophet, hides below deck, silent and in judgment for being so. Both of these perspectives exist in the Old Testament: Israel becoming, in prayer, like the nations; and the nations doing what is appropriate in prayer, as this has been vouchsafed to Israel. In this dialectic of "inside-outside," the significance of prayer as having to do with God's special revelation and election is underscored.

The Old Testament tells us that Moses prayed, that David prayed, and that Israel as a people prayed. Measured against the prayers of Jesus, are we meant to conclude that theirs was likewise a special praying with a special content — in the same way (though, of course, in some preliminary or underdeveloped way) that the praying and prayers of Jesus are central and special and exemplary? Is there something special about the manner of praying and the content of what is prayed in the Hebrew Scriptures that justifies the inclusion of such a discussion within the ecology of prayer, the main sessions of which are devoted to prayer in the New Testament? I believe not. Rather, a discussion of prayer in the Old Testament vis-à-vis prayer in the New Testament only makes sense if it shows how prayer is about the basic theological truth of both testaments — that is, about the identity and disclosure of God as he truly is. And an interest in this theological truth means that our concern will be not only with historical and descriptive matters, but primarily with the abiding and constructive features of prayer as the Old Testament or Hebrew Scriptures present them.

To this end, it will first be established that the witness of the Old Testament is not to prayer as an anthropological distinctive that somehow marks off Israel as God's people. The Old Testament is not a project that sets out to tell us things about Israel as a pre-Jewish *anthropos,* whether in the realm of prayer or in other matters religious. That would make it a handbook of religious practices and ideas, which a people from another period (particularly Jews and Christians today) can open and learn from as one might study (whether out of curiosity or for edification) a certain religion or a body of religious beliefs. This is not to deny that the Old Testament can be read in this way — and, indeed, is generally read this way by many people today, especially by Christian readers who possess a second testament. The very existence of the dual phraseology "Old Testament" and "Hebrew Bible" points to a deeper ambiguity or dialectic that governs the inquiry, and which must be faced right up front.

To state matters somewhat differently, the very first question facing any inquiry into prayer in the Old Testament or Hebrew Bible is form-critical. Just what kind of depiction are we talking about when we turn to a set of Scriptures that was once called by those with a "New Testament Scripture-in-the-making" one thing — that is, "the oracles of God," "the law and prophets," or "the Scriptures" — and then, increasingly, by Christians, by Jews, and by others something else — that is, "Old Testament," "Tanak," or "Hebrew Bible"? What sort of book is this book, which is paired by Christians with another witness, by Jews with another distinctive interpreting lens, and by the simply curious with their own modern or late-modern spectacles?

Given such different perspectives, the opening statement that must be made about prayer is that the depiction of prayer in these Scriptures is not riveted to Israel as a people, but entails a broader, yet more intensive, look at a more privileged reality: the identity of God as he truly is. To say this is to highlight the fact that these Scriptures are making theological statements on the basis of religious ones — that is, they are speaking of Israel's religious experience and the religious experiences attributed to the nations as the means by which to offer testimony to God's very self. And since prayer lies at the heart of all such depictions, the Hebrew Scriptures, which speak most specifically about prayer, are the best place to begin when we want to see how such general religious phenomena have become the media for theological truth about God as he is.

4. Prayer as Universal and Prayer in Israel's Experience

It is bracing to consider how far-reaching and fraught with theological meaning are the depictions of prayer in the Old Testament or Hebrew Bible, particularly when ranged alongside depictions of prayer in the New Testament and the Talmud. If we fail to take into consideration those Old Testament depictions, we will miss the perspective that governs the New Testament's own angle of vision. But there also exists, right alongside of what can be said about Israel's experience, a universal aspect of prayer that guides the self-consciousness of Jesus and forms, under the authority of the Holy Spirit, the early church's emerging identity. And it is this universal understanding of prayer, over against the particular understanding of the Scriptures, that supplies an important key to the portrayals of prayer in the

10

New Testament and sets the mode within which the proclamation of the New Testament plays out its notes and makes its music.

Portrayals in Isaiah and Jeremiah

The universal or generic reality is — like much else in the Old Testament — that prayer can become deeply ironic in God's use of it. When Rabshakeh, the Assyrian general, standing outside the city of Jerusalem with the most powerful army of the day, asked, "Is it without the Lord that Sennacherib has come up against this city?" (Isa. 36:10), he could have been quoting the prophet Isaiah, "Ah, Assyria, rod of my anger, against an ungodly people I send him" (Isa. 10:5). The word of the prophet had, it seems, become genericized. And on the lips of this Assyrian official it constituted a blasphemy calling for divine judgment.

Likewise, prayer may be something of a generic reflex that simply ricochets off God's closed counsel, and so becomes idolatrous. This was God's judgment on Isaiah's generation: "When you stretch out your hands, I will hide my eyes from you; even though you make many prayers, I will not listen" (Isa. 1:15). Israel had become a "sinful nation" (Isa. 1:4; a *goy* or "Gentile-like people"), with prayers to match. Thus a generic "Israel" with generic "prayers" gets a generic "god" *(elohim)* — one comparable to the plural "gods" so boasted about by Rabshakeh (Isa. 36:18), but unworthy of the dignity of God's name and self.

On the other hand, the prayer of a righteous person can reverse the destruction and disgrace of Zion. This is what happened when Hezekiah prayed to God concerning the invasion of Sennacherib and his mocking, defiant letter (Isa. 36:1–37:20). In response, the prophet gives God's verdict: "Because you have prayed to me concerning Sennacherib, king of Assyria, this is the word that the LORD has spoken concerning him" (Isa. 37:21-22a) — with, then, a divine oracle of doom uttered against Sennacherib (Isa. 37:22b-29).

Prayer can also be denied in order to doom an entire generation, as with God's charge to Jeremiah: "You shall not intercede for this people!" (Jer. 7:16; 11:14; 14:11). Or it can go forth with the seeds of its own destruction, as in the case of Sennacherib, who was not killed by an avenging angel outside the city of Jerusalem but by his own sons in an act of worship "in the house of Nisroch his god" (Isa. 37:18). The drama of the siege of

Jerusalem, as portrayed in Isaiah 36–37, is a drama not of military might but of prayer. For the story does not end with the dramatic defeat of an army of 185,000 men, as presented in 37:36, but with the defeat of one man in the silence of his own blasphemous sanctuary, as depicted in 37:38.

The Story of Jonah

The opposite depiction comes in the story of Jonah, where worried, pagan sailors tell Jonah to "call on his god." In a moment of unparalleled self-absorption, Jonah asks to be thrown into the sea (Jon. 1:12; cf. 4:9). The sailors oblige him. But they do so only after offering a prayer that brings about their own salvation — a prayer offered not to their god, nor even to Jonah's god (who, presumably, from their standpoint, was another small "g" god), but to God, the LORD. Under examination, Jonah had earlier, ironically, borne witness to this god as "The LORD, the God of heaven, who made the sea and the dry land" (1:9). Jonah's subsequent prayer in the fish is to "the LORD his God" (2:1-9), who then directs the fish to spit him out when he does, at last, what he was told to do by the sailors (cf. 1:10).

One can see in this story a narrative that conveys a deeply theological truth about prayer: that prayer is not about technique or content, as such, but about naming the name and declaring the honor due that name, by witnessing before the nations to the one God, the LORD, maker of heaven and earth. If Jonah, who is acquainted with God's name, shirks from such a witness, then the nations will bear witness themselves — before God and before Jonah and before heaven and earth, prior to chucking him overboard. It matters not for the sake of the narrative that we be able to assess the moral qualifications of the sailors, their spiritual fitness, or the sheer dice-rolling character of their decision. What matters for the theological force of the narrative is that prayer is about calling on the One God and calling on him by name. Even on the lips of worried sailors with no knowledge of God's ways, God's name is God's self.

All prayer begins with this reality, even if under — and for this narrative precisely when under — forced circumstances. If Jonah persists in his strange piety and religious bearing, it would be just as well if he knew not God's name or called not on God. The consequence would be the same. Any prayer without God's name is as effective as silence. And Jonah tried both before he fell back on what he knew to be true, and what others learned from his stubbornness to be the truth, about prayer.

Prayer, therefore, is to address God by name. And to name God's name is to deal with God as he truly is, without remainder — yet always under the obligation of having invoked the one holy and jealous God. In the story of Jonah, that holiness and jealousy spills out in judgment and salvation, as God sees fit.

The Story of Balaam

Israel's depiction of the generic as testimony to the specific, through the vehicle of prayer, also comes in modified form in the story of Balaam, the hired-gun who was called by Balak, king of Moab, to curse Israel (Num. 22:4-6). While the story is not about prayer as we usually understand it, it is clearly about the reality of God's identity. In the course of the narrative, we see the generic god (22:9-12) become the named LORD God (22:13), become the LORD's angel (22:22), become "the LORD" on the lips of Balaam, the man from the land beyond the Euphrates (23:15), and become acknowledged as "the LORD" even by Balak, his Moabite employer (23:17).

When Balak hired Balaam, a famous foreign curser, to invoke God for his purposes, he did not have it in view that the God who brings judgment on mortals (for a fee) would reveal himself as "the LORD" and make that revelation of himself an occasion for the blessing of Israel and Balaam and the cursing of Moab and Balak. Here, again, we have a story told by Israel about the way that the invocation of God by the nations comes with rather startling and unexpected consequences.

The Story of Job

Job, too, was also not an Israelite, standing as he did on the other side of Sinai. He was a contemporary of Noah, and, like him, was renowned for his intercession (cf. Ezek. 14:14). He was a man from the East, whose "friends" were like him in being removed from the circle of the fully named and known God, as revealed in Exodus 3 and Exodus 6.

It is striking that a man renowned for intercession does so little praying on his own behalf. Form-critically, there is very little in the long dialogue section of chapters 3–26 of the Book of Job that counts as prayer, strictly speaking. Some of that omission may be explicable because of the constraints of the section's form, which is more talk about God than talk to God. But even when Job lays down his famous oath of innocence in chapter 31, while we have talk about God and at God, it is still not prayer. It is not direct "Thou" speech to God in prayer.

Only once does Job name the name of God: "The LORD gave and the LORD has taken away; blessed be the name of the LORD" (1:21). But it is not clear what the narrator means to say by that naming, particularly in view of the full revelation of God's name to Moses in Exod. 3:13-15. At the beginning of the story the narrator tells his readers that the LORD is the God confronted by Satan within his court (1:6–2:6), who forced God to show in the case of Job the possibility of serving God without reward (1:9). And the reader also knows that this LORD is the God who appears in the whirlwind (38:1; 40:6).

Just as the true finale of the contest between Sennacherib and Jerusalem in Isaiah 36–37 did not come until a moment much later than the august military defeat, so, too, the true finale of the Book of Job does not come in chapters 38-41 with the speech of God from the whirlwind. The wager on Job was not determined by sheer divine extrusion into the world of suffering. Rather, it was settled when Job became who he was all along, even on the ash heap — that is, a man of prayer (cf. 42:1-9). So it is at this point the narrator comments: "And the LORD restored the fortunes of Job when he had prayed for his friends" (42:10). And though the narrator does not say it himself, the response of Job to God implies that he had learned something about God in the experience of the whirlwind that he did not know before (42:5), which knowledge was for him akin to the way that God is the same (yet more fully to be known in the events of Sea and Sinai) as the LORD.

Here, then, is a further instance in the Hebrew Scriptures where God demonstrated in a universal manner his sovereignty over how and when he could be known. The consequence in Job's case, however, was overwhelming and compelling. He became a man of prayer — even for those who had not heard his cry. And in so doing, he defeated the evil whose face is hidden, but whose presence is parasitic on all of life.

Here in the Hebrew Scriptures — on the border between the generic and the specific, between the man from the East and God's covenant people at Sea and Sinai — prayer is the place where the truth of God's most essential self is grasped. This truth is that God's self is to be worshiped without any hope for reward. And in Job's confession of 42:5 ("Now my eye sees thee") and prayer of 42:8-9, the forces of evil were rendered mute and helpless — until another Man and another day and another prayer, to the glory of the one Lord.

A Summation

The Old Testament and Hebrew Scriptures reveal that prayer has the widest possible base in God's dealing with the world. What is essentially at stake in prayer is knowledge of God's name. And that knowledge can be mysteriously conveyed, if God so chooses, as with Balaam. It can also be inadvertently and even desperately disclosed, as with Jonah's overtly selfish expostulation to the sailors, which became the means of salvation for them. Prayer, however, is fundamentally about learning that God can be known, as in the case of Job, and that he is one, as he revealed himself to Israel — but that he is also sovereign over his own disclosures, and so is only revealed as he sees fit.

Prayer is not humanity's effort to reach God from below by crying out to him. Rather, it is the consequence of his having made himself known and our faithful response to that prior knowledge. True prayer, therefore, means discourse with the one Lord, and that cannot be taken for granted as covered under some generic deity.

It remains true, however, that naming God's name in prayer, even within Israel, stands under God's sovereignty as well. For if Israel becomes a nation like the other nations, prayer to him will not be heard. In the prophecy of Isaiah, becoming like the other nations (cf. 1:4; a *goy* or "Gentile-like nation") has the consequence of producing — at least externally — a more, not a less, prayerful people (cf. ch. 1 *passim*) — that is, of turning to a proliferation of gods to make up the difference for calling on God by name and not being heard. God holds out his hands all day (65:2), but the people have forsaken him (65:11). And so they become more religious to fill up the void, not less.

5. Prayer within the Covenant

When one looks at prayer within the covenant relationship, what is striking is what one does not find. There is no handbook on prayer, as there is on sacrifice and offerings. The elaborate details that governed Israel's worship have not a single specific word about how to pray or what to pray for. Here again one is thrown up against the reality that prayer in the Old Testament is distinctly nonreligious. Spirituality is religious, phenomenal, and self-conscious. But prayer in the Old Testament lacks the dimension of self-consciousness.

Moses and the Pentateuch

Staying within the realm of Israel's worship and focusing on Moses and the Pentateuch, three things can be said about prayer. First, that the prayer or "Song of Moses" of Exod. 15:1-18 emerges as critical to God's patience and forbearance — not just in the wilderness, but in a much wider sense. Moses intercedes and puts God in mind of his promises to Israel's ancestors. It would not be too much to say that God is blackmailed (in a manner of speaking) by Moses, insofar as his suggestion to build a nation out of Moses or send an angel instead of himself is held hostage, Moses insists, to his own prior promises. Here, again, we see that prayer involves no special techniques, beyond simple truth-telling. Moses does this. God responds. He will build a nation out of the children of the murmurers. And he will go in presence and in name with them, to fulfill his promises to their ancestors.

Second, and akin to this, Deuteronomy, amidst its many worship statements, speaks of prayer in the context of judgment. At the end of the book, blessing and curse are set out before the new generation poised to enter the promised land. Yet the book looks even further into the future, to a time of exile and curse (29:22-29; cf. also 4:25-31; 9:4-5). That is, it reckons with a breaking of the covenant. How can there be a future for God's people? It is prayer, Deuteronomy insists, that reestablishes the relationship (30:1-5). Here we touch upon the fundamental sacrificial reality, which lies just below or alongside the unitive character of sacrificial offering: a broken and contrite heart.

Finally, prayer is understood in Exodus and Deuteronomy as that which interprets and makes clear the unitive, purposeful nature of sacrificial offering (Exod. 34:29-35; cf. 1 Kings 8:22-53). This keeps Israel's cult from devolving into generic religiosity. Why was the worship of Aaron and the people, which they initiated at the foot of the mountain, any less sincere, heartfelt, celebrative, or earnest than what God himself set out? The answer is that their worship was wrong because God was not called upon as he is. And so we return to the fundamental reality that lies behind all prayer: the lifting up of the name of God, which is the *sine qua non* of prayer. Without God's name being lifted up, religion and prayers can flourish and multiply. But curse, not blessing, will ensue — stopped only by the prayer of Moses, which puts God in mind of his prior commitments, and the broken and contrite heart of the people (Deut. 30:1-5; cf. 1 Kings 8:35-53).

Prayer, it would seem, belongs to the realm of truth, from the standpoint of human beings within the covenant, and concerns God's holy self, from the standpoint of the divine. Certain individuals are better at staying with the truth than others. This truth has a twofold character: (1) truth about God's character and self, and (2) truth about the situation of judgment and God's absence or withdrawal from the covenant relationship for a season. The latter is due to the sins of the pray-er and/or the realization that a generation has so turned away from God that he has withdrawn to protect his own name and holy covenant.

Within the covenant a dialectic exists between the prayer of Everyman and the prayer of the one man. Israel retained in its memory the singular role of Moses as a pray-er. This role cannot be underestimated as one looks at prayer more generally.

David and the Psalms

The role of the specific and the general is explicit within the Psalter. Martin Luther worked with an almost modern attitude toward the character of the Old Testament as Christian Scripture, which attitude bears some resemblance to what would later emerge and be called "historical criticism." In the Psalms, however, he recognized what he called "the faithful synagogue." The anachronism "synagogue" may be telling as to Luther's modernity, but more important was his sensitivity to the abiding witness of the Psalter to prayer. The Psalms did not simply tell Luther something about the way a certain people prayed before Jesus showed up. Rather, for Luther the Psalms show us prayer as it eternally is — which is an important corrective to the pernicious habit, whether motivated by practical or mercenary concerns, of printing New Testaments by themselves (though, thankfully, such an inclination often halts at omitting the "Psalms of David").

The faithful synagogue and the Psalms of David? Can both be true? Can the Psalms be prayers of David and prayers of Israel and prayers of Christians all at the same time? The question, of course, is heuristic, since the psalms are manifestly these things anyway. How, then, are they this?

Jesus interpreted Psalm 110 as David's word regarding him (cf. Mark 12:35-37; par.). So the dimension of fulfilled prophecy comes to the fore in many instances of the use of Scripture in the New Testament. And so the psalms of the Hebrew Bible have become prayers for others than Jews. Stated negatively, there are no psalms that represent the wisdom of praying and are universally available in the same way as in the Book of Proverbs, which includes words from Agur or King Lemuel. Unlike the presentation of the Book of Job, the God addressed in the Psalter is not a veiled YHWH. Rather, the God of the Psalms is Israel's God in holy unveiling.

At the same time, it should not be forgotten that the question of "why" Jesus uttered Psalm 22 on the cross is a question that often bypasses a matter of deeper consequence in a Christian apprehension of the Old Testament as Scripture for the Christian church. That God was absent and forsook Jesus in the manner declared by Psalm 22 is a recognition that God — for both Jesus and for Israel before him — could be said to be "my God" in the very strict sense of that term. The heart of Israel's praying is not wrecked on the shoals of either complete presence or complete absence of God for his people. Rather, this heart of Israel's praying is broken open and made accessible by virtue of the relationship that Jesus has with God, thereby tearing open a veil and giving those outside the covenant a relationship to God. And so, by the work of Jesus and being "in him," Gentiles are allowed to enter the sanctuary of the "faithful synagogue" (to use Luther's metaphor) and, further, even to enter into the heart of David himself.

The Suffering Servant and the Prophets

I want to conclude this overview not with Moses or David, but with another figure from the Book of Isaiah who is commonly called the "suffering servant." As we will see, a look at the servant brings us back full circle to Moses, whose prayers saved an Israel in forfeit in the wilderness.

That there is a relationship between the movement of thought within the Book of Isaiah and the movement of thought within the Psalter is a thesis that is highly defensible. For our purposes here, however, it is sufficient to note that Isaiah 40–48 (a subsection of so-called "Deutero-Isaiah") is as concerned with the kingship of God and his sole rule over nations and creation as is Book 4 of the Psalter (Pss. 90–106), and that both sections appear at a similar location in their respective canonical presentations. Furthermore, in both Isaiah 40–48 and Book 4 of the Psalter an explicit mention of God's Messiah falls into the background.

Many have noted also the close association that exists between God's servant in Isaiah 49–53 and the man Moses. Ernst Sellin and Gerhard von Rad are two recent defenders of this view; likewise, Klaus Baltzer pursues this position in his recently published Hermeneia commentary on Isaiah 40–55. Such a view is also consistent with the depiction of Psalm 90, where Moses, in prayer on behalf of David and Israel, is brought back, as it were, from his days as intercessor in the wilderness.

In the movement of thought in Isaiah 40–48, the servant is introduced before the heavenly council in chapter 42. The servant is to have a specific role in relation to the nations. As it is clear in this part of Isaiah that Israel is the servant, we should also expect the role to the nations described in chapter 42 to be that of none other than Israel.

But a change seems to be registered in chapter 49. A more individual figure appears to be commissioned. Moreover, this servant has a role vis-à-vis not just the nations, but also Israel. Jeremiah was commissioned to be a prophet to the nations, and the language that appears here is very similar to what appears in Jeremiah 1. Here, however, the text refers to discouragement and seems to speak of a past vocation that has been frustrated, not one that lies in the future.

Jeremiah was considered by those who shaped the traditions associated with him to be a "prophet like Moses." Such a prophet had been promised in Deut. 18:18 ("I will raise up from among you one like Moses"), and Jeremiah's fulfillment of such a role seems clear. Yet, ironically, with this fulfillment, we may also see a distinctive interpretation of the language of Deuteronomy. For while Jeremiah is a second Moses, he is also the final prophet. With his return to Egypt, the curses of Deuteronomy are brought upon an evil generation. And his command not to intercede is styled on that of Moses — but with the obvious consequence that, without Mosaic prayer, the people are doomed.

Against the backdrop of these experiences of Jeremiah, the language of Isaiah 49 seems to take its bearings. Yet the servant of Isaiah 49 is not discouraged. Like Jeremiah, he suffers and endures persecution — which persecution is described in the third servant poem of 50:4-11. In like manner as Jeremiah, he is assaulted by his own people as well as by others. But the servant's legacy is not lament, as in Jeremiah 11-20; nor is it a withdrawal from the office of prayer, which occasioned such lament. And in the final, dramatic poem of 52:13–53:12, the servant is described as one who "made intercession for the transgressors."

There is every reason to believe that the servant of Isaiah 49–53, unlike Jeremiah, was one whose prayers were salvific because God was doing a truly new thing through him. Intercession was not denied the servant. Even more, the servant gave his life, as well as his petitions, on behalf of the people. That is the explicit verdict rendered by the final tribute of 52:13–53:12.

Now it had been a loosely developed theme that Moses had suffered innocently, which is a theme that one can see especially in the deuteronomic traditions. The people sinned in the wilderness, but Moses interceded and saved them. God said he would make a people out of Moses only, but Moses rejected this and assured through his prayer Israel's ongoing life with God.

Later, however, when the spies returned with a report of giants in the land, God's patience with the people ran out (cf. Numbers 13–14). Again, Moses interceded for them (14:13-19). But God decreed that only the little ones, a new generation, would enter the promised land as a result of Moses' saving intercession. He himself would bear the sins of the people and would suffer God's judgment on a wicked and deserving generation. Yet he would see the promised land from afar and then die in the wilderness, with no one recalling the place of his burial (cf. Isa. 53:9).

The depiction of the servant's saving work in Isa. 52:13–53:12 has been clearly modeled on Moses. He, not Jeremiah, is the awaited "prophet like Moses." Unlike the death of Moses, however, the death of the servant is seen as atoning and bearing sins in the most explicit sense — even to the extent of occasioning an eschatological confession by the nations (52:13-15). Thus through death the servant of Isa. 52:13–53:12 brings to fulfillment the promise made to Jeremiah and to the righteous servant of Isaiah 42 and 49.

6. Conclusion

The Old Testament focuses on key individuals in its presentation of prayer within the covenant. It establishes a clear connection between the election of certain pray-ers and the people at large. These pray-ers and their prayers have the capacity to restore or tear down. In Isaiah, the "one and the many" relationship is extended, quite specifically, to the nations outside of God's covenant. The use of Moses suggests an awareness of his ongoing, figurally real, presence. Yet the "new thing" of Isaiah points to an enlargement of thought: that the servant is a man of prayer. We see into his heart of anguish and find firm resolve there (50:7). His prayer is but the utterance of his life itself, which is given up in obedience — like Moses before him. But his intercession, even though very similar to that of Moses, costs him his life, brings life to a whole generation, and removes their iniquity — something that Moses did not do. And in the context of this vocation, the servant of Isaiah 49–53 sees the final eschatalogical moment released for a split second in the confession of the nations (cf. 52:15).

It is striking, however, that the content, technique, or spirituality of the servant's prayer is hidden. His intercession is known by its results and by its ongoing, dynamic character. Its fruit ("he shall see seed") is encountered in the final chapters of Isaiah in the "servants" who follow where he once walked.

This figural reality — involving the one and the many, the prophet like Moses, the interceding servant, the prayer that unleashes an eschatalogical reality regarding those outside of God's covenant — is crucial to the way that the New Testament forms its central confessions, which are configured in accord with the literal sense of these Scriptures. To speak of prayer in the Old Testament, therefore, is to speak of God's intimate disclosure and the way that disclosure penetrates to the heart of prayer as presented in the New Testament (which is the subject of the present volume of essays in its full form) and to this day.

Selected Bibliography

Balentine, Samuel E. *Prayer in the Hebrew Bible: The Drama of Divine-Human Dialogue* (Overtures to Biblical Theology). Minneapolis: Fortress, 1993.

Baltzer, Klaus. *Deutero-Isaiah* (Hermeneia). Minneapolis: Fortress, 2001.

Barth, Karl. "The True Witness." *Church Dogmatics* IV.3. Edinburgh: T. & T. Clark, 1961, 368-434.

Flusser, David. "Psalms, Hymns, and Prayers." In *Jewish Writings of the Second Temple Period*, ed. M. E. Stone, vol. 2. Assen: Van Gorcum, 1984, 551-78.

Greenberg, Moshe. *Biblical Prose Prayer as a Window to the Popular Religion of Ancient Israel*. Berkeley and Los Angeles: University of California Press, 1983.

Hugenberger, Gordon P. "The Servant of the Lord in the 'Servant Songs' of Isaiah: A Second Moses Figure." In *The Lord's Anointed*, ed. P. E. Satterthwaite, R. S. Hess, and G. J. Wenham. Carlisle: Paternoster; Grand Rapids: Baker, 1995, 105-39.

Jenson, Robert W. *Systematic Theology*, vol. 1. New York: Oxford University Press, 1997.

Miller, Patrick D. *They Cried to the Lord: The Form and Theology of Biblical Prayer*. Minneapolis: Fortress, 1994.

Newman, Judith H. *Praying by the Book: The Scripturalization of Prayer in Second Temple Judaism*. Atlanta: Scholars, 1999.

von Rad, Gerhard. *Old Testament Theology*, vol. 2. Edinburgh: Oliver & Boyd, 1965, 261-62.

Seitz, Christopher R. "Job: Full-Structure, Movement, and Interpretation." *Interpretation* 43 (1989): 5-17.

———. *Zion's Final Destiny: The Development of the Book of Isaiah*. Minneapolis: Fortress, 1991.

———. *Word Without End: The Old Testament as Abiding Theological Witness*. Grand Rapids: Eerdmans, 1998.

———. "Isaiah 40–66" *(New Interpreter's Bible)*. Nashville: Abingdon, 2001.

Sellin, Ernst. *Mose und seine Bedeutung für die israelitisch-jüdische Religionsgeschichte*. Leipzig: Deichert, 1922.

Zimmerli, Walther. *Old Testament Theology in Outline*, trans. D. E. Green. Atlanta: John Knox, 1978.

CHAPTER 2

Prayer in the Greco-Roman World

DAVID E. AUNE

THE PURPOSE OF THIS ARTICLE is to survey the forms, contents, functions, settings, and distinctive features of Greco-Roman prayer, focusing on the late Hellenistic and early Roman periods within the framework of the study of prayer as a phenomenon in the history of religions. A subsidiary concern is the problem of the relationship between "conventional" prayer and "magical" prayer. Given the necessary limitations of the present context, only a general orientation to the subject and focus on some of the more significant issues and problems can be provided.

1. Problematic Perspectives and Methodological Considerations

The study of Greco-Roman prayer is extremely complex, largely because scholarship has been burdened by ideological perspectives that have impeded rather than facilitated an understanding of the phenomenon of prayer in the ancient world. Two perspectives in particular have bedeviled the study of prayer in the Greco-Roman world. The first arises from a tendency in earlier studies to contrast *ritual prayer,* which was public, with *personal prayer,* which was private — regarding the former as mechanical, artificial, and without feeling or devotion, while considering the latter as natural, spontaneous, emotional, and authentic. Ritual prayer was thought to provide no access to the centrally important religious issue of the relationship of the individual to God, since when measured by the yardstick of "religious feeling" it was judged to be lacking.

The main flaws in this perspective lie in (1) the supposition that religion can be reduced to the relationship between an individual and God, and (2) the absolutizing and universalizing of "religious feeling" — a conception most at home in western Christianity — as a standard for judging the vitality and legitimacy of religious experience. Furthermore, our knowledge of private, personal prayer in antiquity is relatively rare and difficult to evaluate.

A second problematic perspective is that which confidently distinguishes between "religious" prayer, which is viewed as supplicative and as using nonempirical means to achieve nonempirical ends, from "magical" prayer, which is judged as coercive and as using nonempirical means to achieve empirical ends — a distinction made by James G. Frazer and others. But attempts to make sharp distinctions between religion and magic, and so to set out mutually exclusive definitions of the essence of each phenomenon, have proven unsuccessful.

Magic can be usefully defined as a form of religious deviance whereby individual or social goals are sought by means that are alternate to those normally sanctioned by the dominant religious institution (cf. D. E. Aune, "Magic in Early Christianity," 1515). But while there are some apparent differences between conventional Greco-Roman prayers and prayers that have been judged for one reason or another to be magical (cf. F. Graf, *Magic in the Ancient World*, 188-213), those differences do not provide a firm basis for distinguishing between religious and magical prayers.

Setting aside the two problematic perspectives critiqued above, it may seem we are left without any theoretical framework within which to interpret the phenomenon of prayer in the Greco-Roman world. Certain things, however, can be said about our subject. And clearly one of the first things to be said is that Greco-Roman prayer must be studied in its own right and not from the perspectives of either Jewish or Christian prayer.

The study of Greco-Roman prayer — like the study of prayer generally and as a phenomenon of the history of religions — has unfortunately suffered from scholarly neglect for reasons not always immediately apparent. Few recent studies have been devoted to the subject. And while older studies tended to focus on prayer in classical Greek literature (i.e., in epic, tragedy, and comedy), they rarely considered seriously the phenomenon in the Hellenistic period.

In our consideration of prayer in the Greco-Roman world, there are some important methodological considerations that need to be made explicit at the outset. First, we will deal with Greco-Roman prayer synchronically. While it is no doubt desirable to treat ancient prayer as a phenomenon that exhibited various changes through time, the fact is that there was a "canonical" structure of prayer that exhibited remarkable stability throughout antiquity. In fact, some of the earliest literary evidence for prayer, the Homeric epics, continued to function as paradigms for prayer throughout antiquity. It is, of course, somewhat problematic to treat Greek and Roman prayer together. Yet it also needs to be noted that there are many common features between them.

Second, since most of the evidence for prayer in antiquity is preserved in fictional literary contexts or in ancient historiography — in which prayers, like speeches, were composed for inclusion in a particular literary setting — our focus will be on these literary and historical materials. Given the formulaic character of most ancient prayers, however, our assumption will be that literary prayers are to be seen as normally imitating the conventions of actual prayers in order to achieve verisimilitude in the narrative — though, of course, prayers attributed to people in earlier historical settings will tend to exhibit anachronistic features. A major exception would be the magical prayers, which are collected in the corpus of the Greek Magical Papyri, where there is little doubt that these "boilerplate" prayers were sold by the owners of the magical recipe books for use by their customers.

Attempts to define and describe the role of prayer in the ancient world must first discuss the phenomenon in its more generic form as a history of religions phenomenon, which is an approach that must necessarily be supplemented by a focus on the particularly sociocultural context of which such prayers are a constituent feature. To begin with, "prayer" in the Greco-Roman world may be defined as the human propensity to communicate with supernatural beings who are regarded as more powerful than those who worship them.

2. Reciprocity

One of the central values of Greek society from its earliest beginnings, which persisted in somewhat altered form into the Roman era, was *reciprocity* — that is, the idea that every gift or service rendered placed a moral obligation (i.e., an informal contract) on the recipient to respond with an equivalent counter-gift or equivalent counter-service (cf. R. Seaford, *Reciprocity and Ritual;* also S. Pulleyn, *Prayer in Greek Religion,* 16-38). The principle of reciprocity in social interaction was naturally assumed to regulate the relationship between worshipers and their gods.

One of the more important terms related to the semantic field of reciprocity is *charis* ("grace, favor"). When a worshiper gives something to a god through sacrifice, he or she gives *charis* in the sense that the offering is pleasing. At the same time, however, the worshiper is storing up a feeling of gratitude on the part of the god, which is also called *charis* (cf. S. Pulleyn, *Prayer in Greek Religion,* 4; B. MacLachian, *Age of Grace,* 6-10). According to Euripides, "when sacrificing to the gods, ask good things" (*Helen* 753-54). And Plato expresses the general view of the relationship between sacrifice and prayer as follows: "The priests, according to law and custom, know how to give the gods, by means of sacrifices, the gifts that please them from us and by prayers to ask for us the gain of good things from them" (*Politicus* 290c).

The gods, like those of high status and in positions of authority, desired "honor" *(timē)*. The verbs "to favor" *(chairō)* and "to honor" *(timeō)* occur together in the epitome prefacing Euripides' *Hippolytus,* where Athena observes: "For there is among the gods this trait, that they enjoy being honored [*timōmenoi chairousin*] by people" (lines 7-8; see also Euripides *Bacchantes* 321; *Alcestis* 53). In essence this concept that "I give that you might give" *(do ut des)* — or "this for that" *(quid pro quo)* — is what scholars have often considered to be magical. In reality, however, what we have here is simply the informal principle of reciprocity in human social interaction applied to the analogous sphere of divine-human relationships.

A regular part of the structure of ancient prayer was a section detailing reasons given why a deity should respond favorably to the request, and it is here that the concept of grace or favor *(charis)* is ubiquitous. In the narrative or argument section of the imprecatory prayer of Chryses in Homer's *Iliad,* which is the earliest prayer in Greek literature, the priest *(arētēr)* calls in his chits, or vouchers of debt, from Apollo, one of the great Olympian gods:

> *Narratio:* Smintheus ['Mouse-god', an epithet for Apollo, for white mice were kept in the temples of Apollo to protect against plagues], if ever it pleased *(charienti)* your heart that I built your temple, if ever it pleased you that I burned all the rich thigh pieces of bulls, of goats,

Request: then bring to pass this wish I pray for: Let your arrows make the Danaans pay for my tears shed. (*Iliad* 1.39-42)

"I give that you might give," however, is not the only reason set out in the narrative or argument sections of ancient Greek prayers. Two other common reasons are (1) because the god had done so in the past, and (2) because it was within his competence to do so now. An example of the "because the god had done so in the past" argument is also to be found in the *Iliad:*

Appeal to Listen: Hear me *(kleuthi meu),*
   Invocation: daughter of Zeus of the aegis,
     Argument: you who forever stand beside me in all hard tasks, nor am I forgotten as I go my ways:
       Request: now give me the best of your love, Athene, and grant that we come back in glory to the strong-benched vessels when we have done a great thing that will sadden the Trojans. (*Iliad* 10.277-82)

And a combination of reasons is used in the following prayer of Diomedes to the goddess Athene (or, Pallas Athene) in the *Iliad,* where Athene's aid in the past to his father Tydeus is supplemented by his vow to offer a sacrifice in the future:

Appeal to Listen: Hear me also,
   Invocation: Atrytone, daughter of great Zeus.
     Argument: Come with me now as you went with my father, brilliant Tydeus, into Thebes, when he went with a message before the Achaians, and left the bronze-armored Achaians beside Asopos while he carried a word of friendship to the Kadmeians in that place; but on his way back he was minded to grim deeds with your aid, divine goddess, since you stood in goodwill beside him.
       Request: So now, again, be willing to stand by me, and watch over me,
     Argument: and I in turn will dedicate you a heifer, broad-browed, one year old, unbroken, that no man ever led yoked. I will drench her horns in gold and offer her to you. (*Iliad* 10.283-94)

27

In general, the narrative or argument in Greek prayers is quite different from Israelite prayers in the Hebrew Bible, where God is frequently reminded of promises he has made in the past (cf. Gen. 32:12; Exod. 32:13; 2 Sam. 7:25; 1 Kings 8:25) and where the answer to prayer serves as a demonstration of God's power and might (cf. 2 Kings 19:19).

3. The Language of Prayer

Many of the most common words for "prayer" in antiquity use the *euch*-root — that is, *euchē, euchetaomai, euchōlē, euchomai, euchos, proseuchē*, and *proseuchomai*, which mean "to speak to God," "to make requests of God," "to ask God for," "to pray," and "prayer." The most general Greek word for prayer is *euchē*. The verb *euchomai*, while its usage is often debated, probably originally meant "to assert solemnly," for it was not restricted exclusively to cultic contexts (cf. S. Pulleyn, *Prayer in Greek Religion*, 59-63). These terms are frequently used in connection with conventional prayers. But they are also used of prayers in the Greek magical papyri. Linguistically, this suggests, at least initially, an overlap between conventional prayers and magical prayers. The verbs *lissomai* (the noun *litē* is used primarily in the plural form *litai*), its cognate *litomai* (cf. *Orphic Hymn* 41.9, *Papyrus Graecae Magicae* 4.947, 2566), and *araomai* (cf. *Iliad* 1.35; 7.176), which signify "to beseech," are used in a more deferential sense than *euchomai*, which means "to pray." The verb *hiketeuō* ("to supplicate, beseech") is used in self-abasing requests, with its noun *hiketēs* signifying "suppliant."

There are also a number of words often translated "to pray" or "prayer," though they do not mean "prayer" in the sense of "speaking to God." These terms belong rather to the subdomain of "ask for" or "request," and include such words as *erōtaō, aiteō, deomai*, and *deēsis*, with their cognates. Since prayers in the Greek world can be formulated in both prose and poetry, and so can be either spoken or sung, it is important to observe that the term *aoidē* ("song") can be used of a prayer of invocation, as in the following Homeric hymn:

> *Address:* Hestia, you who tend the holy house of the lord Apollo,
> the Far-shooter at goodly Pytho, with soft oil dripping
> ever from your locks,

Invocation: come *(ercheō)* now into this house, come *(ercheó)*, having one mind with Zeus the all-wise — draw near, and withal bestow grace upon my song *(aoidē)*. (*Homeric Hymn* 24.5)

The semantically similar term *epaoidai* is used in *Papyri Graecae Magicae* 1.322, with the meaning "songs" rather than "charms": "And may you [Apollo] not be angry at my sacred chants *[epaoidais]*."

Terms based on the stem *hork-* are problematic, for they range in meaning from "to put under oath" to "to strongly implore" (e.g., *hordizō, enorkizō, exorkizō*), and tend to be found in the context of magical prayers. There are, in addition, many semantic subdomains for specific types of prayer, including (1) "blessing" *(eulogeō, eulogia, kateulogeō)*, (2) "cursing" (particularly terms based on the root *ara-*, including *ara* itself, which can mean both prayer and curse: *katara, kataraomai*, as well as *anathema, anathematizō*, and *katathematizō*), (3) "thanksgiving" *(eucharisteō, eucharistia, eucharistos)*, (4) "praise" (many from the *ain-* root, including *aineō, aiknos, ainesis, epaineō*, and *epainos*, as well as such terms as *doxa, doxazō, megalunō, euphēmeō, euphēmia*, and (5) "petitions" *(epikaloumai)*.

4. The Sacrificial Context of Prayer

In Greco-Roman cultic practice, prayer is closely connected with ritual and is nearly always linked to sacrifice (cf. *Iliad* 1.446-56; 2.410-31) or intended sacrifice — so much so that "prayers and sacrifices" *(litai kai thusiai)* is a traditional fixed expression found in many texts. The following example is from the *Olympian Odes* of Pindar, the greatest of the Greek lyric poets: "[Kin] have regaled the herald of the gods [Hermes] with prayerful sacrifices *(litais thusiais)*" (*Olympian Odes* 6.78; cf. W. Burkert, *Greek Religion*, 73).

In other situations, a votive offering (Greek: *anathema;* Latin: *votum*) — that is, a permanent gift to a deity — would be made as a result of a successful prayer (cf. W. H. D. Rouse, *Greek Votive Offerings*). Prayers pronounced aloud by officiating priests were used to ensure the efficacy or success of a variety of important functions or events, such as sacrifices, battles, and public orations. The following, taken from Aristophanes' *Thesmophoriazusae*, is a parody of a prayer spoken before silent citizens prior to the address of orators from the rostrum:

Pray silence, pray silence. Pray to the two Thesmophoroi [Demeter and Persephone], to Ploutos [the god of wealth] and Kalligeneia [Demeter, "bearer of fair offspring"] . . . that this Assembly and gathering of the day may have the most beautiful and beneficial outcome. . . . Address your vows to heaven and pray for your own good fortune. Hail, Paian, hail! Let us rejoice and be glad! (*Thesmophoriazusae* 295-305)

5. The Structure of Prayer

Perhaps the most basic pattern for ancient Greek prayer is the twofold structure of a brief invocation and a short request, as in *Iliad* 7.179-80: "O Zeus, give me good health" (see also Aeschylus *Aegesilaus* 973; Plato *Phaedrus* 279b; cf. Judg. 13:8; 2 Sam. 15:31; 2 Kings 6:17, 20). Another example of this twofold structure is found in the same passage, where (1) the god addressed is briefly named, and (2) the request immediately follows, being expressed with an imperatival infinitive:

> *Invocation:* Father Zeus,
> *Request:* let Aias win the lot, or else Diomedes, Tydeus' son, or the king himself of golden Mykenai. (*Iliad* 7.179-80)

Often, however, Greek prayers exhibit a threefold structure of invocation-argument-request. The following imprecatory prayer from the *Iliad* 1.35-42 is a typical example — with the formal features described in the left margin, including two introductory elements followed by the three structural elements of the body:

> *Narrative:* Over and over the old man [Chryses] prayed
> *Setting:* as he walked in solitude to King Apollo, whom Leto of the lovely hair bore:
> *Request to listen:* Hear me,
> *Invocation:* lord of the silver bow who set your power about Chryses and Killa the sacrosanct, who are lord in strength over Tenedos,
> *Narratio:* Smintheus [i.e., Apollo], if ever it pleased your heart that I built your temple, if ever it pleased you that I burned all the rich thigh pieces of bulls, of goats,

Request: then bring to pass [this wish I pray for]: Let your arrows
make the Danaans pay for my tears shed. (*Iliad* 1.35-42;
see also 5.115-20)

This relatively short prayer exhibits the pattern found in many Greek
prayers: (1) an *invocatio* ("invocation"), which is preceded by a request for
the god to listen (though sometimes omitted), includes the god's name(s),
with a listing of his titles and local associations; (2) a *narratio* ("narrative")
or *argumentum* ("argument"), which consists of special claims on the divinity's favor (mentioned here in the protasis of a conditional sentence: "if ever
it pleased you"); and then (3) the request itself (in the apodosis using an
aorist imperative), which asks for the punishment of the Greeks and so
makes the whole prayer into an imprecatory prayer or curse (note the prayer
in *Iliad* 1.11, where Chryses is called an *arētēr*, that is, a "priest" or "curser").

6. Types and Styles of Prayer

The most common type of Greco-Roman prayer is the request (see "The
Structure of Prayer" above, where several examples of this type of prayer
were given). This central characteristic of ancient prayer is expressed in a
question in Plato's *Euthyphro*: "Is it then the case that sacrificing is making a
gift to the gods and praying is making a request of them?" (14c). The answer,
of course, is positive. The link between prayer and sacrifice is summarized by
S. Pulleyn as follows: "First, prayer for a Greek meant asking the gods for
something. Secondly, one had to give as well as take. One did not customarily
approach the gods empty-handed" (*Prayer in Greek Religion*, 15).

Appeal to Listen or Greeting

Like a herald at a public assembly, worshipers often begin prayers with an
appeal to the divinity or divinities to pay attention. This occurs with some
frequency in Greek prayers, using such words as "hear me" (*kleuthi meu;*
cf. *Iliad* 1.37; 5.115; 10.278) or "hear me now also" (*kekluthi nun kai emeio;*
cf. *Iliad* 10.284). The same phenomenon also appears in purportedly ancient Latin prayers, as in Livy 1.32.10 where imperatives of "hear" (*audi*
and *audite*) are used in a declaration of war:

31

Appeal to Listen: Hear *(audi)*, Jupiter, and you, Janus Quirinus, and hear *(audite)* all heavenly gods, and you, gods of earth, and you of the lower world;

Invocation: I call *(ego vos)* you to witness that this people [naming whatever people it is] is unjust, and does not make just reparation. But of these matters we will take counsel of the elders in our country, how we may obtain our right.

There are also many examples of the regular salutation "hail" *(chaire)*, which was used by Greek speakers to greet one another and as a common salutation in letters, as a salutation that introduces prayers to the gods. This occurs twice in the opening lines of a "magical prayer" in *Papyri Graecae Magicae:*

Salutation: Hail *(chaire)*,
Invocation: serpent, and stout lion, natural sources of fire.
Salutation: And hail *(chaire)*,
Invocation: clear water and lofty-leafed tree, and you who gather clover from golden fields of beans, and who cause gentle foam to gush forth from pure mouths. (*Papyri Graecae Magicae* 4.939-43; see also *Homeric Hymns* 30.17)

Invocations

The gods in Greek religion were frequently invoked to "come" since they were conceptualized as existing in space but not omnipresent, and therefore must "come" in order to be present and actually hear the supplicant. These invocations were customarily expressed using imperative forms of the many Greek verbs meaning "to come" — such as *bathi, deuro* (an adverb used as an imperative), *elthe, eriniseō, herpe, hēke,* and *mole.* It is noteworthy that these verb forms are primarily aorist imperatives. This is in conformity with the general observation that the aorist imperative was used with more frequency in prayers than the present imperative (cf. W. F. Bakker, *The Greek Imperative,* 16-17).

Such invocations were used to dedicate new images and temples of the gods. They were also used for securing a god's presence at sacrifices, oracular consultations, prayers, and in private (magical) rituals. Zeus is the exception. There is no evidence that in public liturgies he was ever invited to come, for he sees and acts from where he is. Such invocations conclude nearly half the late *Orphic Hymns* (e.g., 1.9; 9.11; 11.4, 21; 12.14; 14.12; 27.11; 33.8; 34.1; 35.7; 36.13; 40.8; see also Sappho *Fragments* 1.5, 25; *Papyri Graecae Magicae* 1.296-327; *Homeric Hymns* 24.3).

Invocations to come pervade the magical papyri, which prescribe procedures for procuring revelations through the presence of a supernatural being (cf. *Papyri Graecae Magicae* 1.163; 2.2; 3.51, 129, 481, 564; 4.1171, 1605; 5.249; 7.961-65 [five times]; 62.25). Common invocations are "Come to me Lord" (*deuro moi kurie* or *hēke moi kurie*; cf. *Papyri Graecae Magicae* 12.238 for the first and 13.88, 603 for the second) and "Quickly, by your power now appear on earth to me, yea verily, god!" (cf. *Papyri Graecae Magicae* 1.89-90) — which are phrases very similar to the invocation "Come Lord Jesus" of Rev. 22:20. In dramatic and mythological literature the response pronounced by the invoked deity is at times expressed through "I have come" speeches (cf. Athena in *Iliad* 1.207; Apollo in Euripides *Orestes* 1628; Dionysius in Euripides *Bacchae* 1; a ghost in Euripides *Hecuba* 1; Poseidon in Euripides *Troades* 1; Hermes in Euripides *Ion* 5).

The invocation can be one structural element of a more complex type of prayer. Or it can stand alone as a "cletic" prayer or hymn (from the Greek word *klētikos*, "invocatory"; cf. Menander *Rhetor* 334.25–336.4), appealing to a particular deity to be present (normally at a sacrifice). An example of a prayer of invocation using the verb *lissomai* is found in *Orphic Hymn* 1, which is to be dated in the first to fourth centuries CE:

> *Invocation:* Lovely Hekate of the roads and crossroads I invoke
> *(klēizō);* in heaven, on earth, and in the sea, saffron-
> cloaked, tomb spirit reveling in the souls of the dead,
> daughter of Perses, haunting deserted places, delighting
> in deer, nocturnal, dog-loving, monstrous queen, de-
> vouring wild beasts, ungirt, of repelling countenance.
> You, herder of bulls, queen and mistress of the whole
> world, leader, nymph, mountain roaming nurturer of
> youth,
>
> *Request:* maiden, I beseech *(lissomenos)* you to come *(pareinai)* to
> these holy rites, ever with joyous heart and ever favoring
> the oxherd. (Athanasakis, 5-7)

Here Hekate is addressed by name, followed by a long series of descriptive phrases detailing her particular spheres of competence — including even a brief genealogical element ("daughter of Perses").

Names, Epithets, and Titles

The invocation of a god or gods by name is a regular feature of prayer in both the ancient and modern world. In the polytheistic systems of both Greek and Roman religion, it was necessary to discover which deity one wanted to influence through invoking his or her name (cf. Varro in Augustine *Civitate Dei* 4.22; Horace *Odes* 1.2.25-26). Greek prayers used certain formulas that were intended to insure that the god addressed would not be offended by an incorrect invocation. In the hymn of Zeus in the *Agamemnon* of Aeschylus the formula "whoever he is" *(hostis poti estin)* occurs (Aeschylus *Agamemnon,* line 160). This is similar to the Roman liturgical formulas "whether a god or goddess" *(sive deus sive dea* or *si deus si dea;* cf. Livy 7.26.4; 8.26.4; Aulus Gellius *Noctes Atticae* 2.28.3; Arnobius *Adversus nationes* 3.8) and "by whatever name you want to be called" *(sive quo alio nomine te appellari volueris;* cf. Macrobius *Saturn* 3.9.10; Vergil *Aeneid* 2.351; Servius *Commentary on Vergil's Aeneid* 2.351; Apuleius *Metamorphoses* or *The Golden Ass* 11.2; Catullus 34.21-22).

The problem of knowing the names of the gods is reflected in Plato's *Cratylus:*

> By Zeus, Hermogenes, we, if we are sensible, must recognize that there is one most excellent kind, since of the gods we know nothing, neither of them nor of their names, whatever they may be, by which they call themselves, for it is clear that they use the true names. But there is a second kind of correctness, that we call them, as is customary in prayers, by whatever names and patronymics are pleasing to them since we know no other. (*Cratylus* 400d-e)

In numerous magical texts the deity addressed is said to have a "secret name," which is often followed by a sequence of incomprehensible "magical words" *(voces magicae)* — as, for example, the following from *Papyri Graecae Magicae:*

Invocation: Yes, lord, because I call upon *(epikaloumai)* your secret
name which reaches from the firmament to the earth,
ATHEZOPHOIM ZADEAGEOBEPHIATHEAA AM-
BRAMI ABRAAM THALCHILTHOE ELKOTHOOEE
ACHTHONON SA ISAK CHOEIOURTHASIO IOOSIA
IICHEMEOOOOAOAEI,
    Request: rescue *(anasōson)* me in an hour of need. (*Papyri
Graecae Magicae* 1.216-21)

In another invocation in *Papyri Graecae Magicae* the speaker calls on "your
name" followed by a sequence of *voces magicae,* which are intended to constitute a secret form of the divine name:

> I call *(klēzō)* your name,
> In number equal to the Moirai themselves,
> ACHAIPHOTHOTHOAIEIAEIA
> AIEAIEIAOTHOTHOPHIACHA.
>   (*Papyri Graecae Magicae* 1.325-27; see also *PGM* 21.1)

Secrecy surrounding a divine name, however, was not exclusive to
magic. Though Jupiter Optimus Maximus was the patron god of Rome,
the city itself was regarded as a deity with a carefully concealed name.
Many ancient writers reflect the belief that Rome had a secret name (cf.
Plutarch *Roman Questions* 61; Pliny *Historia naturalis* 28.4.18; Macrobius *Saturn* 3.9.3). Johannes Lydus in the sixth century CE maintained
that Rome actually had three names: (1) *Roma,* the political name
known to all; (2) *Flora,* a hieratic name, which was also widely known;
and (3) a ritual name used only by the Roman priests (*De mensibus*
4.73). Lydus thought that Rome's ritual name was *Amor,* "love" — that is,
Roma spelled backwards. This view had been held by Aelius Aristides in
the mid-second century CE (cf. his *Roman Oration* 8). It is also represented by a graffito on the wall of a house in Pompey, which was destroyed in 79 CE:

```
R O M A
O     M
M     O
A M O R
```

Not only must a divinity be addressed with precision and courtesy, but such invocations must also be accompanied by the formal titles, powers, and attributes of the deity if he or she is to hear the prayer. The following poem by the first-century CE Roman poet Catullus follows the conventions of an invocation directed to Diana (the Latin name for Artemis), who is identified by her divine parents, Latona and Jove, as well as by her aliases, including Juno Lucinia, Trivia, and Moon:

> O child of Latona, great offspring of greatest Jove,
> whom your mother bore by the Delian olive tree,
> that you might be the lady of mountains and green woods,
> and secluded glens and sounding rivers;
> you are called Juno Lucina by mothers in birth pains,
> you are called mighty Trivia and Moon with counterfeit light.
> You, goddess, measure out by monthly course the circuit of the year,
> you fill full with goodly fruits the country home of the farmer.
> Be thou sanctified by whatever name you wish (*sis quocumque tibi
>   placet sancta nomine);*
> and as of old you were accustomed, with good help keep safe the race
>   of Romulus. (Catullus 34)

This is taken a step further in the writings of Livy, the Roman historian of the following generation, where, after calling upon Jupiter and Janus Quirinus, all the gods of heaven, earth, and the underworld are addressed:

> Hear *(audi)*, Jupiter, and thou, Janus Quirinus, and hear *(audite)* all heavenly gods, and you gods of earth, and you of the lower world; I call *(ego vos)* you to witness that this people [naming whatever people it is] is unjust, and does not make just reparation. But of these matters we will take counsel of the elders in our country, how we may obtain our right. (Livy 1.32.10)

Thanksgiving and Votive Offerings

In comparison with the Israelite prayers of the Hebrew Bible and the Christian prayers reflected in the New Testament and early Christian literature, there is a relatively minor emphasis on thanksgiving in ancient Greek and Roman prayers. While prayers of thanksgiving and praise are not unknown in Greco-Roman prayers, by far the most common way of expressing thanksgiving is not by prayer but through an *ex voto* ("from a vow") offering — that is, a votive offering. Votive offerings were voluntary dedications to the gods that consisted of a great variety of objects and were placed in a shrine or temple. They were usually accompanied by an oral *euchē* or prayer, either as a prepayment for expected benefits or in thanksgiving for benefits already received.

Hymns of praise to the gods should be understood not as sung prayers, but rather as offerings or sacrifices. For a hymn of praise was considered a beautiful work of art that was offered to a god as a "smokeless sacrifice" (cf. S. Pulleyn, *Prayer in Greek Religion*, 49-55).

7. Magical Prayer

"Magical prayer" is a problematic category because it merges imperceptibly with conventional prayer. Nevertheless, magical prayer in the Greco-Roman world can be characterized by its antisocial or illegal status.

But is there a particular vocabulary associated with magical prayer? One of the interesting linguistic features is that the aorist imperative, which was used with increasing frequency during the history of the Greek language, tended to be used also more frequently in Greek conventional prayer than the present imperative. The present imperative, however, is often associated with magical prayer. In conventional prayer the present imperative is used when the speaker sees a connection between the existing situation and the action ordered or prayed for — that is, when the action is seen as a perpetual state, or as a repetition of a certain action, or as a process which must be begun now. On the other hand, the aorist imperative is used when the speaker does not see such a connection, but views the action with distance and dispassion as either an absolute fact or an abstraction. The chief difference, therefore, is the perceived presence or absence of a connection between a situation and a person's request (cf. W. F. Bakker, *The Greek Imperative*, 65-66, 98). So the "hortative" present imperative can be seen to have been used with some frequency for the category of prayer that may be designated, as Bakker has called it, "wishes arising from an existing situation" — that is, in prayers that resemble orders more than prayers. Such prayers are based on the person's attitude toward a deity, who is regarded not as a distant, invisible being, but as an assistant who helps the person in all of his or her actions (cf. *ibid.*, 113-14, 127).

One of the primary reasons why scholars have made a distinction between conventional prayer and magical prayer has to do with the rhetoric of "magical" prayer. The religious system that Jewish and Christian prayers share (at least, at a suitably abstract level) is quite different from the religious system presupposed by Greek and Roman prayers. Both Jews and Christians conceptualize God as being distant and sovereign. And they approach him as sinners who are unable to assert their rights, and so must expect everything from him. Pagan Greeks, however, conceived of the gods as being in human form and thought of them as associating with people as helpers and allies. Or as Willem Bakker points out: "The attitude [pagan Greeks] used in approaching [the gods] is often very active whereas Jew and Christian generally show themselves more dependent on the favour and grace of God. It is obvious that such a feeling of dependence practically excludes the use of the direct, urging present stem. The aorist stem, however, is extremely apposite to voicing such feelings" (*ibid.*, 138-39).

Of the two types of magical prayer to be discussed here, one type, which is attested from the fifth century BCE to the end of antiquity, is the binding curse (Greek: *katadesis*, "binding [spell]"; Latin: *defixio*, "fixing [spell]"). These curse prayers were usually written on thin pieces of lead, often pierced with a nail, and concealed in wells or graves. A typical example of such a *defixio*, which was inscribed on a tin tablet about 350-400 CE, is the following:

> To the God Nodens. Silvianus has lost a ring. He has given half of it [i.e., its value] to Nodens. Among those whose name is Senicianus, do not permit health until he brings it to the temple of Nodens. (Gager, *Curse Tablets*, 197, no. 99)

Another example of vaguer date (i.e., second century BCE to second century CE) is the following one inscribed on lead and directed to the goddess Demeter, who was one of the more important chthonic or underworld deities in Greek mythology:

> Lady Demeter, I appeal to you as one who has suffered wrongs. Hear me, goddess, and render justice, so that you bring the most terrible and painful things (on) those who think such things about us and who rejoice to-

gether against us and bring suffering on me and my wife, Epiktesis, and despise us. O Queen, lend an ear to those of us who suffer and punish those who look happily on such as us. (Gager, *Curse Tablets,* 167, no. 75)

The second major type of magical prayer is the prayer for revelation, which sometimes consists of elaborate invocations for the deity to become present. The purpose of these invocations, however, is not simply that the deity will be present at a sacrifice, but that he or she will provide divine revelation. One such prayer, with an elaborate and extended series of appeals to listen and invocations, is as follows:

O lord Apollo, come *(elthe)* with Paian.
Give answer *(chēmatison)* to my questions, lord. O master
Leave *(lipe)* Mount Parnassos and the Delphic Pytho
Whene'er my priestly lips voice secret words,
First angel of [the god], great Zeus, IAO
And you, MICHAEL, who rule heaven's realm,
I call, and you, archangel GABRIEL.
Down from Olympos, ABRASAX, delighting
In dawns, come gracious who view sunset from
The dawn, ADONAI. Father of the world,
All nature quakes in fear of you, PAKERBETH.
I adjure *(horkizō)* God's head, which is Olympos;
I adjure *(horkizō)* God's signet, which is vision;
I adjure *(horkizō)* the right hand you held o'er the world;
I adjure *(horkizō)* God's bowl containing wealth;
I adjure *(horkizō)* eternal god, AION of all;
I adjure *(horkizō)* self-growing Nature, mighty ADONAIOS;
I adjure *(horkizō)* setting and rising ELOAIS;
I adjure *(horkizō)* these holy and divine names that
They send *(pempson)* me the divine spirit and that it
Fulfill what I have in my heart and soul.
Hear *(kluthi)* blessed one, I call *(klēzō)* you who rule heav'n
And earth and Chaos and Hades where dwell
[Daimons of men who once gazed on the light].
Send *(pempson)* me this daimon at my sacred chants,
Who moves by night to orders 'neath your force,
From whose own tend this comes, and let him tell *(phrasatō)* me

39

In total truth all that my mind designs,
And send him gentle, gracious, pondering
No thoughts opposed to me. And may you not
Be angry at my sacred chants *(epaoidais)*. But guard
That my whole body come to light intact,
For you yourself arranged these things among
Mankind for them to learn. I call *(klēzō)* your name,
In number equal to the Moirai themselves,
ACHAIPHOTHOTHOAIEIAEIA
AIEAIEIAOTHOTHOPHIACHA. (*Papyri Graecae Magicae* 1.296-327)

A more literary adaptation of this magical prayer for revelation is found in Vergil's great national epic the *Aeneid:*

O gods who rule all souls! O silent shades!
Phlegethon, Chaos, regions of voiceless night!
Grant me apocalypse! Grant me right and power
to show things buried deep in earth and darkness! (*Aeneid* 6.264-67)

This prayer for revelation is followed by a "descent" *(katabasis)* to the realm of the dead, for it was through such a ritual that the magician was initiated (cf. F. Graf, *Magic in the Ancient World*, 89-117).

8. Conclusions

Within the context of a volume on prayer in the New Testament, it may be helpful to focus in this concluding section on the distinctive features of Greco-Roman prayer when compared with the traditions of prayer in the Hebrew Bible and the Greek New Testament. The basic reason for these differences is the fact that the Greco-Roman and Judeo-Christian religions represent two quite different structures. While various elements within these structures, such as prayer, may appear comparable, it is necessary to assess the role of these individual features in the whole religious structure of which they are part.

Certainly one of the most distinctive features of Greco-Roman prayer is the role played by the idea of reciprocity in the sacrificial setting of nearly all Greek prayers. For while sacrifice was as central to ancient Israel as it was to the ancient Greeks, ancient Israelites never told God that he was obligated to help them because of their past favors or sacrifices rendered to him. Nor were prayer and sacrifice virtually inseparable in the religion of Israel, as they were in the Greek world. Rather, one of the chief reasons why the God of Israel should answer prayer is because he had made certain promises in the past — of which the supplicant, in prayer, reminds him (cf. Gen. 32:12; Exod. 32:12-13). Another striking difference is that thanksgiving and praise, which characterizes the Judeo-Christian prayer tradition, is largely absent from Greco-Roman prayer. Furthermore, the Greek and Roman emphasis on invoking the presence of the deity, particularly at sacrifices, occurs only rarely in Israelite-Jewish prayers. For the God of Israel was conceptualized as being always present — just as Zeus was thought to be always present by the Greeks. The whole spectrum of Greco-Roman prayer, however, which has frequently been categorized as "magical," has little in common with the Judeo-Christian prayer tradition, even though there are occasional examples of the Jewish and Christian use of the ritual curse (e.g., 1 Cor. 16:22; Gal. 1:8-9; Rev. 22:18-19).

Selected Bibliography

Aune, David E. "Magic in Early Christianity." In *Aufstieg und Niedergang der römischen Welt,* ed. H. Temporini and W. Haase, II.23/2. Berlin: de Gruyter, 1980, 1507-57.

———. *The New Testament in Its Literary Environment.* Philadelphia: Westminster, 1987.

———. *Greco-Roman Literature and the New Testament.* Atlanta: Scholars, 1988.

———. "Greco-Roman Antecedents of Modern Secular Spirituality." In *Spirituality and the Secular Quest,* ed. P. Van Ness. New York: Crossroad, 1996, 23-52.

Bakker, Willem F. *The Greek Imperative: An Investigation into the Aspectual Differences between the Present and Aorist Imperatives in Greek Prayer from Homer up to the Present Day.* Amsterdam: Hakkert, 1966.

Burkert, Walter. *Greek Religion.* Cambridge: Harvard University Press, 1985.

Gager, John G., ed. *Curse Tablets and Binding Spells from the Ancient World.* New York: Oxford University Press, 1992.

Graf, Fritz. *Magic in the Ancient World,* trans. F. Philip. Cambridge, Mass.: Harvard University Press, 1997.

Kotansky, Roy. "Incantations and Prayers for Salvation on Inscribed Greek Amulets." In *Magika Hiera: Ancient Greek Magic and Religion,* ed. C. A. Faraone and D. Obbink. New York: Oxford University Press, 1991, 107-37.

MacLachlan, Bonnie. *The Age of Grace: Charis in Early Greek Poetry.* Princeton: Princeton University Press, 1993.

Pulleyn, Simon. *Prayer in Greek Religion.* Oxford: Clarendon, 1997.

Rouse, William H. D. *Greek Votive Offerings: An Essay in the History of Greek Religion.* Cambridge, Mass.: Harvard University Press, 1902.

Saffrey, Henri D. "The Piety and Prayers of Ordinary Men and Women in Late Antiquity." In *Classical Mediterranean Spirituality: Egyptian, Greek, Roman,* ed. A. H. Armstrong. New York: Crossroad, 1986, 195-213.

Seaford, Richard. *Reciprocity and Ritual: Homer and Tragedy in the Developing City-State.* Oxford: Clarendon, 1994.

Versnel, H. S. "Beyond Cursing: The Appeal to Justice in Judicial Prayers." In *Magika Hiera: Ancient Greek Magic and Religion,* ed. C. A. Faraone and D. Obbink. Oxford: Oxford University Press, 1991, 60-106.

————. "Ancient Prayer." In *Faith, Hope and Worship: Aspects of Religious Mentality in the Ancient World,* ed. H. S. Versnel. Leiden: Brill, 1981, 29-30.

Zaidman, Louis B., and Pauline Schmitt Pantel. *Religion in the Ancient Greek City.* Cambridge: Cambridge University Press, 1992.

CHAPTER 3

Prayer in Jewish Life of the First Century as Background to Early Christianity

ASHER FINKEL

THIS ARTICLE EXPLORES the dynamics that affected the phenomenon of prayer in the Jewish world of the first century CE, as reflected in the early sources of the Second Temple period. This seminal prayer tradition laid the foundation for the profound depths and varied aspects of prayer in the experience of Judaism. And it is this prayer tradition that was captured in the teachings of Jesus and the early Christian writings. For Jesus' ministry was conducted in the synagogues of Second Temple Judaism and culminated during a pilgrimage to the temple in Jerusalem for the Passover. He lived a life of prayer and visited the temple as God's abode. His disciples, as portrayed in the Synoptic Gospels, accompanied him as pilgrims "on the road" and celebrated the paschal meal with him prior to his arrest. Furthermore, as presented at the end of Luke's Gospel and the beginning of Acts, they continued to worship in Jerusalem and to offer prayers at the temple, utilizing in their worship traditional Jewish prayers and biblical readings for their understanding of their teacher's ministry.

PART I. THE WORSHIP OF GOD

1. Worship in a Theocratic Society: Avodah

Simeon "the Just," the high priest and head of the Jewish state in the second century BCE, described the theocratic system of Jewish government as follows:

> Upon three foundations the world rests: upon the Torah [the Pentateuch], upon *avodah* [the service and worship of God], and upon acts of *hesed* [loving kindness]. (*Mishnah Aboth* 1:2)

The religio-political governmental system of the Jews during the Second Temple period is depicted by Josephus as a "theocracy" *(theokratia)*, or a system of government that locates "all sovereignty and authority in the hands of God" (*Against Apion* 2.165).

Torah is the constitution of Jewish society. It was formally accepted as constitutive by the founding representatives of the people during the days of Ezra and Nehemiah (cf. Neh. 10:1-39). And while prior to the Great Destruction of 70 CE there emerged various religious groups among the people, all Jews of whatever party or sect enjoyed a common commitment to the Torah and the Prophets, whatever their differences of interpretation and practice.

Torah served as the legal code that governed the people's life *(halakah)*. But Torah also offered paradigmatic stories *(haggadah)* about how God appeared to the patriarchs and Moses in acts of *hesed*. Jews sought to emulate these acts of loving kindness in their lives and society. *Imitatio Dei*, which means the imitation of God or "walking in God's ways," established an absolutist view of altruistic ethics — that is, of an ethic focused on ways of love and *shalom* ("wholesomeness") in human relations. The Torah was read and preached; it was studied and revered. Its laws and values were codified to guide the socio-political order. As stated in Prov. 3:17: "All the paths of Torah lead to *shalom*." Therefore, all areas of human relationship are to be governed for God's people by the Torah: the transpersonal (between God and human beings), the interpersonal (between one person and another person), the intrapersonal (between persons and their own selves), and the subpersonal (between persons and nature).

44

Shalom is the goal of life lived according to the Torah, and it is meant to guide all legislative enactments. *Hesed,* or loving kindness, is reflected in the "thirteen attributes of love" as the way of God, as set out in Exod. 34:6-7a:

> The Lord passed in front of Moses and proclaimed: "The Lord, the Lord, the compassionate and gracious God, slow to anger, abounding in loving kindness [*hesed*] and faithfulness, maintaining loving kindness [*hesed*] to thousands, and forgiving wickedness, rebellion and sin, while he cleanses."

Hesed thereby opens the door to God's redemptive atonement for human error and sin. And in this context of Torah and *hesed,* a theocratic life of worship is intrinsically related to both ethics and education. Consequently, *avodah,* or the service and worship of God, is a transpersonal engagement that affects all of the other areas of human relations as well. So biblically-oriented Jews experience worship *(avodah)* in God's presence as they enter the heavenly kingdom in the acceptance of God's ultimate authority in their lives via God's Torah and *hesed.*

Paul refers to *avodah* in Rom. 9:4-5a, where he lists as the fifth gift among the seven divine gifts given to the people of Israel: "theirs is *the worship"* (v. 4, *hē latreia*). Biblical worship is antithetical to nature worship, which is polytheistic. The God of Israel is transcendental. He is the creator of nature with its multifaceted powers. The human creature, therefore, can approach God only in meekness as a creature. One cannot petition or coerce God for personal gratification, for God is the creator of all that exists in the vast universe. In polytheistic worship one seeks to placate or coerce the gods of nature so that they will do one's own bidding, which relates to magic. Biblical faith, however, rejects this approach as useless. It rests its worship on the purity of one's heart or intention and on one's deep sense of creatureliness. The biblically-oriented person can only approach the Creator by permission in praise and gratefulness, not with a demand but in hope of being granted a gift.

The Bible, therefore, offers key stories and detailed manuals on how to serve God, with prayer formulations incorporated from various religious persons. The gift of "worship" *(latreia)* relates dynamically to the other six gifts that Paul mentions in Rom. 9:4-5a, with those other gifts, conversely, shedding light on the special meaning of *avodah.* From a human perspective, the gift of "sonship" (Greek: *huiothesia* ; Hebrew: *banim*) is most significant, for it speaks of the attitude of a child in meeting the heavenly Father in the act of prayer. From God's perspective, however, the gift of "glory" (Greek: *doxa;* Hebrew: *kabhod*) represents how the divine presence revealed God's thirteen attributes of love to Moses (cf. Exod. 33:18, "Show me your glory," which is to be related to the thirteen attributes of Exod. 34:6-7). Only in this manner can the act of penitential prayer signify a "return" (Hebrew: *teshuvah*) to the unique God of Israel.

So the prodigal son of Jesus' parable in Luke 15:11-32, who returned to the love of his father, reflects a model of Jewish prayer. And it is from such a phenomenological understanding that one can examine the types of *avodah* and ways to God in Judaism as a backdrop to the experience of prayer in the teachings of Jesus and the early Christian church.

2. Sacrificial and Verbal Services: Temple and Synagogue

Avodah represents two distinct forms of the service and worship of God: (1) the sacrificial, which was expressed in the Jerusalem temple, and (2) the verbal, which came to expression mainly in the synagogues. Both of these forms highlight a temporal-spatial setting for "the holy" (Hebrew: *qadosh,* which signifies "set-apartness") in the dimension of human awareness. The temple was the holy abode of God's presence in Jerusalem, where the service was conducted by Levites and priests who followed a strict discipline of purity and holiness. Alongside temple worship, however, there also existed since the time of the Exile communal gatherings for prayer and Torah reading. Jews gathered in cities, towns, and villages, whether in market places or public buildings, for liturgical purposes. Such a gathering was called in Greek a *sunagōgē* or synagogue (Aramaic: *kenishta;* Hebrew: *mo'ade-'el;* cf. Ps. 74:8). Early literary sources and archaeological findings attest to the parallel existence of the temple and the synagogue in the Second Temple period.

Nehemiah 8:1-12 relates how the people, both "men and women and all who were able to understand," gathered "on the first day of the seventh month" at the Temple Mount in Jerusalem, which was adjacent to the temple, from daybreak until noon of the New Year day *(Rosh Hashshanah)* to participate in the verbal service. The Torah lection pertaining to that holiday was read and translated, interpreted and preached, being accompanied by a blessing and communal refrain. Then the people returned in joy to their homes to partake of a festival meal. Here in Nehemiah's account of the people assembling to participate in a verbal *avodah* is the earliest portrayal of a Jewish synagogal gathering, where God's words were read and the community prayed — and where the dictates of the day following the service, as recorded in Neh. 8:13-18, were fulfilled. The focus was on the Torah scroll, which contained God's name. And Ezra blessed the "Great Name," which was reverently acknowledged by the assembly with the response "Amen" and prostration.

Likewise "on the first day of the seventh month," after rebuilding the temple in Jerusalem, the priests carried on a sacrificial service at the temple's altar, as prescribed in Num. 29:1-6. This service was accompanied by levitical singing and instrumental music. It is called in Num. 4:47 an *avodah* (that is, a "priestly service"). The priest's performance in God's presence produced an awesome drama of symbolic meaning that was to be seen "by the assembled pilgrims three times a year" (Deut. 16:16).

Jewish pilgrims prepared themselves for the sacrificial *avodah* through their experiences "on the road" to Jerusalem. They set aside all the activities of their secular lives in order to enter the sacred site of the temple. Prayers and refrains were then said by the crowds in the temple courts. At the end of the service the Aaronic blessing of Num. 6:24-26 was offered by the priests:

> *The Lord* (YHWH) bless you and keep you.
> *The Lord* (YHWH) make his face to shine upon you, and be gracious to you.
> *The Lord* (YHWH) lift up his countenance upon you, and give you peace.

The highlight of the service was the pronouncement of the unspoken name of God, the "tetragrammaton" (i.e., the four sacred letters YHWH), which is repeated three times in the Aaronic benediction. And on hearing the tetragrammaton thrice-repeated, the crowds fell and hid their faces as a reverential act in the presence of the holy and they recited a doxological proclamation of God's kingdom.

Both the sacrificial service of the temple and the verbal services in the synagogues focused on God's presence as revealed in his name. The service itself was offered "in God's name" and had to be endowed by a proper intention. A priest could invalidate the sacrificial service by an improper intent. In the same way, a verbal service was not true prayer if the words spoken were not in harmony with the person's inner thought. "Prayer without intention (Hebrew: *kawannah*)," as the rabbis later said, "is like a body without a soul." In tannaitic lore, prayer represents *avodah* of the heart.

Kawannah in Jewish thought consists of three parts: *the person* who faces *God* with *a service.* Prayer represents the hyphen between the person and God in the verbal service. The service is rendered with "purity of the heart" when the inner self is in unison with the words spoken — that is, when the words are directed by true intent.

Prayer among Jews consists of (1) a proper address, (2) words of praise at the beginning, (3) words of thanks at the end, and (4) personal petitions of need and penance, hope or despair, which are inserted in the middle. On sacred days the particular experience being commemorated is introduced into the middle. Coined phrases drawn from the Scriptures, which were formulated by the prophets or priests of the past, are used. In addition, certain addresses and prayers of contemporary charismatic teachers are sometimes acknowledged as being appropriate for public usage.

The liturgy of the Jerusalem temple was collected and kept in the biblical psalms, where musical notations are still to be found and antiphonal or doxological refrains have been retained. The use of instruments to accompany the choral singing is referred to in Ps. 150:3-5. The Dead Sea scroll of the psalms also shows us, in particular, how the Psalter was used. Certain psalms were chanted on particular days, during the festivals, and at some sacrificial services.

The services of the Levites and priests, which were carried out in accordance with the Torah manuals, produced an awesome impact on pilgrims worshiping at the temple. The Levites and priests acted as the people's agents before God, with their actions being symbolic representations on behalf of the people. In their worship, the Levites and priests — by means of oracular gazing and paradoxical wonderment — seem to have experienced a mystical connection with angelic hymnology and enjoyed a spiritual sense of being in correspondence with the heavenly hosts. And as was the case with the covenanters of the Dead Sea community, who also followed a strict discipline of purity and holiness, the Levites and priests of the Jerusalem temple were trained from childhood in the proper use of intent, lived a secluded and strict life, and properly pronounced God's name in the Aaronic blessing.

The liturgy of the people was developed by the scribes, who first appeared in the company of Ezra and Nehemiah as members of "the Great Assembly." It was the scribes who determined the proper forms of address in prayer and who fixed the key phrases having to do with creation, revelation, and redemption, as drawn from passages in the Torah. In addition, they established the proper order for the verbal services. This same council was responsible for the careful transmission of the sacred text for public reading. Under Ezra, however, the scribes produced a significant change in the use of the Assyrian script for the canonical text. A cycle of sabbatical and festival readings emerged in connection with the calendar of the temple and the synagogues, with particular selections — such as the Shema, which is recited twice daily — being designated for both the temple and the synagogue services.

In this manner, the scribes restored the Torah and the Prophets to the center of Jewish life during the Second Temple period. Furthermore, they democratized the service in the Jerusalem temple by their introduction of the *Ma'amadot,* which were weekly "stations" consisting of representative Israelites gathered from various towns and villages to stand watch over the sacrificial services of the priests. It was through their influence that the synagogal tradition of prayer begins with *Ma'amadot* gatherings in a market place for the public reading of the Torah and public prayers. These representatives fasted and offered intercessory prayers for the sick and needy of their communities, which they did as acts of *hesed.*

3. The Ways of Awe and Love in God's Service

The Torah describes *avodah* in two ways: the way of awe and the way of love. Both ways are prescriptively set forth in Scripture and tradition for the worship and service of God.

The Way of Awe

Deuteronomy 6:13 states: "You shall have awe of the Lord your God and you shall serve him." Service, therefore, is rooted in an awe experience of the *mysterium tremendum.* One stands as a creature before the majestic, transcendental Creator with the sense of "I am nothing but dust and ashes" (Gen. 18:27). The person perceives himself in prayer as a "servant" (*'eved*), a human subject doing God's will. The scribal phraseology of this attitude is captured in the opening and/or closing words of petitionary prayer: "*Let it be thy will, O Heavenly Father.*" So also Jesus at Gethsemane: "Abba, Father . . . *not what I will, but what you will*" (Mark 14:36; Luke 22:42). Furthermore, the Pharisees adopted the formula *baruch* ("blessed be") to introduce all prayer petitions. For the Hebrew passive "blessed be" signifies that God is the ground or source of all blessings. It also captures the related word *berech* ("knee") to express how we face God in the act of kneeling as creatures in his service.

The way of awe was experienced in the Jerusalem temple as Jews acknowledged God at the beginning of the year (cf. *Mishnah Rosh Hashshanah* 4:5). "Coronation" texts from the Torah, the Prophets, and the Psalms were proclaimed as human subjects faced the Creator. These texts were then followed by "remembrance" texts from the tripartite canon to recall how Israel had enjoyed God's providence through his revelatory acts. Finally, the "shofar" ("horn blast") texts were recited to celebrate the significant redemptive occasions in the nation's history. These three sets of texts related to the theological construct of biblical thought that perceived God as Creator, Provider, and Redeemer, and so a theistic awareness was deepened for both pilgrims at the temple and worshipers in the synagogues.

Jewish pilgrims entered into the arena of the sacred as they witnessed a priestly procession at sunrise on each of the festival days. This procession was, in actuality, a march that protested against idolatry. As the priests moved from the Eastern Gate to the temple, the Holy Sanctuary, they turned away from the rising sun, which was the focus of Roman heliocentric worship. They faced west toward the Holy of Holies, proclaiming, "Our forefathers worshipped the sun, but we worship the Lord and our eyes are focused only on him" (*Mishnah Sukkah* 5:4).

Biblical faith, therefore, is a religion that protests against all forms of mythopoeic thought and astral worship. *Avodah* in the temple was, in fact, a symbolic protest against every kind of religion that was based on fears of natural forces and human powers. Instead, it generated a transformative knowledge of the transcendental God and evoked inner dread and a sense of awe before the Ultimate Reality.

This is why the Gospel of Matthew juxtaposes the last scene of the Temptation story (4:8-11) with the beginning of Jesus' ministry in Galilee

(4:12-17). For in the last scene of confrontation between Jesus and the devil, Jesus cites Deut. 6:13 ("Worship the Lord your God; *serve him only!*") as a denial of the words of Satan, who had shown him the glory of the world's power. In Jesus' days, the world's power was represented by the Roman empire with its heliocentric worship. In the Matthean text, however, the deuteronomic and scribal liturgical formulation — "Worship the Lord your God; *serve him only!*" — lays stress on the uniqueness of God in Jewish worship. In this manner, a new "light has dawned" for the Gentiles in Galilee to receive Jesus' proclamation: "Repent, for the kingdom of heaven is at hand." The focus is on a transcendental ultimate authority.

The Way of Love

Avodah of the heart is introduced in Deut. 11:13, where it is said that to obey God's commands faithfully is "to love the Lord your God and to serve him with all your heart and with all your soul." True prayer expresses love for God. It results from a paradoxical mixture of inner joy mingled with trembling (cf. Ps. 2:12). Such an experience reflects the *mysterium tremendum et fascinans* that Rudolph Otto spoke about in describing the numinous event of humanity's highest relations with the Divine.

True prayer generates a yearning love for God's elusive presence. The way of awe evokes the response of a servant who is subject to the almighty King. The way of love, however, results in childlike response to a merciful Father in heaven. Both sobriquets for God's name — that is, "King" and "Father" — appear in Jewish prayers. Jesus in the Gospels is presented as building on this attitudinal difference, reserving for his disciples the way of love with its appeal to God as *Abba,* that is, "Father."

PART II. THE EXPERIENCE OF PRAYER

4. God's Name: Focus and Address

God's name cannot be pronounced by an individual, for it is "set apart" and hidden. This phenomenon represents a transcendental reality. The four letters of the tetragrammaton (YHWH) produce theistic meanings: "the One who causes all to be," that is, the Creator; and "the One who exists in all situations," that is, the Provider. They also connote that God is beyond all time and space — that he is "the One who is, was, and will be." Furthermore, God's being is unknown. He is beyond all human thought and affection. Great care, therefore, is given by Jews to pronounce the full name of God with all of its connotations.

In the early Jewish mystical tradition, the tetragrammaton enjoyed seventy-two permutations of vocalized words. Oracular insight could be gained from the way one gazed on — and received on the screen of one's mind the impression of — God's name. Such knowledge was related to the particular readings that the priest received when he viewed the illuminated letters on the twelve precious stones of the Urim and Thummim (i.e., "Lights" and "Completions"), which were on his breast plate. Such an interpretative approach to Scripture, it seems, governed the priestly exegesis.

Public use of God's name was limited to the sobriquets "King" and "Father." The four letters YHWH were substituted by the vocalized term "the Lord" (Hebrew *Adonay;* Greek *Kyrios*). Prayers were addressed to "the Lord (YHWH) our God *(Elohim),*" with each name receiving a sobriquet — that is, *YHWH* representing the attribute of love (related to "Father"); *Elohim* representing the attribute of judgment (related to "King").

Jesus, who instructed those who would follow him to be like children, taught his disciples to address God as "Father" *(Abba).* The appellative "Father" is also found in Jewish prayers, particularly when one seeks forgiveness from the Lord or prays out of despair in time of crisis — as in Isaiah's prayer (Isa. 63:16), Ben Sira's prayer (*Sirach* or *Ecclesiasticus* 51:10), and the petition for forgiveness in the *Amidah* (petition 6).

Jews begin the *Amidah,* the major prayer of the synagogue, with the words "O Lord, our God" *(YHWH Elohenu).* The first formulation of praise and prayer in the *Amidah* describes God in terms of his love: God is the God of the patriarchs, "who shows his mercy to them and their descendants." The second formulation focuses on God, who, through his creative powers *(dunamis),* sustains all life, heals, and provides the final act of resurrection. In this second formulation there is attested the Pharisees' belief in life after death, as described by Josephus and as testified to by the tannaitic rabbis. Since the Creator can heal, he can also restore to life: "See now that I myself am he! There is no god besides me. I put to death and I bring to life; I have wounded and I will heal" (Deut. 32:39). Jesus, too, taught his disciples to relate to God as Father when they appealed to his mercy and sought his forgiveness. Yet he also — as is true in Jewish practice as well — associated God's power *(dunamis)* with resurrection (cf. Matt. 22:29-30) as well as with physical healing (cf. Mark 5:30).

5. Pilgrimages and Festivals: The Passover in the Days of Jesus

Deuteronomy 31:10-13 records God's words to the people to gather "at the end of every seven years, at the set time of the year of release, at the feast of booths . . . at the place which he [God] will choose . . . in order to hear [the Torah] and learn how to revere the Lord your God, and to observe all the words of this law." Central to the sabbatical year gathering was a pilgrimage, which is commanded in verse 12: "Assemble the people — men, women and children; also the alien-residents [the converts] who are living in your towns."

Pilgrimage transforms people "on the road" into a cohesive, holy, religious body. It was practiced by multitudes of Jews from near and far, especially for the Passover celebration at Jerusalem, in accordance with the biblical mandate: "Three times a year shall your males be seen by the Lord your God at the place that he [the Lord] will choose" (Deut. 16:16). The expression "the place that he will choose" of Deut. 16:16 and 31:11 refers to Jerusalem. "The place" also designates the temple in Jerusalem, which was located on Mount Moriah (cf. Acts 6:13-14). Paschal celebration requires that the paschal lamb be eaten in Jerusalem. As sacrificial or "sacred" food, it cannot be eaten anywhere else but in Jerusalem.

Jesus lived in a socioeconomic order governed by a religious calendar that determined for every individual the proper times for the celebration of the sabbath and the celebration of the festivals. It also determined for the nation the proper times for celebrating the sabbatical years and the year of Jubilee. Such sacred or "set-apart" time is distinct from secular time, for it offers an opportunity to relate to God's presence affectively — that is, it invites both the individual during the week and the entire society during the septennial year to pass into "serenity and peacefulness" by a release from the usual material and physical order, which is filled with work, stress, and anxiety. Such is the invitation of the sabbath day and the significance of the sabbatical year. No wonder the great pilgrimage to Jerusalem occurred in the fall, after the sabbatical year was completed.

Annual pilgrimages and the great pilgrimage were oriented toward a sacred space and enjoyed by means of a passage into sacred time. It was an experience that transformed the individual, for by it human awareness was deepened through a qualitative change that affected everything in a person's life. Pilgrimage, of course, generated a religious vocabulary associated with time and space. Such time-space language, however, should not be read as merely geographical or directional language, but as language symbolizing spiritual significance. Thus the fifteen "Songs of Ascent" of Psalms 120–134 depict the movement of pilgrims from their homes, family, and properties toward the temple at Jerusalem. The term "ascent," or "going up," signifies "elevation," which the pilgrims enjoyed as they experienced *shalom* ("wholesomeness") — that is, trust in God, equality and fellowship with others, and acts of loving kindness — and as they gained a sense of redemption. This experience, which was transformational, prepared the pilgrims to enter the discipline of purity and holiness at the Jerusalem temple and to share in the sacred meal of the temple sacrifice with their families or particular groups.

The last part of Jesus' ministry is portrayed in the Synoptic Gospels as commencing with Jesus and his disciples on the road "going up to Jerusalem" (Mark 10:32; Matt. 20:17; Luke 18:31a) — with such a depiction of "going up" (i.e., pilgrimage) introducing Jesus' third prediction of his death and resurrection (Mark 10:33-34; Matt. 20:18-19; Luke 18:31b-33). The intention of all three of the evangelists, it seems, was to link Jesus' pilgrimage experience to the kerygmatic meaning of his coming. For the early Christian tradition saw Jesus typologically as the "holy abode" of the temple (cf. the use of "temple," היכל or ναός, for Jesus' body in John 2:21-22) and as the ground of serenity (cf. Matt. 11:28-30). Furthermore, the discipline of pilgrimage (cf. *Mishnah Berakot* 9:5) guided Jesus' disciples as they carried out their ministries on their "road of mission," just as their teacher had instructed them (cf. Mark 6:8-9; Matt. 10:9-10; Luke 9:3). And it was also such vectors of time and space in relation to the holy that affected the earliest disciples of Jesus in their understanding of his person, for he is depicted as a paschal lamb in early Christian writings as well as in early Christian preaching (cf., e.g., Melito of Sardis's *Homily on the Passion*).

In setting out a Christian calendar of Holy Week, Mark's Gospel presents three pilgrimage scenes. The first is in Mark 11:9, which portrays Jesus' entry into Jerusalem on Palm Sunday. This scene reflects how pilgrims were received by the Jerusalemites: they were welcomed by the residents of the city with the psalmic song, "We bless you in the name of the Lord" (Ps. 129:8b), which was preceded by the acclamation "Hosanna" (Ps.

118:25-26). The second scene is in Mark 13:1-3, which describes how Jesus and his disciples engaged in the circumambulatory experience of pilgrims, who would walk around and view the sacred buildings of the Jerusalem temple. They entered from the South Gate of the Temple Mount, whose stairway has recently been excavated, and then left through the Eastern Gate, which led down to Gethsemane. In this act of marching around the sacred precincts they acknowledged the majestic presence of God in the temple, as parabolically depicted by Jesus in his lament, "Like a hen who gathers her brood under her wings" (Matt. 23:37//Luke 13:34).

This circumambulatory experience of pilgrims is portrayed in Ps. 48:12-15, where it produces a lasting impression of beauty and grandeur:

> Walk about Zion and go round about her;
>   count her towers.
> Consider well her ramparts;
>   view her citadels.
> That you may tell it until the final generations.
> For this is overwhelming!
> Our God exists forever,
>   and he will lead us beyond death.

After leaving the city through the Eastern Gate and passing over to Gethsemane, Jesus used the occasion of walking about the temple precincts with his disciples to predict the imminent destruction of Jerusalem and to offer his teaching about the End (cf. Mark 13:3ff.; Matt. 24:3ff.; Luke 21:7ff.).

The third pilgrimage scene is in Mark 14:12-16, which portrays the preparations made on the eve of Passover for the celebration of the Passover. The paschal lambs were slaughtered in the temple and then taken by those living in Jerusalem to their homes to be eaten, with the quantity of meat taken regulated by the number of participants expected to be at the meal. Jerusalemites extended invitations to all pilgrims to use the upper chambers of their homes for their celebrations of the paschal meal. So Jesus, who from his early youth had often visited Jerusalem during Passover with his parents (cf. Luke 2:41-42), knew what to expect and how to select the particular house where he might eat the Passover with his disciples. He was looking for a person who kept the strict rule of purity in his quarters — that is, "a man carrying a jar full of water." There in the man's upper room his disciples ate the paschal lamb, but he declined (cf. Luke 22:15). Rather, he offered his disciples wine and bread, which were symbolic prospects of God's kingdom: symbolic representations of the "sacred" always governed the sacrificial tradition.

Eucharistic worship in the early church as "anaphora" (i.e., an "offering," see Ps. 50 [51]:21 LXX) relates the significance of the items to "epiclesis" (i.e., the bestowal of the Holy Spirit). Sacrificial items in the temple, being holy, were "set apart" by an appeal to the Spirit. So the eucharistic celebrations of the early church reflect the temple tradition of prayer — though in a new christological form. For at the Last Supper Jesus offered his disciples a new symbolic meaning: "Do this in remembrance of me" (Luke 22:19). Among Jews, the sacred meal of Passover relates the story of the Exodus and invites participants to reenter the experience of that initial generation in sensing God's redemption. For the disciples of Jesus and Christians generally, however, the symbols of the meal now point to Jesus, who provides the invitation to redemptive transformation.

Most significantly, Jesus concluded the Last Supper by chanting the Hallel ("praise") psalms — that is, Psalms 113-118, which Mark 14:26 and Matt. 26:30 refer to as "the Hymn." Psalms 113–114 reflect the redemptive experience of Israel in the past and were sung before partaking of the meal, with a designated "wine-cup of salvation" being also present. Psalms 115–118 were sung after the meal as a psycho-dramatic reading, with both the head of the family or group and those at the meal participating. The *pater familias* ("father of the family") assumed the role of the Messiah while chanting Psalm 116 — which relates the Messiah's love for God (vv. 1-2), his suffering ending in death (v. 3), but expresses, as well, confidence in God (vv. 5-8) and holds out the prospect that "I shall walk before God's presence in the land of the living" (v. 9). The psalm also relates how the Messiah's death is perceived by God — that is, as the passing of the pious one *(hasid)*, God's "servant, the son of your [God's] maidservant" (v. 16). In the early memory of his disciples, Jesus identified himself as "the son of Mary." This was in addition to his words of symbolic identification at the Last Supper, which the early church took to be the institution of the Eucharist offering — that is, the *todah* offering of v. 17a, "I will sacrifice a thank offering to you."

Psalm 118, the last of the Hallel psalms, has antiphonal readings, which were used by the participants at the Last Supper, who played the roles of the companions of the Messiah. Especially significant is verse 22, which Jesus recited at the table: "The stone that the builders despised has became the chief corner-stone." This verse was introduced by the evangelists into their Gospels to explain the delivery of Jesus by the priests and scribes to the Roman procurator (cf. Mark 12:10; Matt. 21:42; Luke 20:17). Likewise, the companions of Jesus recalled how perplexed they were at the time of his arrest — that they ran away, that Peter denied him, and that they were not present at the crucifixion. They also recalled how they responded to Jesus when he spoke of "the stone," using the refrain of Ps. 118:23: "It happened so from the Lord and it is astonishing in our eyes."

All of this led Jesus' disciples after his crucifixion to seek from their canonical Scriptures an understanding of their "wonderment." And this scriptural search led them to the Song of the Suffering Servant of Isa. 52:13–53:12, where the servant is depicted as "causing astonishment to the many" (52:14-15) and the question is asked: "Who can believe what God has unveiled?" (53:1). Such a kerygmatic view of Jesus' death was, therefore, based on Scriptures that speak of sacrificial atonement (cf. Mark 10:45; 1 Cor. 15:3).

6. Public Readings and Daily Recitations

Since the days of Ezra, the canonical text of Scripture was read and preached. The focus of the Torah, which was viewed as a "set-apart" book, was perceived to be the covenant that God made with Israel in the days of Moses. Torah, therefore, became the guiding constitution that affected all of the educational, legislative, and judicial institutions of the Jewish nation. In the elementary schools children learned to read and write Hebrew, the "set-apart" language of Torah. Such a school was called a "House of the Book." A higher school of learning became known as a "House of Midrash" (i.e., "interpretation of the Book"). In the synagogues a Torah scroll was placed in an ark, whether on wheels or in a fixed niche, and it became the focus of Jewish worship.

Public Readings

Torah was read publicly in the synagogues every sabbath and at festivals, in addition to every Monday and Thursday during the week. The congregational experience was by means of hearing God's words, which were correctly and affectively rendered for proper reception. The written text of Scripture contains only consonants. Therefore the text needed to be vocalized and punctuated, with particular stresses and pauses in the reading. An oral tradition — originally, the *Massorah* — fixed the meaning of the biblical texts for the hearers. The community came to hear and receive the words of God, which came to them through the canonical Torah and Prophets and by means of correlative interpretations.

Torah represents the tradition of the past, which was received by Moses, the greatest prophet. The Prophets represent words describing the future, as transmitted until the Persian period. A reading in the synagogues of a Torah lection, which presents the covenant of a correlative past, was followed by a reading of the Prophets, which held the promise of the future. Such public readings affected the people's lives here and now. Their conviction was expressed in the prayer that concludes the public reading: "The words of God are true and righteous, . . . their prospect will be fulfilled, . . . none of the words of the past will become void."

The people's trust in and commitment to the Lord God was displayed in their hearing the words of Torah. But their trust and commitment was also fortified by public preaching. Didactic preaching prescribed a way of life of both praxis and faith, while proemic preaching sought to demonstrate scriptural fulfillment in the people's historical setting. The latter form of preaching proclaimed "good news" for communal hearing, especially when it was correlated with particular persons and events. Such preaching, in fact, promoted a consciousness of eschatological reality — as witness, for example, the *pesher* commentaries of the Qumran community.

The preaching of Jesus and his followers embraced this latter approach to scriptural preaching. According to Papias, as recorded by Eusebius (*Ecclesiastical History* III.39), the Gospel of Mark was based on the preaching of Peter in the synagogues, which preaching would have followed the sabbath and festival readings. Mark himself, according to Papias (cf. Eusebius, *Ecclesiastical History* II.15), was a *Meturgemman* or "public translator-orator" (Greek *hermēneutēs*). No wonder, then, that Mark's Gospel opens in 1:2-3 with a collating of a text from the Torah (Exod. 23:20a, "Behold, I am sending my angel before you to protect you on the road") and a text from the Prophets (Isa. 40:3, "A voice crying in the wilderness, clear the way of the Lord"). Such a collation of biblical texts was the mark of proemic preaching. And it was in this manner that Mark, at the beginning of his work, linked his "good news" (*euangelion*, "gospel") to the Jewish canon.

Luke 4:16-21 portrays a synagogal setting for the initial proclamation of Jesus to his people at Nazareth. In the synagogue at Nazareth he was called on to conclude a reading from the Pentateuch with a prophetic portion from Isaiah 61 that began with the words: "The Spirit of the Lord God is upon me" (v. 18). And, according to Luke's depiction of this event, Jesus inserted the words of a Torah lection into his proemic preaching — that is, he explicated the purpose of his proclamation of "a favorable year of the Lord" by reference to the sabbatical teaching of Lev. 25:10a, "to proclaim liberty on the land to all inhabitants" (v. 19). In so doing, he was proclaiming the kingdom of God as a sabbatical fulfillment for the people. Furthermore, by saying "Today this Scripture is fulfilled in your hearing" (v. 21) — which statement captures the essence of his preaching — Jesus used a *pesher* interpretation of the Scriptures in formulating the agenda of his ministry.

Daily Recitations

In addition to public readings of Scripture, four Torah selections were used by the Jewish worshiping community as didactic forms of prayer — with all adult Jews commanded to repeat these texts both morning and evening, thereby bracketing their waking day by the principal teachings of the Torah. The four passages to be recited daily from the Torah are (1) the Decalogue of Deut. 5:1-21, (2) the Shema of Deut. 6:4-9, (3) the portion on Rewards and Punishments of Deut. 11:13-21, and (4) the concluding lection of Num. 15:32-41 (cf. *Mishnah Tamid* 4:3 [end]–5:1). The recitation opened and closed with the signature, "I am the Lord your God." This is the nuptial formulation of God's covenant, which captures in prophetic thought the marital form of the covenant (cf. Hos. 2:4, whose wording was the original form for the dissolution of a marriage). Daily recitation reaffirms the covenantal experience of the people's forefathers (cf. Exod. 19:6; see also Deut. 5:3 and 29:12). In this manner Jews perform the act of receiving God's kingdom and God's commandments into their lives (cf. *Mishnah Berakoth* 2:2).

The significance of this practice of a daily recitation of these four Torah passages, which were to be recited both in the home and in the synagogue, is to be seen by the way that the practice entered the daily sacrificial service of the Levites and priests in the Jerusalem temple. For the sacrificial service in the temple came to be interrupted by this recitation, which was performed away from the altar — that is, in the lower chamber of the Hewn Stones, where the Supreme Court of Israel sat in session. The Decalogue of Deut. 5:1-21 was recited to portray how the laws of God govern all areas of human relationship. The Shema of Deut. 6:4-9 declared that ultimate authority rests in the transcendental God of Israel. The reciter accepted such a relationship to God in love as he welcomed the kingdom affectively in his life. The other two selections of Deut. 11:13-21 and Num. 15:32-41 highlight a believer's awareness of eternal rewards and punishments by one's choice of action — and of how one can trigger God's awareness by the use of blue fringes on his garment as a mantra.

Luke's Gospel presents the case of a Jewish scribe who once asked Jesus: "Teacher, what shall I do to inherit eternal life?" (10:25). In reply, Jesus appealed to the daily recitation of the Shema and the Decalogue: "What is written in the Torah and how do you recite?" (10:26). The scribe answered by first quoting the words of Deut. 6:5, "You shall love the Lord your God with all your heart, and with all your soul, and with all your might" — which are the opening words of the Shema — and then he continued with the Decalogue of Deut. 5:1-21, which concludes with the words "your neighbor as yourself." The citing of familiar texts by reference to the opening and closing words of those texts, with the intent that those texts be understood in full, was common in the world of Judaism. Jesus confirmed that the scribe's recitation held the key to a person's right praxis and eternal reward by his reply: "You have answered correctly. Do this and you will live" (10:28).

In Mark 12:28-34, in response to Jesus' summation of the commandments as being "to love God" and "to love one's neighbor" (vv. 29-31), a scribe is presented as answering in a manner reminiscent of Hillel, the great Jewish rabbi:

> Well said, teacher. You are right in saying that God is one and there is no other but him. To love him with all your heart, with all your understanding and with all your strength, and to love your neighbor as yourself is more important than all burnt offerings and sacrifice. (vv. 32-33)

The transpersonal (i.e., relations between God and human beings) in Judaism is to be conditioned by the interpersonal (i.e., relations between one person and another person), with acts of loving kindness taking priority in the fulfillment of one's transpersonal obligation of pilgrimage.

A particularly interesting illustration of this principle of interpersonal acts of loving kindness taking priority in fulfilling one's transpersonal obligations is to be found in the parable of the Good Samaritan in Luke 10:29-37. In that parable, even a Samaritan, who was "on the road" to fulfill his own transpersonal obligation of pilgrimage to the city of Shechem, breaks the levitical rule of purity to take care of a seemingly dead body, even though such an interpersonal act of kindness would contaminate him.

In Mark 12:33 the Jewish scribe adds: "To love your neighbor as yourself is more important than all burnt offerings and sacrifice." In so doing he echoes Hos. 6:6, "For I desire mercy, not sacrifice, and the acknowledgment of God rather than burnt offerings." Rabban Yochanan ben Zakkai, a disciple of Hillel, applied this passage to the situation of the Jewish people after the destruction of Jerusalem, and so is understood by some to have changed and revolutionized Judaism after the destruction of Judaism by laying stress on the ethical significance of synagogal prayer over the atoning, sacrificial service of the temple. It was not Yochanan ben Zakkai, however, who first used Hos. 6:6 in this manner, as has been claimed by Jacob Neusner (cf. his *Rabban Yochanan* [Leiden: Brill, 1970]). The testimony of Mark 12:33b-34a — both in the statement of the scribe and the response of Jesus — is a clear pre-destruction witness that reveals how the Shema was understood by pre-destruction Hillelites, with whom Jesus seems to have agreed (as I have pointed out in my *The Pharisees and the Teacher of Nazareth* [Leiden: Brill, 1972]).

7. Long and Brief Prayers: The Order of Petitions

Daily prayer during the period of Second Temple Judaism consisted of a chain of petitions, with each petition focused on a particular theme and preceded by the opening formula "Blessed art Thou, O Lord." Psalm 136, which is called "the Great Hallel Psalm," consists of twenty-six petitions, with each petition sealed by the repetitive phrase "The whole world is full of his mercy" (my trans.). Likewise *Sirach* (or, *Ecclesiasticus*) 51:12, in an extended verse existing only in Hebrew, sets out a chain of sixteen petitions — most of which begin with an opening formula that expresses thanksgiving to God and conclude with a repeated phrase that extols his mercy (most often, "For his mercy endures for ever"). Furthermore, each of the sixteen petitions of

61

Sirach 51:12 echoes a construct of Pharisaic daily prayer, which constructs became fixed at the Hillelian academy of Yavneh (or Jabneh; Greek: Jamnia) toward the end of the first century CE.

The order of daily prayer was standardized in the eighteen petitions of the *Shemoneh Esreh:* (1) three petitions at the beginning expressing praise; (2) three petitions at the end offering thanksgiving; and (3) the middle part consisting of six existential petitions followed by six formulations of eschatological expectation. This order reflects the way of prayer in synagogal worship while standing (thus the name *Amidah,* which means "standing") before God. It opens with an address to God that recalls his redemptive dealings with the *patriarchs,* which is followed by an address to God the Creator in terms of his *powers.* It closes with an address to the *thrice holy* or "set-apart" God, which is an expression of his transcendental reality.

Communal prayer in times of crisis and individual prayers to be said daily are in the Jewish liturgies usually long prayers. The longest prayer has twenty-four petitions. The *Shemoneh Esreh,* which is the standard prayer of Judaism, consists of eighteen petitions, with these eighteen expanded to nineteen petitions for Jews in Babylonia. There are, however, brief formulas of prayer to be used on the road or in times of danger, which sought to capture the essential appeal made to the "Hearer of Prayer" by travelers and those in danger. Such appeals were worded by charismatic teachers and used by their followers. A later development strung together all the themes of the longer prayers into an encapsulated, brief prayer.

Jesus was asked by his disciples to teach them a prayer for the road as they embarked on their mission (cf. Luke 11:1, which follows the return of the seventy [or seventy-two] in 10:17-24). In the Lucan version of Jesus' prayer in 11:2-4 there are five petitions. The second one, evidently, was originally an epicletic appeal: "Let thy Holy Spirit come and purify us." For this formulation is echoed in the Lucan juxtaposed parabolic lesson of how "the heavenly Father gives the Holy Spirit to those who ask him" in 11:11-13. To ask, of course, is to pray (so 11:9). The important point to note for our purposes here, however, is that in Luke's Gospel Jesus is portrayed as offering a prayer to guide his apostles on the road, and that he is depicted as doing so without the inclusion of two of the petitions found in Matthew's Pater Noster.

Matthew's version of Jesus' prayer in Matt. 6:9-13 consists of seven petitions. The first part of the prayer opens with "Our Father who art in heaven" (v. 9a) and closes with the first missing petition in Luke: "Thy will be done as in heaven so on earth" (v. 10b). This first part relates to the transpersonal in prayer with three petitions to God, the eternal Thou. The second part of Jesus' prayer shifts to the plural "us" (vv. 11-13). The fourth petition of this latter part of the prayer relates to the subpersonal need of daily bread (v. 11); the fifth relates to the interpersonal need for forgiveness (v. 12); and the final two relate to the intrapersonal needs for the removal of trial and the release from evil (v. 13). The concluding petition regarding release from evil is also not found in Luke. Matthew's version of Jesus' prayer is given to the *ecclesia* as instruction on how to pray corporately, and not to individual apostles "on the road." Yet even in the Gospel of Matthew, Jesus' formulation of prayer is relatively brief and is contrasted with the long prayers of the synagogue (cf. 6:5-8; see also *Didache* 8:2).

The formulation of ecclesiastical prayer in Matt. 6:9-13, while brief, touches on all the major areas of human relationships. It begins with the collective address "Our Father," and then from the perspective of this transpersonal focus it goes on to petitions dealing with the areas of nature, humanity, and self. This is in line with how Matthew understands relations between the transpersonal and all other matters to be prayed about, as expressed later in this same chapter in verse 33: "Seek first his kingdom and his righteousness, and then all these will be yours as well." Thus Jesus is presented as inviting the community in time of crisis to pray for their existential needs from the perspective of realized eschatology — that is, from the perspective of God's love and the eschatological realization of his kingdom, whose coming on earth is to correspond to the heavenly reality that fulfills God's will.

The arrangement of Jewish intercessory prayer at Yavneh (cf. *Babylonian Talmud Megillah* 17b and *Berakoth* 28b) was related to the people's experiences of suffering under and subjugation to the Roman empire. The rabbis viewed the Jewish people as the Suffering Servant and their exilic situation as their mission to be a "light to the nations." They lived in a yet unredeemed world, and so they anticipated a messianic coming in the future. Thus their collective hopes, as formulated in their petitions, follow their prayers regarding their existential needs. Both Jews and Christians, however, await the final coming of the Messiah at the end of days.

Selected Bibliography

Bradshaw, Paul F. *Daily Prayer in the Early Church*. New York: Oxford University Press, 1982.

Charlesworth, James H., Mark Harding, and Mark Kiley, eds. *The Lord's Prayer*. Valley Forge, Penn.: Trinity, 1994.

Finkel, Asher. *The Pharisees and the Teacher of Nazareth*. Second ed. Leiden: Brill, 1964, 1974.

———. "The Pesher of Dreams and Scriptures." *Revue de Qumran* 4 (1964): 357-70.

———. "The Passover Story and the Last Supper." In *Root and Branch*, ed. M. Zeik and M. Siegel. Williston Park, N.Y.: Roth, 1973.

———. "Midrash and the Synoptic Gospels," *Society of Biblical Literature 1977 Seminar Papers*, ed. P. J. Achtemeier. Missoula, Mont.: Scholars, 1977, 251-56.

———. "The Theme of God's Presence and the Qumran Temple Scrolls." In *God and His Temple*, ed. L. Frizzell. South Orange, N.J.: Institute of Judaeo-Christian Studies, 1981.

———. "The Prayer of Jesus in Matthew." In *Standing Before God: Studies on Prayer in Scriptures and in Tradition with Essays* (In Honor of John M. Oesterreicher), ed. A. Finkel and L. Frizzell. New York: KTAV, 1981, 131-70.

———. "Jesus' Preaching in the Synagogue on the Sabbath (Lk 4:16-28)." In *The Gospels and the Scriptures of Israel*, ed. C. A. Evans and W. R. Stegner. Sheffield: Sheffield Academic Press, 1994.

———. "Biblical, Rabbinic and Early Christian Ethics." In *Jewish-Christian Encounters over the Centuries*, ed. M. Perry and F. M. Schweitzer. New York: Peter Lang, 1994.

Haran, Menahem. *Temple and Temple Service in Ancient Israel*. Oxford: Clarendon, 1978.

Kadushin, Max. *Worship and Ethics*. New York: Bloch, 1963.

Levine, Lee I., ed. *The Synagogue in Late Antiquity*. Philadelphia: American Schools of Oriental Research, 1987.

Longenecker, Richard N. *Biblical Exegesis in the Apostolic Period*. Grand Rapids: Eerdmans, 1975, 1999.

Millgram, Abraham. *Jewish Worship*. Philadelphia: Jewish Publishing Society, 1971.

Otto, Rudolph. *The Idea of the Holy*. Penguin, 1959.

Petuchowski, Jakob J., ed. *Contributions to the Scientific Study of Jewish Liturgy.* New York: KTAV, 1970.

Turner, Victor, and Edith Turner. *Image and Pilgrimage in Christian Culture.* New York: Columbia University Press, 1978.

Werner, Eric. *The Sacred Bridge.* New York: Schocken, 1970.

CHAPTER 4

Prayer in the Dead Sea Scrolls

EILEEN M. SCHULLER

1. Introductory Comments

General Orientation

The Dead Sea Scrolls are an important source of information about prayer in Judaism in the Second Temple period. Among the approximately 850 scrolls or their remnants found to date, there are texts of almost two hundred prayers, hymns, psalms, and liturgies. The majority of these are compositions that were not known at all before 1947. The Dead Sea Scrolls are significant if for no other reason than for the amount of "new" material they have supplied.

The Scrolls contain the earliest copies that have been preserved of 126 of the 150 psalms that are known to us from the Massoretic Psalter — plus the original Hebrew text of Psalm 151, which was previously known only from the Greek Psalter, and Psalms 154 and 155, which were known from the Syriac Psalter. There are also copies of some prayers and psalms from the Apocrypha/Pseudepigrapha that were previously only known in translation (e.g., *Sirach* 51:13-25, *Tobit* 13, *1 Enoch* 84). And in addition to the actual texts of prayers and psalms, there are explicit statements *about* praying, regulations regarding how and when to pray, and indirect references to the practice of prayer and other acts that were part of the worship (*avodah*) of God.

At first glance, it might appear that the prayers and psalms of a sectarian Jewish group, which existed only for about two hundred years (c. 150 BCE to 68 CE) and then disappeared, are of rather limited significance for an understanding of the development of either Rabbinic Judaism or early Christianity. This brings us immediately to a host of questions about the identity of the authors of these scrolls and their place within the "map" of Second Temple Judaism. Should we think in terms of a numerically small, rather esoteric group, fanatically preoccupied with preparations for an imminent eschatological battle, who had withdrawn from the mainstream of society to the desert site of Qumran, to live "without women . . . without money . . . and having for company only the palm trees" (Pliny *Natural History* 5.17.73)? Are the authors of the Dead Sea Scrolls to be identified with the Essenes described by Josephus (*War* 2.119-161, *Antiquities* 18.18-22) and Philo (*Quod omnis probus liber sit* 12.75-91), so that we can draw on these more extended sources as a supplementary fund of information? Or can we still say no more than that these scrolls come from "an unknown Jewish sect," as Louis Ginzberg described the authors of the Cairo Damascus Document (*Eine unbekannte jüdische Sekte* [New York, 1922]; in English: *An Unknown Jewish Sect* [New York: Jewish Theological Seminary, 1976])? Or is Hartmut Stegemann correct in his reconstruction of this "union" or "community" *(yaḥad)*, which he regards as "the most numerous religious group in the Judean heartland of Israel," a group that enjoyed "particularly high esteem as the most praiseworthy representative of Jewish piety" (*The Library of Qumran*, 153, 140)?

This is not the time or place to go into any of these questions in detail. Yet some basic assumptions must be made and a working framework for our discussion proposed. So I will assume in this presentation a relationship that is close — though perhaps not identical — between the Scrolls and the Essenes, and will therefore draw occasionally on Josephus to supplement or reinforce material in the Scrolls themselves. And since we do not know exactly how the authors of these scrolls identified themselves, I will call them by the Greek term "Essenes" or by the designation "the community," which is a translation of the Hebrew word *yaḥad*. I will, however, avoid using "Qumran community," for I want our thinking to be orientated toward all the members of the group — many of whom were married and lived "in all the towns and cities" (cf. Josephus *War* 2.124; Philo *Quod omnis* 12.76) — and not just toward the much smaller number who lived at any given time at the site of Qumran.

Relevance of the Material

Having established some general framework, it is necessary to return to our earlier question of how this material is relevant for the broader study of prayer, which is the focus of our present volume. Putting aside for a moment the two hundred or so scrolls that are copies of the books of the Hebrew Bible, it has been common in recent scholarship to distinguish between two basic categories of texts in the Dead Sea Scrolls: (1) "sectarian" writings, which were authored by the Essenes (some, perhaps, even by the Teacher of Righteousness) and which express the group's distinctive religious outlook with its cosmic dualism, strict determinism, and sharp eschatological/apocalyptic sense of living "at the end of days"; and (2) "nonsectarian" writings, which were composed earlier in the Persian and Hellenistic periods — certainly before we can talk of a separate "sect" — and so may have been read and shared broadly across the spectrum of Second Temple Judaism, but are known to us only because they happen to have been preserved in the caves at Qumran.

We have prayers and psalms of both types in the Dead Sea Scrolls — though the separation of the writings into two categories is particularly difficult in this genre because of the very nature of the material. The language of prayer is traditional, stereotypical, and biblically-based, and many of the distinguishing features of a sectarian composition (for example, their organizational terminology) are not likely to be found in prayers. Prayers that are usually identified as sectarian include the *Thanksgiving Psalms* or *Hodayot* (1QH^a and 4QH^{a-f}), the *Blessings* or *Berakot* (4Q286-290, 1QSb), and the *Blessings for Purification* (4Q512, 4Q414). Examples of nonsectarian compositions are the *Words of the Luminaries* (4Q504) and the "apocryphal" psalms in 11QPs^a and 4QPs^f. There are, however, some compositions that are very difficult (at least given present research) to categorize — for example, the *Songs of the Sabbath Sacrifice* (4Q400-407) and the *Barki Naphshi* psalms (4Q434-438).

The sectarian material enables us to see how prayers and psalms were formulated in this specific branch of Judaism — especially how this community's distinctive theological perspective expressed itself in prayer (as distinct from *halakah,* or "directives for living"). The nonsectarian material gives us knowledge of how other Jews prayed, though the specific authors and original contexts of these compositions are quite nebulous. One thing that is particularly noteworthy in this material is that the Essenes seemed to have had little hesitation in putting their prayers and religious poetry into written form, in contrast to the practices of both Pharisaic and Rabbinic Judaism, where the setting down of prayers in writing was discouraged (cf. *Tosephta Shabbath* 13:4). Although there are scattered references to prayers — occasionally even the text of certain blessings — in the Mishnah and the Talmuds, the earliest preserved copies of a Jewish prayer book (the *Siddur*) can be dated only to the ninth century CE, the *Seder Rab Amran Gaon*. So the Dead Sea Scrolls fill in, at least in part, a stage in the development of Jewish forms of prayer that had largely been bereft of written texts. And the Scrolls are virtually our only source for a knowledge of Jewish prayers contemporaneous with the beginnings of Christianity.

Terminology and Scope

As a final introductory comment, let me say something about terminology and the scope of this presentation. Terms like "prayer," "psalm," "hymn," "liturgy," "liturgical," and "cultic" tend to be used in Scrolls scholarship very imprecisely — even in somewhat contradictory ways. "Prayer" is sometimes a generic term that can include almost any religious sentiment or any address to God, no matter what its content (whether praise, thanksgiving, or petition). At other times, "prayer" is limited to compositions in prose (rather than poetry) where the content is petition (rather than praise). In what follows I will speak of prayer in the more expansive sense. Likewise, "hymn" is sometimes used for any religious poetic composition; at other times, it is limited to a composition of praise that speaks of God in the third person. In order to keep closer to the classic biblical form-critical usage, I will here use the term "psalm" for poetic compositions that are modeled on the language or style of the biblical psalms.

Because the material from the Dead Sea Scrolls is not generally as familiar as biblical material, our presentation will be somewhat more descriptive than would be necessary if we were treating well-known and long-studied sources. And though it is far from comprehensive and makes no claim to mention, much less discuss, every relevant text, the material that follows will hopefully give a sense of both the richness and the complexity of these relatively "new" sources for the study of prayer.

2. The Nature of the Evidence

Although there is a wealth of material, detailed study of the prayers and liturgy in the Dead Sea Scrolls is at a preliminary stage, being very much a "work in progress." Most of this material is quite fragmentary — though, of course, one could make the same lament about most of the material in the Scrolls. The 313 little pieces of the *Festival Prayers* (4Q509) or the 215 little bits of the *Song of the Sage* (4Q511) supply only a portion of what was once contained in the original scrolls. And when only isolated words and phrases are preserved, there is always the problem of trying to reconstruct missing material according to the determination of set formulas. The most recent official listing of the Dead Sea Scrolls compiled by Emanuel Tov (*The Dead Sea Scrolls after Fifty Years: A Comprehensive Assessment*, ed. P. W. Flint and J. C. VanderKam [Leiden: Brill, 1999], vol. 2, 669-717) lists by title a rather large number of scrolls only recently published (e.g., 4Q291-293, *Work Containing Prayers A, B, C;* and 4Q441-457b, various works entitled *Prayer, Lament,* or *Hymn*). Many are very fragmentary, often identified as a "prayer" only on the basis of some second person address to what seems to be God or an isolated word or phrase that seems vaguely psalm-like. And what we can learn from these fragmentary portions will probably always be quite limited.

Furthermore, the publication of the prayers and hymns from Qumran has been a long and drawn-out process, made perhaps more difficult because of how the material was allotted and subdivided at various stages. Some of the key texts have been available for study for over forty years — for example, the *editio princeps* of the major collection of *Thanksgiving Psalms* or *Hodayot* (1QH^a), which appeared in Hebrew in 1954 and in English in 1955 (*The Dead Sea Scrolls of the Hebrew University*, ed. E. L. Sukenik). 1QH^b was published by J. T. Milik in 1955 (*Qumran Cave I*, ed. D. Barthélemy and J. T. Milik). Milik worked independently in Jerusalem on the other side of the Mandelbaum Gate, and so it took some time to realize that 1QH^a and 1QH^b were actually two copies of the same collection and not different parts of the same scroll, as had first been proposed. The next major publication was in 1965, with the edition of a large but very puzzling scroll that contained many of the biblical psalms (though arranged in quite a different order than in the Massoretic text) plus nine or ten "non-canonical" psalms (*The Psalms Scroll of Qumran Cave 11*, ed. J. Sanders). Debate has raged now for over thirty-five years as to whether this scroll should be classified with the biblical manuscripts as a "Psalter" or be viewed as an independent "prayer book" — a question that is almost impossible to resolve until all of the biblical Psalter manuscripts are not only published but also fully studied.

The first major publication of prose prayers from the Qumran texts (*Daily Prayers, Festival Prayers,* and *Words of the Luminaries*) and other liturgies (e.g., 4Q502, the *Marriage Ritual*) did not appear until 1982 (*Qumrân Grotte 4.III*, ed. M. Baillet). Other texts were made available, at least in preliminary form, in the later 1980s, at which time the diversity and complexity of this type of material became apparent (C. Newsom, *The Songs of the Sabbath Sacrifice: A Critical Edition* [Atlanta: Scholars, 1984]; E. M. Schuller, *The Non-Canonical Psalms: A Pseudepigraphic Collection* [Atlanta: Scholars, 1986]). The recently published volumes XI *(Qumran Cave 4.VI: Poetical and Liturgical Texts, Part 1)* and XXIX *(Qumran Cave 4.II: Poetical and Liturgical Texts, Part 2)* in the *Discoveries in the Judaean Desert* series are devoted to prayers, hymns, and liturgies of the Dead Sea Scrolls. The latter volume includes six more copies of the *Thanksgiving Psalms* or *Hodayot* from cave 4 (4Q427-432), almost forty-five years after these psalms from cave 1 were first published, and so will allow us to re-study this important collection in a totally new way — drawing on the evidence of all the copies, some of which are quite different than what has been available up to this point.

The first full book-length study of the prayers and hymns of Qumran did not appear until 1994 (B. Nitzan, *Qumran Prayer and Religious Poetry*). There is only one other recent study of this material, which was published in 1998 (D. Falk, *Daily, Festival and Sabbath Prayers from Qumran*). Because so much of this work is still ongoing, the broad, comprehensive sketch that I will attempt to present here can be only tentative and may well need to be revised in light of further study and reflection.

3. The Place of Prayer in the Life of the Essenes

Prayer played a central role in the worship life *(avodah)* of the Essenes. Indeed, one of the distinctive components of the ideology of this community is the radical claim that prayer — in conjunction, of course, with a way of life lived strictly according to Torah, as interpreted "properly" within the community — was "like" the sacrifices of the temple and could function as a means of atonement in its own right. Thus the vocabulary that originated in the sacrificial system of the temple came to be applied to prayer — for example, in 1QS 9.5, "the offering of the lips for judgment is as an acceptable fragrance of righteousness, and a perfect way of life as a freewill offering of favor." Prov. 15:8 is alluded to here and quoted explicitly in CD 11.20-21 as scriptural justification, "the sacrifice of the wicked is an abomination, but the prayer of the just is like an agreeable offering."

This understanding of the cultic and atoning function that prayer could exercise seems to have developed largely as a pragmatic response to the Essenes' conviction that the sacrifices in the present Jerusalem temple under the existing priesthood were being carried out according to misguided halakic practice (cf. 4QMMT, *Miqsat Ma'ase ha-Torah* or "Works of the Law"), and — perhaps even more seriously — according to the wrong calendar, that is, a lunar calendar rather than the "proper" solar calendar. Thus the Essenes could not take part in the regular fixed daily, sabbath, and festival sacrifices. But in looking ahead to the final days of the great eschatological battle of the Sons of Light over the Sons of Darkness, the first stage of victory after seven years would involve the restoration of temple worship in Jerusalem (cf. 1QM 2.1-6). Prayer, therefore, was not to replace ultimately the sacrificial system ordained by God for all eternity in the Torah. For the covenantors, only in the present "time of Belial" did it need to take on that role.

Prayer in the Dead Sea Scrolls is a corporate activity. The *Rule of the Community* stipulates that "they shall eat together, they shall bless together, and they shall take counsel together" (1QS 6.2-4). The "many" *(rabbim)* are to come together — the next phrase admits of two interpretations, either one-third of the nights of the year *or* one-third of each night — "to read the book, to explain the regulation and to bless together" (1QS 6.7-8). Thus prayers are formulated in the first person plural. And there are some hints of a dialogical or antiphonal style, as, for example, the response "Amen, amen" in the *Berakot* (4Q287 1 4) and the *Words of the Luminaries* (4Q504 3 ii 3).

Of course, personal words of devotion and petition — the spontaneous turning to God in times of crisis or joy — are not precluded. We can assume that these must have been part of the life of the pious, even if such words are not preserved in the Scrolls themselves. Perhaps this more spontaneous type of prayer is what is referred to in the first part of the *Hymn about the Times of Prayer,* where it specifies "[and in distr]ess he shall bless his Creator and in all that happens he shall rec[ount] . . ." (1QS 9.26). As the passage goes on, however, the emphasis is on the fixed times of prayer, as in 1QS 9.26–10.1: "with the offering of his lips he will bless him [God] during the set times that he prescribed." A similar listing of fixed times for prayer appears in 1QH[a] 20.7-14 (or 12.4-11 in Sukenik's *editio princeps*). These times are set in accordance with the order of the cosmos — that is, the regular cycle of morning and evening, the beginnings of the months, the festivals, the sabbatical years, and the jubilee years (1QS 10.1b-7). Thus through prayer the community is brought into harmony with the whole of the cosmos and with all of the angels of the heavenly world who praise God at these regular intervals (cf. 11QPs[a] 26.11-12 of the *Hymn to the Creator:* "Separating light from darkness, by the knowledge of his mind he established the dawn. When all his angels had witnessed it, they sang aloud").

Although this survey will concentrate on the actual texts of prayers, perhaps a few words can still be said about some of the practical details, such as where the people prayed. The Essenes living in towns and cities presumably had places to gather for prayer, but there are few texts and no archaeological evidence to support such an assumption. Since the basic unit for a Jewish assembly was ten (cf. 1QS 6.3, 6), we need not think in terms of large, separate or public buildings. There is one passage in the *Damascus Document* that refers to the "house of prostration" (*beth hishtaḥut,* CD 11.21-22). This may, of course, be a reference to the Jerusalem temple, where people prostrated themselves in worship. But it has recently been argued that "house of prostration" is an Essene term for local centers of worship (cf. A. Steudel, "The Houses of Prostration CD xi,21–xii,1 — Duplicates of the Temple," *Revue Qumran* 16 [1993]: 49-68). And if this is the case, then many features of temple worship — including prostration, ritual purification before entrance, and the blowing of trumpets — should be seen as having been extended to these non-temple settings, which developed in a way very different than the way the synagogue developed during the Rabbinic period.

For Essenes who lived at the site of Qumran, their place of prayer was probably the main dining hall. It is, in fact, on the basis of how many people could prostrate themselves in the community's dining room that Hartmut Stegemann argues that the group that lived there normally numbered only about 50 people — though if prostration was not an intrinsic part of their worship, closer to 150 people could have gathered for prayer in this room (*The Library of Qumran*, 46).

4. Set Prayers for Fixed Occasions

Prayer at Morning and Evening

Sunrise (dawn) and sunset (late afternoon/evening) were specific times of prayer. Josephus says of the Essenes, "before sunrise they speak no profane word but recite certain ancestral prayers to/towards the sun as though entreating it to rise" (*War* 2.128). The hymn-like text at the end of the *Rule of the Community* expresses this more poetically: "At the beginning of the rule of light in its time, and when it is gathered to its appointed place . . . when the lights shine out of the holy vault, when they retire to the abode of glory . . ." (1QS 10.1-3). It has sometimes been argued that this passage is speaking of up to six separate times of prayer, but this is probably too literal a reading of a poetic calendar.

From a combination of descriptive statements and actual prayer texts we can deduce at least some components of these daily times of prayer. "With the arrival of day and night I will enter the covenant of God, and at the exit of evening and morning I will speak of his laws" (1QS 10.10) probably alludes to the recitation of some form of the Shema along with the Decalogue, a practice that was fairly standard throughout Judaism at this time. It is more uncertain whether the statement "I will bless his name" (1QS 10.13) can be taken as evidence that blessings were already being linked to the recitation of the Shema, as are attested later in the daily liturgy.

In terms of actual prayer texts, there are at least two collections of short prose prayers that are associated with morning and evening. *Daily Prayers* (4Q503), preserved in only one copy, is a collection of blessings for each day of one of the months in the Jewish calendar — either the month *Nisan* or the month *Tishrei,* though which month is still disputed and depends on complex calendrical calculation. There is a standard rubrical notation, "on the X-day of the month in the evening, they shall bless and answer and say," and then "when the sun goes forth to illumine the earth they will bless and answer and say. . . ." Each prayer seems to begin (or can be so reconstructed) with a blessing formula in the third person: "Blessed be the

God of Israel who. . . ." And the unit may conclude with a second person blessing, though few examples have been preserved: "Blessed be you/your name, O God of Israel . . ." (col. 10:20, frgs. 14 2, 68 2). Someone, perhaps a priest, then addresses the congregation directly with the words "Peace upon you, Israel" (cf. Ps. 125:5; 128:6). These blessings praise God for creation and for the daily cycle of both the sun and the moon in their progressive phases.

An important and recurrent theme in the *Daily Prayers* is the joining of the prayers on earth with those of the angels in heaven — as in the expressions "we with the holy ones" (frgs. 1-6 20) and "those praising with us" (frgs. 37-38 20). In the study of the development of the daily rabbinic liturgy there has been considerable dispute as to the origins of this motif of praise with the angels, both in terms of date and as to whether it began as a distinctive feature of Sabbath prayer that was then extended to the daily *Qedushat Yoṣer.* 4Q503 gives evidence of the early occurrence of this theme in non-Sabbath prayers. The manuscript was copied about 100-75 BCE, and the composition is generally considered to be nonsectarian in origin.

Another set of prayers is usually associated with the morning and evening recitations because of the title written on the outside of one copy, that is on 4Q504: *Words of the Luminaries (divrei hame'orot).* This is a collection of petitionary prayers for each day of the week (for the Sabbath section, see below). As the scroll has been reconstructed by Esther Chazon (unpublished dissertation, Hebrew University, 1991), these prayers follow a set structure and are written as a literary whole. There is a superscription "Prayer for X-day"; an imperative "Remember, O Lord"; an extended historical narrative that is divided over the consecutive days of the week, from the creation of Adam (Sunday) to the postexilic time of tribulation and distress (Friday); an extended petition rising in some sense from the narrative; and a concluding blessing in which God is praised in relationship to the theme of the prayer (e.g., "Blessed be the Lord who taught us . . ."; frg. 4 14). The communal response "Amen, amen" is further evidence of a liturgical usage. The early paleographic date of 4Q504 (that is, the middle of the second century BCE) and the traditional vocabulary and content indicate that these prayers predate the founding of the Essene community. All this implies that already in the second century BCE there was a practice, at least among some pious groups, of saying set prayers on each day of the week — a practice that was presumably continued by the Essenes, since copies were found at Qumran.

There are other prayer compositions that refer to morning and evening, but it is very unclear how they relate to the above sets of prayers. For example, there are blessings on the theme of the creation of morning and evening in 4Q408, but these overlap in part with a longer, puzzling liturgy that also deals with the discovery of the false prophet (as preserved in 4Q375/376). There is also a liturgical calendar (4Q334) that prescribes a set number of "songs" and "words of praise" (though no actual texts are given) to be recited on the evening and morning of consecutive days of the month. But it is not clear whether these are prayers of angels or of humans, or both.

Sabbath Prayer

Prayer giving praise to God was especially emphasized on the Sabbath. In the *Daily Prayers* (4Q503), the Sabbath prayers are not particularly distinctive in structure, though the content emphasizes specific themes of rest, delight, and election (as in the wording "the appointed time of rest and delight . . . who chose us from all the nations"; frgs. 24-25). In the *Words of the Luminaries* (4Q504), the Sabbath prayer is radically different from that for the other days of the week. It is formulated in parallel poetic lines rather than as prose, focuses on themes of creation and covenant, and is totally doxological with no supplication. Thus there seems to be a basic continuity between these second-century BCE prayers and later rabbinic (tannaitic and amoraic) texts, which have restrictions on "crying out" with petitions on the Sabbath.

Another type of prayer for the Sabbath is exemplified by the *Songs of the Sabbath Sacrifice*. The presence of nine copies of this work at Qumran (4Q400-407, 11Q17) and another copy at Masada points to the importance of these songs. There are thirteen compositions for consecutive Sabbaths, each beginning with a heading — for example, "By the *Maskil* [Instructor]: Song of the sacrifice of the X-sabbath on the x-day of the x-month." The assumption is that the cycle was repeated for the 52 Sabbaths of the solar calendar.

Praise is the dominant motif of all of these songs, though the specific content is quite varied. Only in the first five songs is there an actual address to God by humans who speak in the first person plural ("how shall we be considered"; "let us exalt"). Songs 6-8 are repetitious formulaic accounts of the praises and blessings offered by "seven chief princes" and the "seven deputy princes" and summonses to the seven priestly councils to give praise (but no actual texts for the angelic songs are given). The final section, songs 9-13, works its way through an elaborate description of the heavenly temple, including the *merkabah* ("chariot-throne") and the dress and worship of the angelic priesthood.

There has been considerable debate as to the origin of these songs. Many have assumed that they must be Essene compositions. The designation "By/For the *Maskil*" is a rubric found in other sectarian works (cf. 1QS 3.13; 9.12, 21; 1QH^a 20.7 [or 12.4 in Sukenik's *editio princeps*]; 25.34 [frg. 8 10]; 4Q298 11, *Words of the Maskil to the Sons of Dawn*). Some of the vocabulary is certainly shared with the sectarian texts, though it is not limited to them. And the strong sense of correspondence between the earthly realm and the heavenly realm is a recurrent theme in the *Hodayot*. But it is also possible that these were much older songs from priestly circles — perhaps related to the composers of *Jubilees* and the Aramaic *Testament of Levi*, with which there are many parallels.

The purpose of these songs is equally unclear. Were they understood to be an accompaniment to the Sabbath sacrifice as offered at Jerusalem or in the heavens? Or were they to be a replacement or a substitute? Carol Newsom, the principal editor of *Song of the Sabbath Sacrifice*, has suggested that the repetitive, almost hypnotic language, which is reminiscent of later *Hekalot* hymns, was intended to produce a kind of "communal mysticism" — that is, to give the reciters an experiential sense of participating in the heavenly cult, even if they were shut out from the earthly temple.

Festival Prayer

The cycle of festivals marked divinely ordained times for prayer and song. In addition to the regular Torah festivals — the Day of Atonement, *Sukkot*, Passover, *Shavuot*, and the beginning of each new month — the Essenes celebrated the festivals of the First Fruits of New Wine, Oil, and Wood, as specified in the *Temple Scroll* (11QTemple 19.11–25.2) and some of the calendrical texts (4Q325, 4Q327). This expanded calendar of feasts finds liturgical expression in a short work identified as 4Q409, or the *Times for Praising*: "Praise and bless in the days of [   ]; praise and bless and give thanks . . . in the day of remembrance . . . the wood for the burnt offerings." The repeated calls for praise become the very substance of praise (cf. Ps. 150:1-6, *The Praise of the Three Young Men*).

There was an extensive collection of prayers for various festivals, but only four or five copies remain and all of them are very poorly preserved (*Festival Prayers*, 1Q34, 4Q507-509, perhaps also 4Q505). The structure of these prayers is very similar to that of the *Words of the Luminaries*, which suggests that they may have had a similar nonsectarian origin. Also, the festivals that can be identified in this collection by name (i.e., Day of Atonement, First Fruits) or by theme (e.g., Passover) are all biblical festivals. The prayers are a mixture of praise and petition. Lawrence Schiffman has pointed out that the specific theme of "assemble our banished . . . and gather our dispersed ones" (4Q509 3.1.3-4) appears in the festival *Musaf* of later rabbinic tradition, which means that "the prayer for the restoration of the Diaspora to the Land of Israel recited on festivals may go back as early as first century BCE" ("The Dead Sea Scrolls and the Early History of Jewish Liturgy," 42).

The Annual Covenant Ceremony

A distinctive liturgy was developed by the Dead Sea covenantors for the annual ceremony of the Renewal of the Covenant, which was held during the Feast of Weeks (Pentecost) on the fifteenth day of the third month (4Q*Damascus*ᵃ 11.17). At this time new members took their solemn oath, and all members renewed their commitment and received their ranking (1QS 2.21-23). The ritual is described in some detail in 1QS 1.18–2.18, which includes some of the actual words to be said. Two other manuscripts, 5Q13 and 4Q275, also seem to deal with this ceremony, though these texts are very fragmentary. A section of the *Damascus Document* preserved in 4Q266 11 also gives the words of the liturgical pronouncement that were said at the expulsion of a member who had rejected the discipline of the community.

This ceremony for the Renewal of the Covenant illustrates both (1) that new rituals of prayer were developed for specific purposes and (2) that the new forms were based on adaptations of earlier biblical models. The priests and Levites first "bless the God of victories and all the works of his faithfulness," and all those who enter the covenant give their assent with a double "Amen, amen" (1QS 1.19-20). Those who enter the covenant confess their sins: "We have acted sinfully, we have transgressed, we have sinned, we have committed evil" (1QS 1.24-25); and they declare God's justice — thus following a pattern of prayer that was developed and is attested in various penitential prayers throughout the postexilic period (cf. Dan. 9, Neh. 9, Ezra 9, 1 Kings 8). The blessings for those of God's lot and the curses for those of the lot of Belial follow the pattern of blessings and curses on Mt. Gerizim and Mt. Ebal (cf. Deut. 27–29; Josh. 8:30-35). The blessings are a version of the priestly blessing of Numbers 6, which are expanded in accordance with the community's dualistic outlook, "May he bless you *with everything good* and may he keep you *from everything bad*," and lay emphasis on the salvific role of knowledge, "May he illuminate your heart *with the discernment of life* and be gracious to you *with eternal knowledge*" (1QS 2.2-4; expansions in italics).

Other Collections

The Scrolls preserve at least remnants of many other collections of short prose prayers. Some of these seem to be liturgies for specific occasions, though where specific rubrics are absent it can be exceedingly difficult to deduce the occasion. The fragmentary blessings and rubrics in 4Q502, for example, have been variously associated with a marriage ritual (M. Baillet, *Qumran Grotte 4.III*), a "Golden Age Ritual" for elderly men and women (J. M. Baumgarten, "4Q502, Marriage or Golden Age Ritual?" *Journal of Jewish Studies* 34 [1983]: 125-35), or the celebration of the new year (M. L. Satlow, "4Q502, A New Year Festival?" *Dead Sea Discoveries* 5 [1998]: 57-68). Other short prose prayers are of the nature of blessings to be recited in conjunction with purificatory washings after the incurrence of various types of impurity (related to bodily functions or contact with the dead), as well as purification in preparation for Sabbaths and festivals (4Q512 and 4Q414). That is, both the action (washing) and the pronouncement of words (blessing) were part of the ritual of purification, with the blessing, in contrast to rabbinic practice, to be said, it seems, *after* rather than *before* the action.

It is to be noted that most of these prayers are formulated as blessings — that is, they begin with "blessed/praised" *(baruk)*, either in the third-person "blessed be God," as is more common in the biblical material, or with the second-person formulary "blessed are you" *(baruk atah)*, as became the norm in rabbinic blessings. The formulary "blessed are you" was, it seems, becoming dominant among the Essenes. Perhaps it was the normative way to formulate a prayer during the Second Temple period. Yet no set form had been standardized, and considerable diversity was allowable even within the same community.

In the listing of occasions for praising God, 1QS 10.15a includes "and before I extend my hand to enjoy the pleasure of the world's produce," which probably refers to the practice of reciting a prayer or blessing before meals. Other texts, such as 1QS 6.5 and 1QSa 2.18-19, mention the blessing of bread and wine at the start of a meal, first by the priest and then by individual participants. Only in Josephus is there mention of a blessing at the end of a meal ("at the beginning and at the end they bless God as the Giver of life," *War* 2.131). No actual text of such a blessing, however, is extant in the Scrolls.

5. The Corpus of Religious Poetry

There is a considerable corpus of religious poetry in the Dead Sea Scrolls that should be included under "prayer" in the broader sense. These writings are evidence that the art of composing religious poetry continued to flourish throughout the Second Temple period. Much of this poetry was explicitly modeled on the biblical psalms, not only on the level of genre but also in the extensive reuse of biblical phraseology and language, so that new composition involved a virtual *relecture* of earlier texts.

Some of the poetry is clearly sectarian in origin, most notably the *Hodayot* (see below). But there are a number of psalms preserved in the Scrolls that were probably composed in the Persian and early Hellenistic periods, though it is notoriously difficult to reconstruct anything very specific about their authors or their *Sitz-im-Leben*. Some are psalms of lament and petition (e.g., the *Plea for Deliverance* in 11QPs^a 19.1-18). Others are wisdom-oriented (e.g., Psalms 154 and 155 in 11QPs^a 18.1-16 and 24.3-17, which are also found in the Syriac Psalter). And there are poems addressing praise directly to Zion (11QPs^a 22.1-15) and to Judah (4QPs^f 10.4-15). In at least one collection the psalms are attributed pseudepigraphically to various biblical figures — not only to King David, but also to prophetic figures such as Obadiah (4Q380 1 ii 8) and to various kings of Judah. The

80

name of the king is unfortunately missing in one of the psalms ("[Prayer of   k]ing of Judah"; 4Q381 31 4). But another psalm (4Q381 33 8) is clearly attributed to King Manasseh, apparently following the tradition in 2 Chronicles 36-37 that the wicked king repented and prayed to God.

Still another collection is given the title *Barki Naphshi*, "Bless the Lord, my soul," after the opening line (4Q434 1 i 1), which takes up this phrase from Psalms 103 and 104. These are generalized psalms of thanksgiving and praise for divine deliverance and grace. The presence of five copies of *Barki Naphshi* suggests that the collection had some importance within the community. But it is very difficult to propose any context for these psalms, or even to come to a decision whether they are sectarian or nonsectarian in origin.

Finally there are hymns/psalms where the content and purpose is much more specific — in particular, to ward off evil spirits (11QapocrPs, 4Q444, 8Q5, 4Q510-511). A few are incantations that address the evil spirits directly. Most of them, however, are true hymns — that is, words of praise about God and directed to God, which were considered to have the power to "frighten and to terrify all the spirits of the angels of destruction and the spirits of bastards, demons, Lilith, howling creatures . . ." (4Q510 1 4-5).

In focusing on all this "new" psalmic material, it is important to remember that there are also thirty-seven scrolls found at Qumran containing at least some portion of the biblical psalms. This is far more than any other biblical book (as compared with twenty-nine copies of Deuteronomy, twenty-one copies of Isaiah, and two to four copies of many of the wisdom and historical books). The Essenes considered the Psalms to be words of prophecy whose fulfillment was taking place in the events associated with the foundation of their community. Thus the Psalms were studied along with the prophetic books. And commentaries *(pesher)* were written on the Psalter (4Q171, 173), just as they were on the words of Isaiah, Hosea, or Habakkuk. But it is generally assumed that the biblical psalms also functioned liturgically in the group's communal worship.

There is, however, little concrete evidence about how psalmody was actually used in worship other than at the Jerusalem temple. There are occasional references in the Dead Sea Scrolls to singing. 1QS 10.9, for example, reads: "I will sing with knowledge and all my music shall be for the glory of God; my lyre and my harp should sound for his holy order." But this could simply be a reuse of traditional biblical language in a metaphorical sense. In one of the psalm copies, 2QPs, the first two lines — that is, the opening lines of Ps. 103:1-4 — are written in red ink. This may have been done for liturgical purposes to alert the reader or singer, as, apparently, the use of red ink in one manuscript of the Book of Numbers [4QNum[b]] was meant to introduce pericopes for liturgical reading.

There is a long-standing debate among scholars about whether certain of these psalm scrolls are actually a very early "prayer book." Do we have here a collection of materials that had been put together as a resource for communal worship — that is, some psalms considered scriptural (though their order is rearranged for liturgical purposes; e.g., in 11QPs[a] the order is Psalms 101–103, 109, 11, 104, 147, 105, 146, 178, 121, 132, 119, 135–136, 145) combined with other religious poetry that the community wanted to use for their devotions (e.g., the *Plea for Deliverance*, the *Apostrophe to Zion*, the *Hymn to the Creator*)? Or are scrolls like 11QPs[a, b], 4QPs[e], and 4QPs[f] actually editions of the biblical Psalter that had not yet taken on a fixed order or content, especially in the final third portion of the Psalter (as argued with great intensity by Peter Flint, *The Dead Sea Psalms Scrolls and the Book of Psalms*)? In either case, the regular use of the Psalter would have been an important component shaping the piety of the community. The numerous psalms of lament, for example, would sustain an element of plea and petition before God that is relatively rare in the sectarian compositions.

6. The Thanksgiving Psalms *(Hodayot)*

The most important sectarian poetry discovered at Qumran is a collection of between thirty and forty *Thanksgiving Psalms* or *Hodayot* preserved in two copies in cave 1 (1QH[a], 1QH[b]) and six copies in cave 4 (4Q427-432). At least one of the cave 4 manuscripts (4QH[a]) has the psalms in a totally different order than the largest and most complete manuscript from cave 1 (1QH[a]), and there is some evidence that other manuscripts from cave 4 (4QH[c], 4QH[f]) may have originally contained only a part of this collection. The size of this collection, the number of copies, their presence in cave 1 with the other foundational compositions of the community, and the possibility that some of them may have been written by the Teacher of Righteousness himself (see below) justify our paying special attention to this collection.

The psalms of this collection address God directly in the second person. There is a first-person singular speaker, but, as in the biblical psalms, the "I" may be corporate, that is, the voice of the community. In a few places the speaker is the plural "we." Unlike the biblical psalms of thanksgiving, however, where the psalms can begin in quite different ways, these psalms all start with a set introductory formula: either "I thank you, O Lord," or "Blessed are you, Lord." It is not clear that there is any real distinction between these two introductions, and in one case (1QH^a 13.22 [5.20]) the first is erased and the second written in above the line. The psalmist then states his reason for offering praise by recounting what God has done for him: "because you have placed my soul in the bundle of the living" (1QH^a 10.22 [2.20]); "because you have redeemed my soul from the pit" (1QH^a 11.20 [3.19]); "for you have illumined my face by your covenant" (1QH^a 12.6 [4.5]); "because you have dealt wondrously with dust and mightily with a creature of clay" (1QH^a 19.6 [11.3]). Other reasons frequently cited for giving thanks are that God has granted the psalmist knowledge of marvelous mysteries (e.g., 1QH^a 12.28-29 [4.27-28]) and brought him into the community (the *yaḥad*), giving him fellowship with the elect on earth and the angels in heaven (e.g., 1QH^a 11.23-24 [3.22-23]).

The main body of the psalm can be quite varied in form and content. There might be an extended and elaborate development of a specific image or motif — for example, a tree planted in a garden (1QH^a 16.5-27 [8.4-26]); a fortified city (1QH^a 14.28-32 [6.25-29]); or a woman in labor (1QH^a 11.8-14 [3.7-13]). In some psalms there are extended descriptions of the events to come in the eschatological future, with particular emphasis on the destruction of Belial and all the spirits of wickedness (1QH^a 11.26-37 [3.25-36]; 25.3-16 [frg. 5.1-14]). As in the biblical psalms of thanksgiving, there are very few petitions, although there are occasionally imperative verbs and requests to God (e.g., 1QH^a 19.33 [11.30]; 8.29-30 [16.11-12]). There is no standard concluding formula. In the biblical psalms of thanksgiving there was often mention in the concluding section of offering sacrifice and fulfilling vows in the temple (e.g., Ps. 107:22; 116:17-18), but this element is not found in any of these texts.

Many scholars, beginning with the first editor, Eliezer Sukenik, have suggested that this entire collection of psalms was a unified work and was authored by the Teacher of Righteousness, the founder of the *yaḥad*. Here, it was thought, we could find the Teacher's personal devotional piety, an account of how God had given him a special revelation that he was to share with the members of his community (1QH^a 12.28 [4.27]), and, at least obliquely, references to his persecution and exile by the Wicked Priest (e.g., 1QH^a 12.10-12 [4.9-10]: "They have banished me from my land like a bird from the nest"; cf. 1QpHab 11.6). Other scholars have found evidence for two distinct types of psalms. In one group of psalms, the "I" seems highly personal — representing, it seems, a person with an exalted position who functions as a mediator of revelation to others and who describes at length his enemies and persecution. At least six to eight psalms of this collection (perhaps as many as twelve) fall into this category of *Hymns of the Teacher.* In the other psalms, the so-called *Hymns of the Community,* the "I" seems more the corporate voice of the community. These psalms are characterized by an explicit confession of God's salvific action and justice (e.g., 1QH^a 19.20-21 [11.17-18]: "I know that righteousness is yours") and by extended reflections about the sinful condition and misery of humankind, which are often expressed in the form of rhetorical questions (e.g., 1QH^a 5.31-33 [13.14-16]: "What is one born of a woman in the midst of all your awesome works? He is a construction of dust and kneaded with water; his foundation is sinful guilt, and ignominious shame, and a source of uncleanness; a spirit of perversity rules over him").

The authorship of these latter psalms has not been defined with any precision, beyond the observation that they are sectarian in worldview (e.g., dualistic, deterministic), that they use sectarian vocabulary and organizational terminology (e.g., *maskil*), and that they completely avoid the use of the tetragrammaton. It has been suggested that these so-called *Hymns of the Community* originated within the context of the liturgy for Covenant Renewal (see above), and then thereafter came to be part of the daily "entering the Covenant of God" (1QS 10.10). There are some themes in common with the morning blessings in later rabbinic prayer (e.g., thanksgiving for knowledge; thanksgiving for creation), but the links are general rather than specific.

The picture is further complicated because there are some compositions that do not fit neatly into either category. One psalm (1QH^a 9.1–10.4 [1.1–2.2]) is distinctive because it contains an extended wisdom-like reflection on creation and divine determinism, and because it concludes with an exhortation to a plural audience: "Hear, O you wise, and you who meditate on knowledge. . . . O you righteous, put an end to wickedness." Another psalm, which is best preserved in 4Q427 7, though with some smaller overlapping fragments in 4Q431 and 1QH^a 25.34–26.41, is much more liturgical in style. It contains an extended series of imperative calls to give praise: "Sing, O beloved ones, rejoice . . . ring forth . . . give praise, extol." It also contains confessional statements in the first person plural, "we have known you, O God of righteousness," and a series of summonses to "proclaim and say, Great is God/blessed is God." Toward the beginning of the psalm, the speaker describes himself in exalted language as "beloved of the king, a companion of the holy ones" and one who is "with the heavenly beings" (the *'elim*).

A version of this latter passage, though a distinct recension, appears in another fragment that may be part of a copy of the War Scroll (4Q491 11 i), or perhaps is an independent composition. This is significant because it is one of the very few instances where a passage appears both in the *Hodayot* and in another scroll — which suggests that the author or authors of these psalms may have drawn on existing compositions. When all is said and done, however, there is still a great deal that we do not know about the origin and use of these poems.

7. Concluding Remarks

The caves at Qumran have provided us with important materials for the study of prayer in the time of Second Temple Judaism. Virtually all of these texts are now, since the end of 1999, available in standard published form, including photographs of the originals.

Some of these materials, however, still require much more work at the basic textual level. This is especially true for the *Thanksgiving Psalms,* where there is an urgent need for a new edition. Since Sukenik's edition of 1QH[a] in 1955, the whole scroll has been reconstructed, with the fragments arranged in a quite different order. Better photos have enabled us to read more letters in certain places, and the evidence of the six manuscripts from cave 4 needs to be incorporated into a composite text. Similar reconstructive work remains to be done on a number of the other scrolls.

But as the technical work in the study of these manuscripts is completed, the focus must turn more and more to broader issues. There is still much work to be done, for example, at the foundational level of form-critical and linguistic analysis. It may seem obvious that prayers and psalms are an important resource for the study of "the religion of the Dead Sea Scrolls." Yet surprisingly little study has been devoted to a theological reading of these texts. In addition to specialists in the Scrolls *per se,* it is to be hoped that scholars in Hebrew Bible, New Testament, and Early Judaism, plus scholars with expertise in the study of liturgy and ritual, will become familiar with this corpus and contribute their expertise. There is, in fact, still much to be learned about prayer from the Dead Sea Scrolls.

Selected Bibliography

A. *Primary Editions of Major Texts*

The Dead Sea Scrolls of the Hebrew University, ed. Eliezer L. Sukenik. Jerusalem: Magnes, 1954 Hebrew edition; 1955 English edition. (Transcription and photos of 1QH^a.)

Qumran Cave I [*Discoveries in the Judaean Desert* I], ed. D. Barthélemy and J. T. Milik. Oxford: Clarendon, 1955.

The Psalms Scroll of Qumran Cave 11 (11QPs^a) [*Discoveries in the Judaean Desert* IV], ed. James A. Sanders. Oxford: Clarendon, 1965.

Qumrân Grotte 4.III (4Q482-4Q520) [*Discoveries in the Judaean Desert* VII], ed. Maurice Baillet. Oxford: Clarendon, 1982. (Includes *Daily Prayers, Festival Prayers, Words of the Luminaries,* and some small texts.)

Qumran Cave 4.VI: Poetical and Liturgical Texts, Part 1 [*Discoveries in the Judaean Desert* XI], ed. Esther Eshel, Hanan Eshel, Carol Newsom, Bilhah Nitzan, Eileen Schuller, and Ada Yardeni. Oxford: Clarendon, 1998. (Includes *Berakot, Songs of the Sabbath Sacrifice,* non-canonical Psalms, and 4Q448, an apocryphal psalm and prayer.)

Qumran Cave 4.XX: Poetical and Liturgical Texts, Part 2 [*Discoveries in the Judaean Desert* XXIX], ed. Esther Chazon, *et al.* Oxford: Clarendon, 1999. (Includes 4Q*Hodayot* manuscripts, *Barki Naphshi,* and many short and fragmentary compositions.)

B. *Studies*

Chazon, Esther. "Prayers from Qumran and Their Historical Implications." *Dead Sea Discoveries* 1 (1994): 758-72.

————. "On the Special Character of Sabbath Prayer: New Data from Qumran." *Journal of Jewish Music and Liturgy* 15 (1992): 1-21.

————. "Hymns and Prayers in the Dead Sea Scrolls." In *The Dead Sea*

Scrolls After Fifty Years: A Comprehensive Assessment, vol. 1, ed. P. W. Flint and J. C. VanderKam. Leiden: Brill, 1998, 244-70.

Falk, Daniel K. *Daily, Festival and Sabbath Prayers from Qumran* [*Studies on the Texts of the Desert of Judah* 27]. Leiden: Brill, 1998.

Flint, Peter W. *The Dead Sea Psalms Scrolls and the Book of Psalms.* [*Studies on the Texts of the Desert of Judah* 17]. Leiden: Brill, 1997.

Flusser, David. "Psalms, Hymns and Prayers." In *Jewish Writings of the Second Temple Period, Apocrypha, Pseudepigrapha, Qumran Sectarian Writings, Philo, Josephus* [*Compendia Rerum Iudaicarum ad Novum Testamentum*], vol. 2, ed. M. E. Stone. Assen: Van Gorcum, 1984, 551-77.

Holm-Nielsen, Svend. *Hodayot: Psalms from Qumran* [*Acta Theologica Danica* II]. Aarhus: Universitetsforlaget, 1960.

Nitzan, Bilhah. *Qumran Prayer and Religious Poetry* [*Studies on the Texts of the Desert of Judah* 12]. Leiden: Brill, 1994.

Schiffman, Lawrence. "The Dead Sea Scrolls and the Early History of Jewish Liturgy." In *The Synagogue in Late Antiquity,* ed. L. I. Levine. Philadelphia: JTSA/ASOR, 1987, 33-48.

Schuller, Eileen M. *Non-Canonical Psalms from Qumran: A Pseudepigraphic Collection.* Atlanta: Scholars, 1986.

———. "Some Observations on Blessings of God in Texts from Qumran." In *Of Scribes and Scrolls: Studies on the Hebrew Bible, Intertestamental Judaism, and Christian Origins* [*Festschrift* John Strugnell], ed. H. Attridge, J. J. Collins, and T. F. Tobin. Lanham: University Press of America, 1990, 133-43.

———. "The Psalm of Joseph Within the Context of Second Temple Prayer." *Catholic Biblical Quarterly* 54 (1992): 67-79.

———. "4Q380 and 4Q381: Non-Canonical Psalms from Qumran." In *The Dead Sea Scrolls: Forty Years of Research,* ed. D. Dimant and U. Rappaport. Leiden: Brill, 1992, 90-99.

———. "A Hymn from a Cave Four *Hodayot* Manuscript: 4Q427 7 i + ii." *Journal of Biblical Literature* 112 (1993): 651-74.

———. "The Cave Four *Hodayot* Manuscripts: A Preliminary Description." *Jewish Quarterly Review* 85 (1994): 137-50.

———. "Prayers, Hymns and Liturgical Texts from Qumran." In *Community of the Renewed Covenant: The Notre Dame Symposium on the Dead Sea Scrolls,* ed. E. Ulrich and J. C. VanderKam. Notre Dame: University of Notre Dame Press, 1994, 153-74.

————. "A Thanksgiving Hymn from 4QHodayot[b] (4Q428 7)." *Revue de Qumran* 16 (1995): 517-32.

————. "Confession," "Doxology," "Glorify," "Laments," "Liturgy," "Poetry," "Prayer," and "Psalms." In *Dictionary of Judaism in the Biblical Period*, ed. J. Neusner and W. S. Green. New York: Macmillan, 1996.

————. "The Use of Biblical Terms as Designations for Non-Biblical Hymnic and Prayer Compositions." In *Biblical Perspectives: Proceedings of the First Orion Center Conference on the Dead Sea Scrolls*, ed. E. Chazon and M. Stone. Leiden: Brill, 1997, 205-20.

Schuller, Eileen M. and L. Ditommaso. "A Bibliography of the *Hodayot*, 1948-1996." *Dead Sea Discoveries* 4 (1997): 55-101.

Schuller, Eileen M. and J. Strugnell. "Further *Hodayot* Manuscripts from Qumran?" In *Antikes Judentum und Frühes Christentum. Festschrift für Hartmut Stegemann*, ed. B. Kollmann, W. Reinhold, A. Steudel. Berlin: de Gruyter, 1999, 51-72.

Stegemann, Hartmut. *The Library of Qumran: On the Essenes, Qumran, John the Baptist and Jesus.* Leiden: Brill; Grand Rapids: Eerdmans, 1998.

Talmon, Shemonyahu. "Emergence of Institutionalized Prayer in Israel in Light of the Qumran Literature." In *World of Qumran from Within*. Jerusalem: Magnes; Leiden: Brill, 1989, 200-243.

Weinfeld, Moshe. "Prayer and Liturgical Practice in the Qumran Sect." In *The Dead Sea Scrolls: Forty Years of Research* [*Studies on the Texts of the Desert of Judah* 10]. Leiden: Brill; Jerusalem: Magnes, 1992, 241-58.

VanderKam, James C. *The Dead Sea Scrolls Today.* Grand Rapids: Eerdmans, 1994.

Jesus and the Gospels

CHAPTER 5

The Canticles of Luke's Infancy Narrative: The Appropriation of a Biblical Tradition

STEPHEN FARRIS

THE CANTICLES OF LUKE'S infancy narrative are particularly lovely windows into the worship of the earliest Christian churches. Such a statement, however, will hardly pass unchallenged among students of Luke's Gospel. For almost every conceivable question surrounding the hymns of Luke 1 and 2 has given rise, at some point, to rather hot scholarly debate. In what follows, therefore, we will deal with (1) distinctive and overlapping features of hymns and prayers and (2) some basic critical questions regarding the Lucan canticles; then turn to (3) an analysis of the hymns themselves and (4) discussion of relations between the old and the new in Christian worship; and finally offer (5) a few concluding statements regarding the importance of the canticles of Luke's infancy narrative for the church today.

1. On Hymns and Prayers

The canticles of Luke's infancy narrative are pretty clearly hymns rather than prayers. One might, therefore, reasonably ask, "Why, then, an essay on hymns in a volume on prayer?" The two categories are certainly distinguishable. Prayer is speech addressed to God that contains praise or petition — in many cases both. Some prayers are cast in poetry, but this is by no means characteristic of prayer language as a whole. Most prayers are in the form of prose, whether expressed in an artful fashion or blurted out almost inarticulately.

Hymns, on the other hand, most commonly speak not to God but about God. Though some hymns address God directly, they characteristically use the third person singular when speaking of God. So we read in Luke's infancy narrative, "My soul magnifies the Lord" (1:46) and "Blessed be the Lord, the God of Israel" (1:68). A brief glance at the Psalter will confirm the preponderance of third person speech in hymns. They offer praise for what God has done, for what he does repeatedly, or even for what he will do — but they do not normally urge or beg God to do anything. Finally, hymns are always poetry; they have a lyrical quality to them.

The great German expert on the psalms, Hermann Gunkel, defined a hymn simply as "a song of praise" (*The Psalms: A Form-Critical Introduction,* trans. T. M. Horner [Philadelphia: Fortress, 1967], 10). To this we might add the slightly longer definition offered in the fourth century by St. Ambrose of Milan, who was himself a noted composer of hymns:

> A hymn is a song containing praise of God. If you praise God but without song you do not have a hymn. If you praise anything that does not pertain to the glory of God, even if you sing it, you do not have a hymn. Hence a hymn contains the three elements: *song* and *praise* of *God*. (*De cantu et musica sacra,* I.14, as translated by E. Werner, *The Sacred Bridge* [New York: Schocken, 1970], 207)

It is clear under these definitions that the canticles of Luke 1 and 2 are hymns.

But while the categories can be distinguished, they also overlap. We can see this in the way we use the words "hymn" and "prayer" in common speech. A typical "hymnbook," for example, contains poetry or "hymns" that are actually "prayers." The nineteenth-century hymn "Spirit of God! Descend upon my Heart!" is a hymn that is actually a prayer, as its first verse (as well as all of its other verses) amply illustrates:

> Spirit of God! descend upon my heart!
>   Wean it from earth; thru' all its pulses move.
> Stoop to my weakness, mighty as Thou art.
>   And make me love Thee as I ought to love.

It addresses God in the second person singular and begs of God the gift of the Holy Spirit. It is in technical terms an *epiklesis*.

Nor are scholars necessarily more precise than the editors of hymnbooks. *The Oxford Book of Earliest Christian Prayers,* for example, contains some materials that look a good deal more like hymns than prayers. For example, the editors identify Eph. 1:3-23, which begins "Blessed be the God and Father of our Lord Jesus Christ who hath blessed us with every spiritual gift," as a prayer.

This overlap of categories is rooted in something more significant than simply the imprecision of speech. Hymns and prayers overlap in reality as well as in our language. Hymns always contain praise, and prayer often does. So the Benedictus of Luke 1:68-79, which is a hymn, begins "Blessed be the Lord, the God of Israel." And the ancient Jewish prayer of blessing over one's daily bread, the *birkhat ha mazon,* begins "Blessed art Thou, Lord our God, King of the Universe." The point at which a prayer that offers praise to God becomes a hymn is very difficult to determine. What is clear, however, is that the common ground between hymns and prayers lies in the concept of praise.

At the heart of both hymns and prayers is recognition of who God is and what God has done. This is obvious with respect to hymns. But in a profound way it is also true of prayers that contain only petitions. When we petition God we are in that very action recognizing both God's capacity and God's willingness to act for us — in other words, both God's power and God's benevolence toward us.

This is hardly a novel insight. Perhaps the reader will forgive a Presbyterian minister quoting John Calvin at this point. According to Calvin, God "wills indeed, as is just, that due honour be paid him by acknowledging that all which men desire or feel to be useful, and pray to obtain, is derived from him" (*Institutes of the Christian Religion* III.20.3). Praise and petition are two aspects of the same reality. Praise and prayer, all mixed together, are the primary linguistic response to God. They are what religion is all about.

It is no surprise, therefore, that the language of hymnody and the language of prayer are often mixed together. Psalm 9 is a classic example. At one moment the psalmist is using classic hymnic language:

> Sing praise to the Lord who dwells in Zion.
> Declare his deeds among the people.

For he who avenges blood is mindful of them;
  he does not forget the cry of the afflicted. (vv. 11-12 NRSV)

The next moment, however, there is prayer: "Be gracious to me, O Lord. See what I suffer from those who hate me" (v. 13 NRSV).

Prayers likewise regularly break into praise. The common ending of the Lord's Prayer, "For thine is the kingdom and the power and the glory forever," is merely the most familiar example of this phenomenon. The doxology is likely an addition to the original text, but a concluding doxology was characteristic of early Christian prayer.

This phenomenon may also be seen in Luke's infancy narrative. The Magnificat of 1:46b-55 and the Benedictus of 1:68-79 are clearly hymns. But the Nunc Dimittis of 2:29-32 is a mixed type. Unlike the two former hymns, it addresses God in the second person singular. Indeed, if the noble translation of the King James Version is followed, it directs what is, in effect, a petition to God and therefore *is* a prayer: "Now lettest Thou Thy servant depart in peace according to Thy word." I do not believe that this is the best translation of these words, but it does demonstrate how close prayer can be to hymnody.

2. Some Basic Critical Questions

That the hymns of Luke 1 and 2 are examples of the praise of the earliest Christian churches cannot, however, be merely stated. The claim must be argued. And since the purpose of this article is to say something about the language of praise in the early Christian church, before that can be done a number of critical questions must first be discussed, at least briefly.

Authorship

There are several theories regarding the authorship of the hymns of Luke's infancy narrative. Two of the most obvious will be mentioned here. Two others will be considered later — including that which the author of this article espouses — since their defense requires a prior determination of the original language of the hymns and more extensive elaboration.

1. Luke as the Author

One theory is that Luke himself was the author. It is known that the composition of speeches for various characters in a narrative was practiced by Greek historians and that Luke patterned himself, at least in part, after Greek historiography. Moreover, Luke's great model, the Septuagint, is replete with hymns and speeches of all sorts. So, it is argued, Luke composed the hymns of the first two chapters of his Gospel in order to enrich his narrative and give it a "biblical" air. This position is held, for the most part, by what might be called "big picture" students of Luke-Acts — that is, by scholars who concern themselves with Luke's literary strategies in the writing of his two-volume work as a whole. This is true of the originator of the theory, the German scholar Adolf von Harnack; of its popularizer in the English-speaking world, Henry J. Cadbury; and of such contemporary advocates as John Drury, Michael Goulder, and Robert Tannehill.

Now it is certainly true that the hymns of Luke 1 and 2 ought not be considered in isolation from Luke's theological intention in writing Luke-Acts as a whole. It is also beyond debate that Luke intended that his writings in general — and his infancy narrative in particular — should remind the reader of the Scriptures of Israel. But considerations like these can hardly determine the question. Authors may quote materials drawn from other sources for their own theological purposes, with such quotations made in order to fit into their own literary strategies. After all, the famous citation of Isa. 6:1-2a in the Nazareth synagogue, "The Spirit of the Lord is upon me . . ." (Luke 4:18-19), obviously suits Luke's purposes. And yet Luke did not compose that quotation. [One wonders, however, if we did not already possess the text of Isaiah 61 whether scholars would argue that Luke had, indeed, composed even these words himself.]

Luke's quotation of Israel's Scriptures certainly suggests a motivation for including hymnic materials, but it tells us nothing about the origin of those materials. A careful study of Luke's strategy, I believe, shows that the hymns of the first two chapters of the evangelist's Gospel are used in a manner more similar to his quotation of Isa 61:1-2a than to what we find with regard to the speeches of Acts, which Luke may well have composed himself. Moreover, a sticky question remains: If Luke did, indeed, compose the three hymns that appear in the infancy narrative of his Gospel, why did he stop with only three? Why aren't there similar hymns scattered throughout his two volumes? But this is almost beside the point. The issue can only, in the end, be decided by a careful and thorough study of the hymns themselves and of their contexts. And those who have carried out such studies have, for the most part, rejected the theory of Lucan authorship.

2. Mary, Zechariah, and Simeon as the Authors

Others, however, have attributed the composition of the hymns of Luke 1 and 2 to Mary, Zechariah, and Simeon themselves. Mary, it is argued, was the source of the information in Luke 1–2, and so that narrative, including its three hymns, was passed on to Luke by her. It seems unlikely, however, that this is the case, at least with respect to the hymns. It is more probable that the hymns were inserted by Luke into his narrative to express the theological significance of the births of John the Baptist and of Jesus. In any case, many of the arguments against the theory that Luke composed the hymns are equally telling against this proposal.

The Nunc Dimittis fits rather neatly into its narrative context. But this is not equally the case with the other two hymns. With the exceptions of 1:48 in the Magnificat and 1:76-77 in the Benedictus, those two hymns are surprisingly general in their praise. Neither offers praise that is specific to the situation of the two speakers. Furthermore, the Magnificat, with its talk of pulling down the mighty from their thrones and lifting up the poor, is, for a young, newly pregnant girl, surprisingly vigorous — even warlike in its language. The nearest parallel to the Benedictus as a whole is the "Hymn of the Return" found in the *War Scroll* at Qumran (i.e., 1QM 14.4-8), which is the hymn of the triumphant warriors after their ultimate battle with God's enemies.

One scholar, Paul Winter, spent most of his life trying to prove that the canticles of Luke's infancy narrative were originally songs of triumph, which had been composed by victorious Jews during the Maccabean wars. This proposal has won few, if any, supporters. But the fact that it could be made at all is testimony to our point. It is also noteworthy that there has been, over the years, a rather heated debate regarding the text of 1:46a, "And Mary said," where a few old Latin manuscripts attribute the Magnificat not to Mary but to Elizabeth — a debate that Raymond Brown has called "eloquent proof of the non-specific nature of the canticle" (*Birth of the Messiah,* 348).

One could easily read Luke 1 without either of the two hymns. Indeed, the narrative would read slightly more smoothly without the Magnificat. For whereas 1:56 reads, "And Mary remained with her," this would follow very nicely after 1:45. But it is slightly awkward following the Magnificat. One would instead expect to read, "And she remained with Elizabeth."

More significantly, Luke's hand can be seen clearly only in those verses that link the hymns to their context. Luke 1:48 is a clear example, for it contains two of Luke's characteristic phrases, or so-called "Lucanisms": "for behold" and "from now on." It has the only two explicitly maternal allusions of the hymns — to the praise of the mothers Hannah and Leah. Likewise, 1:76-77 draws its vocabulary from the description of John the Baptist found in the prologues of the Synoptic Gospels, including their Old Testament references. The most reasonable explanation of all this is that Luke adapted preexisting hymns to their present contexts by means of these short insertions.

It would be easier to argue that Luke composed the Nunc Dimittis of 2:29-32 himself. But the extensive stylistic similarities between the Magnificat and the Benedictus of chapter 1 and the Nunc Dimittis of chapter 2 suggest that all three hymns shared a common origin. This point, however, will be taken up again later in this article.

The Original Language of the Hymns

Connected with the question of authorship is the matter of the original language of the hymns. The questions are not the same. One could believe, as did Raymond Brown, that the hymns were composed in Greek but not by Luke. But if it could be shown that the hymns are really translations of Semitic originals — probably, in fact, originally written in Hebrew — it would be conclusive evidence that Luke did not compose them. This is an immensely technical matter, which time and space forbids being reviewed in detail here. In my 1985 work on *The Hymns of Luke's Infancy Narrative*, I applied a statistical method developed by Raymond A. Martin for determining the presence of translation Greek. These studies have convinced me that the hymns of Luke 1–2 are, indeed, to be seen as translation phenomena, and that they were probably translated into Greek from Hebrew originals. And nothing in more recent scholarship has changed my mind on this issue.

The Community of the Hymns

In our search for the provenance of the hymns of Luke 1 and 2, we need to look for a community in which the hymns originated. If our determination regarding the original language of the hymns is accurate, we can say with confidence that the community of origin was Jewish — indeed, even Palestinian. Other than the proponents of the Lucan composition theory, I know of no scholar who would deny their having been originally composed within a Jewish or Jewish-Christian milieu. But the consensus disappears at that point, with two main options proposed: (1) a community of disciples of John the Baptist, some of whom may even have revered their master as the Messiah, and (2) a circle of early Jewish-Christians.

1. Disciples of John the Baptist

The theory that a community of John the Baptist disciples originally composed the hymns now found in Luke's infancy narrative was widely popular earlier in the century, especially in Germany. According to this theory, the narrative in Luke 1 that deals with John derives from a "Baptist" source. Luke integrated this material into his Gospel to show the disciples of John that their master, though worthy of immense respect, had been overshadowed by One who was greater still. It was a narrative way of saying of John the Baptist, as does John 1:8, "he was not the light, but came to bear witness to the light."

Now it does, indeed, appear that there were in the first century followers of John the Baptist. And it seems that Luke knew that it was possible to attract them into Christianity (cf. Acts 18:24-28). But is there any positive evidence that the hymns of Luke 1 and 2 originated in those circles? Aside from their position in a narrative that has been identified as "Baptist" in its origins, there is nothing in the hymns themselves to suggest a John the Baptist origin. On the contrary, as we will see later, there are certain references to a Davidic Messiah that are very difficult to explain under this theory.

If the theory is largely dependent on the hymns themselves being an integral part of a preexisting John the Baptist narrative, the evidence of their insertion into the narrative by Luke is also evidence against such a Baptist origin theory. I have shown above that there is some evidence that this is the case. Even aside from this point, the present position of the hymns is a problem for the proponents of this theory. The Nunc Dimittis of chapter 2, which is so similar in form to the two hymns of chapter 1, is completely outside any proposed John the Baptist source. Indeed, I know of no scholar who has claimed this hymn for such a Baptist theory. And the position of the Magnificat is also a problem.

Luke 1 and 2 is a diptych — that is, a work made up of two matching parts — which is marked by a subordinating parallelism between the stories about John the Baptist and the stories about Jesus. One angelic annunciation is paralleled by another; one birth by a second; one hymn by a pious old man is followed by another; and so on. They are obviously parallel. But equally obvious is the fact that Luke has tilted the balance in favor of Jesus. For whereas John is born of aged parents, Jesus is born of a virgin; whereas John is "great before the Lord," Jesus is simply "great." The exaltation of Jesus over John is most explicitly emphasized in the visitation scene in which Mary visits the aged Elizabeth — where John, *in utero*, foreshadows his role in the Gospel by leaping in the womb to greet Jesus, and Elizabeth hails Mary as "the mother of my Lord."

The Magnificat is the climax of this key visitation scene. In other words, this hymn is an integral part of a scene explicitly designed to demonstrate the superiority of Jesus over John the Baptist. Merely attributing the hymn to Elizabeth, as is sometimes proposed, is not only a textually suspect maneuver, it does not change the nature of the scene as a whole. In fact, this scene could not have been part of any supposed Baptist source, for it runs contrary to the veneration of such a worthy figure.

Recognizing this conflict, some scholars have attempted to place the Magnificat elsewhere in the hypothetical Baptist source — after what is now 1:25 or 1:42, for example. But the hymn is so general in its praise that there is not the least reason to suppose that it belongs at any of its other proposed locations. If it were cut loose from its present mooring, why would it wash up on those particular shores?

The whole weight of the theory that the Lucan canticles were originally composed within a community of John the Baptist disciples ultimately rests on the identification of the Benedictus as a Baptist hymn. Yet, ironically, it is the Benedictus that contains the clearest reference to the advent of a Messiah of David's line. There has been an attempt to turn John the Baptist into a Davidide. But that is contradicted by the evidence of the so-called "Baptist source" itself, which identifies John's father as a priest (cf. Luke 1:5-25). Jesus, on the other hand, was identified as a descendent of David from the earliest days. This is witnessed to not only by the genealogies of Matt. 1:1-17 and Luke 3:23-38 but also by the confessional formulation of Rom. 1:3-4, which probably antedates Paul. In all of these sources Jesus is identified as "the son of David according to the flesh."

The Davidic references in the Benedictus seem abundantly clear. The most compelling is 1:69, "He has raised up a horn of salvation in the house of David his servant." A horn is a symbol of strength and power and "horn of salvation" is a reference to the Messiah. The fifteenth benediction of the Babylonian version of the *Shemoneh Esreh,* the great prayer of the synagogue, reads: "Let the shoot of David your servant speedily spring up and raise his horn in your salvation. . . . May you be blessed, O Lord, who lets the horn of salvation flourish." It is difficult to determine the age of this prayer. But certainly it demonstrates a climate of expectation and the use of key vocabulary. The Benedictus, in fact, sounds like the kind of hymn sung by a person who would have prayed in this manner and who has now seen the answer to those prayers.

There may also be a Davidic allusion in the introductory blessing itself. One might hear in it an allusion to the words of the aged David at the time of the enthronement of his son Solomon: "Blessed be the Lord, the God of Israel, who today has granted one of my offspring to sit on my throne and permitted me to witness it" (1 Kings 1:48). Inasmuch as the formula also appears three times in the Psalter, this identification must remain hypothetical but it is suggestive.

A more important Davidic allusion may be found in the Benedictus at 1:78, "in the heartfelt mercy of our God, through which the *rising light* from on high has visited us." The Greek word rendered "rising light" *(anatolē)* is used in the LXX to translate the Hebrew word צמח, which is rendered in our English translations as "branch," "root," or "sprout." The word "branch," in fact, is used in the writings of the Old Testament prophets as a title for "the one who is to come." So, for example, Jer. 23:5 reads:

> The days are surely coming, says the Lord,
>   when I will raise up for David a righteous Branch;
> and he shall reign as king and deal wisely,
>   and shall execute justice and righteousness in the land.

A similar use of this title appears in Jer. 33:15 ("righteous Branch"), Zech. 3:8 ("the Branch"), and Zech. 6:12 ("the Branch").

Here in the Benedictus, however, it is not a plant that rises up but an astronomical object — the common ground between "rising lights" and "branches" or "sprouts" being that they are things that rise up or sprout up. This combination of ideas is not strange to the New Testament, as witness the statement of the glorified Jesus in Rev. 22:16: "It is I, Jesus . . . I am the root and the descendant of David, the bright morning star." The metaphor may be mixed, but it is understandable. The "rising light," therefore, is the Messiah of David's line. But why would a hymn composed by disciples of John the Baptist, who supposedly thought of John more highly than they did of Jesus, praise Jesus' advent in such terms?

Some supporters of the Baptist source theory have adopted a somewhat different and more plausible approach. Following Hermann Gunkel in identifying the Benedictus as an "eschatological hymn," they posit that such hymns as were later incorporated into Luke's infancy narrative originally looked forward to the triumph of God with such confidence that they could speak of that triumph as if it had already happened. Examples of this type of proleptically fulfilled eschatological hymns can be found most easily in Deutero-Isaiah — for instance, in Isa. 52:9:

> Break forth together into singing,
>   you ruins of Jerusalem;
> for the Lord has comforted his people,
>   he has redeemed Jerusalem.

But if the hymns now found in Luke 1–2 were originally eschatological in this sense of the word, there would seem to have been no necessity to attach them to the actual advent of a Davidic Messiah — and, according to this argument, it is only the expectation of a Davidic Messiah that they bear witness to. It may, of course, be argued (as has been done) that the Lucan hymns stemmed from a Baptist source despite their Davidic references. On such a thesis, however, all that is being asserted is that the hymns were originally simply Jewish and that they were only preserved for Luke in a Baptist source. But, again, it may be asked: Why would hymns that speak about the expectation of a Messiah of David's line be preserved in such a Baptist community? And if they were hymns that arose within the matrix of a common Jewish heritage, why would one suppose that they come to us from a hypothetical Baptist circle rather than from the community to which the not-at-all hypothetical Luke belonged, which was a community that revered the Davidic Messiah? The theory of a community of John the Baptist disciples as the original source for the Lucan canticles begins, in fact, to collapse from a series of accumulated improbabilities.

In any case, the hymns of Luke 1 and 2 do not appear to be eschatological hymns at all. They look, rather, like hymns that praise God for some actual event that has already occurred. Admittedly, this event has eschatological consequences. The world will be turned upside down because of it. In principle, however, the great redemption — the consolation of Israel; the reversal of all things — has already happened. What could make people suppose that this is the case? I believe the only reasonable answer is the life, death, and resurrection of the One who was hailed by the early church as the Messiah of David's line. The hymns of Luke 1 and 2 are best understood as Jewish-Christian hymns that praised the coming of Jesus the Christ. And taking such a stance, it seems natural to find them in what is, after all, a Christian account of the Messiah's birth.

2. Early Jewish Christians

A number of scholars — including Raymond Brown, author of the standard work on the infancy narratives, and Ulrike Mittmann-Richert, author of the most recent (and remarkably thorough) study of the Lucan infancy hymns — are willing to be even more precise than this. They believe that the hymns of Luke 1 and 2 may well have originated in the Jewish-Christian church of Jerusalem itself. I would not venture so far myself. But it certainly seems likely, as translations of Semitic (perhaps even Hebrew) originals, that they are Palestinian in origin. Their triumphant tone indicates that they predate the tragic destruction of Jerusalem in AD 70. The completely unself-conscious identification of the hymnist's people with Israel makes it likely that they were composed in the very early years of the Christian church. There is no hint of any separation between the church and Israel in these hymns.

If these remarkable hymns were, indeed, compositions of the early Jewish-Christian church — whether written by believers in Jesus within the Jerusalem church or by Jewish believers more generally — they open for us a window into the piety of the earliest Christians. That piety appears to have been shaped primarily by an inherited familiarity with the worship of Israel. For these hymns stand in almost complete continuity with the traditions of Israel and give evidence of having been shaped by those traditions in a number of ways. Scholars such as Hermann Gunkel, Sigmund Mowinckel, and Claus Westermann, who are steeped in the poetry of the Old Testament, have recognized in these hymns old friends. It is, therefore, of first importance that we understand the hymns of Luke's infancy narrative as being part of a living history of praise.

This is true, in the first place, of the form of the hymns, which is quite characteristic of Hebrew psalmody. It is also true, however, with respect to their content. While we have spoken of them as "hymns," and will continue to do so in what follows, they are also in Old Testament parlance "songs of thanksgiving" (using the classification of H. Gunkel) or "declarative psalms of praise" (in the scheme of C. Westermann). Such canticles praise God for particular blessings rendered to an individual or to the people.

Westermann has added another category: "descriptive psalms of praise," which are psalms that praise God for who he is or what he regularly does. The Magnificat has certain features of this latter type, as in its statement: "Holy is his name, his mercy is from generation to generation upon those who fear him" (1:49b-50). One ought not to expect in hymns or psalms too great a purity of type. The categories are only rough guides for the student. As a whole, however, the Magnificat, like the other two hymns, fits most nearly the category of a "declarative psalm of praise."

3. An Analysis of the Hymns

There are two characteristic features in each of the hymns of Luke 1 and 2. First, there appears a word of praise: "My soul magnifies the Lord, and my spirit rejoices in God my Savior" (1:46, which begins the Magnificat); "Blessed is the Lord God of Israel" (1:68, which begins the Benedictus); and "Now you are letting your servant depart in peace, as you have promised" (2:29, which begins the Nunc Dimittis). Second, reasons for praise are given. These reasons commonly appear in the past tense and take up the remainder of the hymns. These features are also common in both the canonical psalms and the extrabiblical psalmody of Second Temple Judaism. And their presence in the hymns of Luke 1 and 2 are evidence that the Lucan canticles are to be seen as part-and-parcel of Israel's ancient, yet still vigorous, liturgical tradition.

STEPHEN FARRIS

Corporate and Individual Emphases

It is immediately apparent that the Benedictus looks like a "song of thanksgiving" of the people. It is hard to miss its emphasis on the collective:

> Blessed is the Lord the God of *Israel,*
>> for he has visited and redeemed his *people.*
> He has raised up a horn of salvation for *us,*
>> in the house of his servant David; etc.
>>> (as Zechariah's hymn begins in 1:68-69)

On the other hand, both the Magnificat and the Nunc Dimittis appear, at first sight, to be "songs of thanksgiving" of individuals:

> *My* soul magnifies the Lord,
>> and *my* spirit rejoices in God my Savior.
> For he has regarded the low estate of *his handmaiden;*
>> henceforth all generations will call *me* blessed.
> For the Mighty One has done great things for *me,*
>> and holy is his name; etc.   (as Mary's hymn begins in 1:46-49)

and

> Now you are letting *your* servant go in peace, according to your
>> word,
> for *my* eyes have seen your salvation.
>>> (as Simeon's hymn begins in 2:29-30)

Such a first impression, however, is not entirely accurate. In both of these latter cases, the hymns move from the individual to the corporate. So the Magnificat ends with the words: "He [God] has helped *Israel* his servant, in remembrance of his mercy, as he said to *our fathers,* to *Abraham and his seed* forever" (1:54-55). And the Nunc Dimittis displays a similar movement toward the corporate when it speaks of the birth of the Savior as being "a light for revelation to the *Gentiles* and for glory to your *people Israel*" (2:32).

Moreover, the persons singing these hymns are to be taken, to a considerable degree, as representative figures. Some Roman Catholic scholars

104

have seen in Mary the figure of the "Daughter of Zion," who was antici-pated in various Old Testament prophecies (cf. Mic. 1:13; 4:8, 10, 13; Zech. 3:14-17). Raymond Brown, however, has effectively demolished this argu-ment (*Birth of the Messiah*, 320-28). Nonetheless, Brown sees Mary as rep-resenting the piety of a group he identifies as the *Anawim*, or "the poor" of Israel, who were beloved by the psalmist (*Birth of the Messiah*, 353 n. 45).

Brown's identification of Mary with "the poor" is compelling. But even if that identification be denied, it is clear that the hymn of 1:46-55 is not the hymn of a solitary individual. The singer moves seamlessly from what God has done for "me" (v. 49) to what God has done for "those of low estate" (v. 52), for "the hungry" (v. 53), and eventually for "his servant Israel" (v. 54). There is no late second millennium individualism here. The singer identifies completely with the people.

And what is true of the Magnificat is also true of the Nunc Dimittis, where Simeon is also to be seen as a representative figure. The opening words of Simeon's hymn in 2:29-30 ("Now you are letting your servant go in peace . . . for my eyes have seen your salvation") hearken back to the words of the aged Jacob as he greets his long-lost son Joseph in Gen. 46:30: "I can die now, having seen for myself that you are still alive." The resem-blance is even more striking in the expanded account of this same event of Jacob at last meeting Joseph in *Jubilees* 45:3, which is an early writing of the Second Temple period:

> Let me die now that I have seen you. And now let the Lord, the God of Israel, be blessed, the God of Abraham and the God of Isaac, who did not withhold his mercy and his kindness from his servant Jacob.

Here Jacob speaks as *Israel*, the representative of the whole people. Like-wise, the singer of the Nunc Dimittis is seized by a sense that what was done for him is part of a much wider blessing of God. It is, in fact, not merely a personal salvation that he has witnessed, but one "prepared be-fore the face of all the peoples" (2:31).

The Language of Israel's Sacred Traditions

Not only the form of the hymns of Luke's infancy narrative, but also their vocabulary has been supplied by the sacred traditions of Israel. They are, in truth, mosaics of allusions to the canonical psalms and prophets. Raymond Brown has shown how it is possible to parallel every line of the three Lucan hymns to one or more texts from the Old Testament and/or the writings of Second Temple Judaism (cf. *Birth of the Messiah*, 358-60 [for the Magnificat], 386-89 [for the Benedictus], and 458 [for the Nunc Dimittis]). It is impossible to reproduce all of those parallels here. But in order to gain a sense of how completely these hymns were formed by the language of Scripture, at least the following parallels from the Old Testament should be noted.

1. The Magnificat (1:46-55)

Most commentaries argue that the Magnificat is based on Hannah's hymn of praise in 1 Sam. 2:1-10. This is, however, an oversimplification, for the Magnificat is more than an imitation of only one Old Testament passage. As a whole, it does, indeed, resemble Hannah's hymn. But most of the individual lines and phrases more closely resemble other parts of the Old Testament.

Mary's hymn begins, "My soul magnifies the Lord and my spirit has rejoiced in God my Savior." That line is somewhat similar to Hannah's hymn: "My heart exults in the Lord; my strength (horn) is exulted in my God. My mouth derides my enemies, because I rejoice in my victory" (1 Sam. 2:1). Rather more comparable, however, is Hab. 3:18: "I will rejoice in the Lord; I will exult in the God of my salvation." It is also comparable to Ps. 35:9, "My soul shall rejoice in the Lord, exulting in his deliverance."

The reasons stated in 1:48 for Mary's praise — "For he has looked upon the low estate of his handmaiden; for behold from now on all generations will call me happy" — contain allusions to the prayers and praise of various representative Old Testament mothers. Behind this verse may, indeed, be Hannah's prayer (not her hymn) of 1 Sam. 1:11:

> O Lord of hosts, if you will indeed look on the affliction of your maid-servant, and remember me, and not forget your maidservant, but give to your maidservant a son, then I will give him to the Lord all the days of his life, and no razor shall touch his head.

But the wording of Mary's praise also contains an allusion to the rejoicing of Leah, an ancestor of David, at the birth of her son Reuben, as given in

Gen. 29:32: "The Lord has looked upon my affliction." It also seems to reflect Leah's further rejoicing at the birth of Asher, whom Zilpah, Leah's maid, bore to Jacob, as expressed in Gen. 30:13: "Happy am I! For the women will call me happy." The only words not supplied by these texts are the "Lucanisms" identified earlier — that is, the words "for behold" and "from now on."

In 1:49b of the Magnificat we read, "Holy is his name." The background to this ascription of praise is Ps. 111:9: "He has sent redemption to his people; he has commanded his covenant forever. Holy and awesome is his name." What is particularly interesting is that the first half of Ps. 111:9 is also the background to a phrase in the Benedictus, "he has redeemed his people" (or, more literally, "he has made or performed redemption for his people" (1:68). This verse of the Magnificat (i.e., 1:49b) also introduces the key word "covenant," which will reappear later in the Benedictus. This is an important feature to note, for it serves to highlight the facts that the method of composition and the style of language in the Magnificat and Benedictus are remarkably similar. It may be, in fact, that we should speak not just of a community from which these two hymns have come, but of an individual composer.

2. The Benedictus (1:68-79)

We have already seen several examples of Davidic allusions in the Benedictus. The remainder of the hymn also hearkens back to the Old Testament. So, for example, we read in verses 71-73 of God granting "salvation from our enemies, and from the hand of those who hate us, showing mercy to our fathers and remembering his covenant, the oath which he swore to Abraham." Are there not echoes of the Psalter in those words? Witness, for example:

> "So he saved them from the hand of the foe, and delivered them from the hand of the enemy" (Ps. 106:10);
> "For their sake, he remembered the covenant" (Ps. 106:45);
> "He is mindful of his covenant forever . . . the covenant he made with Abraham" (Ps. 105:8-9).

The composer (or composers) of both the Magnificat and the Benedictus was (or were) immersed, it seems, in a river that flows from the

Old Testament. The primary source of that river was the Psalter. But there were also other canonical sources. The prophets, most notably Isaiah, also give words to the hymns. And there are occasional allusions to the Pentateuch.

3. The Nunc Dimittis (2:29-32)

The Nunc Dimittis, on the other hand, depends primarily on Deutero-Isaiah. Here we hear echoes of various passages from that major Israelite prophet:

> "Then the glory of the Lord shall be revealed and all people shall see it" (Isa. 40:5);
> "I have given you as a covenant to the people, as a light to the nations" (Isa. 42:6);
> "The Lord has bared his holy arm before the eyes of all the nations; and all the earth shall see the salvation of our God" (Isa. 52:10).

It is as though the author (or authors) of these hymns was (or were) immersed in a mighty river of scriptural praise, which had come down to him (or them) from olden times. Nor does the river disappear unnoticed into the ground with the completion of what we now recognize as the Old Testament canon. Portions of the Lucan hymns also have certain similarities to some of the writings of Second Temple Judaism. *Psalms of Solomon* 10:4 ("The Lord will remember his servants in mercy"), for example, reminds us of Luke 1:54 ("He has helped his servant Israel, in remembrance of his mercy") and Luke 1:72 (". . . to perform the mercy promised to our father, and to remember his holy covenant") — though this may be too general a resemblance to be classed as an allusion.

Echoes can also be found in the Dead Sea Scrolls and in certain passages from the *Testaments of the Twelve Patriarchs*. Likewise, to cite again the standard prayer of Judaism, the fifteenth benediction of the *Shemoneh Esreh* reads: "Let the shoot of David your servant speedily spring up and raise his horn in your salvation. . . . May you be blessed, O Lord, who lets the horn of salvation flourish." Such verbal parallels to features within the hymns of Luke 1 and 2 may not, however, indicate any direct genealogical relationship, but only that all of the authors in question were dependent on a common and vibrant tradition.

4. On Relations between the Old and the New

Luke used the three hymns that he incorporated into his infancy narrative, as suggested above, in a manner he learned from the Old Testament. Psalms in the Old Testament are found not only in the Psalter, but also at key points throughout the entire biblical narrative. One thinks not only of Hannah's song of 1 Sam. 2:1-10, but also of the song of Moses in Exod. 15:1-15, the song of Miriam in Exod. 15:21, the song of Deborah in Judg. 5:1-31, and many others. Undoubtedly, Luke wanted to give his narrative a biblical air through the use of these hymns. And in this purpose he succeeded brilliantly.

Indeed, the coming of Christ was a new thing. It turned the world upside down. But the coming of Christ, through the fulfillment of prophecy, was also a continuation of the history of God's gracious and mighty deeds. In my work on *The Hymns of Luke's Infancy Narrative,* I highlighted Luke's use of the "prophecy and fulfillment" motif in his Gospel. I would not wish to abandon that concept. But perhaps a better phrase for what is taking place in Luke's infancy narrative would be "prophecy and pattern," as suggested by Darrell Bock in his helpful 1987 book entitled *Proclamation from Prophecy and Pattern.* For as Luke evidently saw it, that new thing that was in Christ "fit" the pattern established in the history of God's gracious and mighty deeds on behalf of his people.

It was not Luke's wish, I believe, to distinguish completely the Christian church from Israel. Jakob Jervell, the Norwegian scholar, was substantially correct when he declared that the evangelist did not so much picture an Israel that as a whole rejected the gospel, but rather one that was split by the gospel. The Israel that accepted the gospel was as pious as was Mary or Zechariah or Simeon — all of whom welcomed Jesus as the fulfillment of God's long history of promise. That faithful Jewish church was the foundation of the mission that was now reaching out to the Gentiles. The hymns of Luke 1 and 2 express a theology of continuity marvelously well, and the circles from whom he obtained them were the evidence for Luke that such a theology was not a fantasy.

5. Conclusion

In a society that gives high marks to "innovation" and "originality," some may wish to demean the aesthetic and spiritual value of the hymns of

Luke's infancy narrative. John Drury, for example, considers them only a pastiche or stylistic imitation of a hodgepodge of Old Testament fragments. He argues that these imitations of biblical hymns were created by Luke, and, in disparaging fashion, goes on to say that "to suggest that Luke wrote these is not to posit any very great skill on his part" (*Tradition and Design in Luke's Gospel*, 49). More to be commended than Drury for their aesthetic judgments, however, are Johann Sebastian Bach and Antonio Lucio Vivaldi, to name only two great artists who have been inspired by the Magnificat.

But "pastiche" may not, in any case, be the right word for these hymns. Rather, their author or authors were so absorbed into the spiritual and liturgical life of their tradition that their praise for the new thing God had done in Jesus Christ could not do other than express itself in the revered language they had come to know so well. Far wiser than Drury is Robert Tannehill in saying that

> the use of the language of tradition is not necessarily a sign that creative ability is lacking. Traditional language is language already heavy with meaning. It carries the weight of its use in the past, and a skilled poet can awaken this past meaning and use it for his own purposes. . . . This act of praise gains in power because in it reverberate Israel's many acts of praise in response to God's deeds. ("The Magnificat as Poem," 265)

One of the main things to be said about the hymns of Luke's infancy narrative is, quite simply, that they are exceedingly beautiful. It is true that the unadorned but sincere praise of people caught up in seemingly inexpressible gratitude to God is to be preferred to the merely artful use of words. But one of the glories of the praise tradition of Israel and the Christian church is that this gratitude often finds expression in works of beauty that make the soul ache with delight. The praise of God need not be beautiful to be spiritually valuable. But it helps when it is.

Admiration for the new and the innovative may not only affect our estimate of the value of these ancient hymns, it may also lead us to value only the new in the hymns and prayers of our day. The hymns of Luke's infancy narrative tell us that it is perfectly possible to express joy in the new using the language of the old. The revered language of our tradition has had a rough go of it in recent years. The language of tradition is sometimes spurned as an impediment to effective communication. Hymns and prayers in many of our churches are now full of language that is new — sometimes even shocking. The example of the hymns of Luke 1 and 2 certainly does not tell us that it is impossible to praise except in the language of the tradition. Surely there is room for new language in our liturgies. But the beauty, elegance, and deep spiritual power of the language of tradition can also spring to new and vigorous life. The praise of Israel and the Christian church is still a mighty river — and we, if we learn its cadences as thoroughly as did the singers of the Lucan infancy hymns, may still be baptized into it.

The key word in all of this is continuity. The hymns of Luke 1 and 2 are marked in every aspect by continuity rather than innovation. Insofar as they speak to us about prayer and praise in the New Testament, they remind us that prayer and praise are to be expressed within a tradition — that is, they follow the forms and express themselves in the language of a particular tradition *religiously*. In this respect, prayer and praise as we see them in the New Testament are actually remarkably old.

Selected Bibliography

Bemile, Paul. *The Magnificat Within the Context and Framework of Lukan Theology*. Frankfurt: Peter Lang, 1986.

Bock, Darrell L. *Proclamation from Prophecy and Pattern: Lucan Old Testament Christology*. Sheffield: JSOT, 1987.

Brown, Raymond E. *The Birth of the Messiah: A Commentary on the Infancy Narratives in Matthew and Luke*. Garden City: Doubleday, 1976. (Note: Brown's book gives remarkably complete bibliographical information up to 1976.)

————. "Gospel Infancy Research from 1976 to 1986: Part II (Luke)." *Catholic Biblical Quarterly* 48 (1986): 660-80. (Note: Brown's review article extends the bibliographical information found in his *Birth of the Messiah* to 1986.)

Coleridge, Mark. *The Birth of the Lukan Narrative: Narrative as Christology in Luke 1–2*. Sheffield: JSOT, 1993.

Drury, John. *Tradition and Design in Luke's Gospel*. London: Longman & Todd, 1976.

Farris, Stephen C. *The Hymns of Luke's Infancy Narratives: Their Origin, Meaning and Significance*. Sheffield: JSOT, 1985.

Horsley, Richard A. *The Liberation of Christmas: The Infancy Narratives in Social Context.* New York: Crossroad, 1989.

Jones, Douglas R. "The Background and Character of the Lukan Psalms (Lk 1:46-55, 68-79)." *Journal of Theological Studies* 19 (1968): 19-50.

Manns, F. "Une prière juive reprise en Luc 1, 68-69." *Ephemeridies Liturgicae* 106 (1992): 162-66.

Mittmann-Richert, Ulrike. *Magnifikat und Benediktus. Die ältisten Zeugnisse der jüdenchristlichen Tradition von der Geburt des Messias.* Tübingen: Mohr, 1996. (Note: Mittmann-Richert's book provides more recent bibliographical information, beyond that set out by R. E. Brown in 1976 and 1986.)

Ravens, David. *Luke and the Restoration of Israel.* Sheffield: JSOT, 1995.

Strauss, Mark L. *The Davidic Messiah in Luke-Acts.* Sheffield: JSOT, 1995.

Tannehill, Robert C. "The Magnificat as Poem." *Journal of Biblical Literature* 93 (1974): 263-75.

CHAPTER 6

Jesus — Example and Teacher of Prayer in the Synoptic Gospels

I. HOWARD MARSHALL

A COMPREHENSIVE STUDY of prayer in the Synoptic Gospels must include the practice of Jesus himself, the practices of other people in the story, and the teaching of Jesus regarding prayer. Since, however, other authors in this volume are dealing with the Canticles of Luke 1–2 (see chapter 5) and the Lord's Prayer (see chapter 7), these two matters will not be treated at any length in this chapter.

1. The Material for Discussion

Prayer occupies a prominent place in the Synoptic Gospels. This can immediately be seen by a survey of the words used: the verb "to pray" (*proseuchomai;* about 44 times), the noun "prayer" (*proseuchē;* 7 times), the verb "to ask" (*deomai;* used of prayer 4 times), the verb "to bless" (*eulogeō;* used of prayer about 7 times; also *kateulogeō,* once), the verb "to thank" (*eucharisteō;* used of prayer 7 times), and the verb "to ask" (*aiteō;* used of prayer 8 times). We must also, however, consider passages where the vocabulary may be absent but the theme is nevertheless present. What we are doing in this article, therefore, is not simply a word-study but a study of the concept of prayer, to which we are often guided by the vocabulary that is used.

Prayer is mentioned in about a dozen passages in the Gospel of Mark. In 1:35 and 6:46 Jesus prays by himself. In 14:32-39 he prays and talks about prayer to his companions in Gethsemane. In 6:41 and 8:6-7 he gives thanks before food, as also in 14:22-23 before the Last Supper. In 9:29 he tells his disciples that some demons can be cast out only by prayer. In 11:17 he reminds the people that the temple is meant to be a house of prayer "for all nations." In 11:24-25 he gives his disciples teaching on prayer, involving the need for faith and a readiness to forgive others. In 12:40 he warns against people who pray at great length, but whose conduct is inconsistent with their apparently pious demeanor. In 13:18 he tells his disciples that they will need to pray that the future tribulation does not come in the winter, when conditions would make the situation all the worse. And in 15:34 he cries out to God from the cross: "My God, my God, why have you forsaken me?"

Assuming that Matthew used Mark and a collection of sayings of Jesus generally designated "Q" (i.e., *logia* or "sayings," which he and Luke derived from the same source or sources), it appears that the evangelist Matthew was generally dependent on his sources for material that he included in his Gospel about prayer. For virtually every occurrence of prayer material in Matthew has a parallel in Mark or Luke, and so can be viewed as having been derived from either Mark or Q.

Matthew took over most of the prayer material listed above that appears in Mark's Gospel, but he tended to abbreviate it. Thus he omitted Mark 1:35, along with the whole of Mark 1:35-38, probably because of his recasting of the order of that material and his inclusion of other material at this point. He also omitted Mark 9:29, the saying about casting out demons by prayer, and replaced it in 17:20 by a statement about the need for faith (cf. Luke 17:6). This latter statement may be an isolated saying that Matthew and Luke each placed separately in what probably seemed to them a more appropriate setting. Furthermore, Mark 12:40, the saying about scribes who make long prayers, disappeared in Matthew's presentation, being replaced by an extensive series of "woes" on the "scribes and Pharisees" in chapter 23 — a series of denunciations that was evidently drawn from non-Marcan material. Matthew 6:7 also deals with long prayers, but from a different angle. In all of this, however, no significant difference in the treatment of prayer, as compared with Mark's treatment, can be detected.

Matthew shares with Luke the saying about praying for persecutors

(5:44; cf. Luke 6:27), the so-called Lord's Prayer (6:9-13; cf. Luke 11:2-4), parabolic teaching about prayer (7:7-11; cf. Luke 11:9-13), and the injunction to pray to the Lord of the harvest for laborers (9:38; cf. Luke 10:2). Matthew and Luke both include, as well, Jesus' prayer thanking God for the revelation of himself to the unlearned (Matt. 11:25-26; Luke 10:21). But Jesus' teaching and warning about lengthy, public prayers in 6:5-8 seems not to have been drawn from either Mark or Q, but from some other "special" source. In the expansive reading of 19:13, "that he [Jesus] might lay his hands on them [the children] and pray for them," the evangelist correctly explained what Mark 10:13 means by "that he might touch them"; and in 26:44 he filled out what is implied in the Gethsemane story in Mark. Furthermore, in 26:42 we are presented with an interesting account of Jesus' second prayer in Gethsemane, which marks a further stage of acceptance beyond what is given in his first prayer: "My Father, if it is not possible for this cup to be taken away unless I drink it, may your will be done."

There is, however, nothing in any of this to suggest an independent development of the topic of prayer in Matthew's Gospel. Nevertheless, it is significant that prayer is a topic in its own right in Matt. 6:5-15 — a passage that Joachim Jeremias has characterized as "instructions on how to pray for people who do pray," whereas the corresponding material in Luke 11:1-13 is more in the nature of "an encouragement to people who do not pray to do so" (*New Testament Theology*, 193-95). Moreover, in Matt. 18:19-20 there is an important saying about God answering the prayers of two people who are in agreement in their petition.

Luke took over much of the material in Mark's Gospel, although sometimes he omitted a verse and added something equivalent elsewhere (cf. 5:16; 9:18; see also 21:36). Luke also shares with Matthew the material already noted above (cf. 6:28; 11:2-4, 9-13). But Luke has more material on prayer than either Mark or Matthew, additional material which fits into two categories: (1) Luke's editorial insertions into his Marcan source material, as seen in 3:21; 6:12; 9:28f.; 22:32, 44 (if authentic); and 23:34 (if authentic), 46; and (2) Luke's use of other sources, as in 1:10; 11:1, 5-8; 18:1-14; and 24:30. In these latter verses, of course, it is a matter of speculation whether the material was drawn from another source or sources or is to be credited to Luke himself.

Both the quantity and content of the material on prayer in Luke's Gospel suggests that the third evangelist was consciously aware of the significance of prayer in Jesus' ministry and teaching. The total picture regarding prayer in Luke, in fact, goes much beyond what we find in either Mark or Matthew — so much so that "prayer" is usually regarded by commentators as one of the distinctive facets of Luke's Gospel.

2. Jesus at Prayer

The Gospels, both explicitly and implicitly, refer to the fact that Jesus prayed. They do not usually record such normal occurrences of life as that Jesus ate meals or that he went to sleep at night or that he washed himself. Such occurrences may be taken for granted. They become interesting only when something unusual occurs — as, for example, a deliberate fast or sleep at an unusual time. Prayer for Jews was a normal practice of everyday life — that is, set prayers in the synagogue, the saying of grace before meals, and the saying of personal prayers in the morning, in the afternoon (i.e., at the time of sacrifice in the temple), and in the evening (cf. J. Jeremias, *New Testament Theology*, 185-88; see also J. D. G. Dunn, "Prayer," 617-18). Because Jesus did everything that was normal for a Jew and more, it should not be considered startling that references to his prayers in the Synoptic Gospels are not more abundant. When prayer by Jesus is highlighted by the Synoptic evangelists, it must be for special reasons, and we are entitled to ask in each case why.

In Mark's Gospel the evangelist specifically says in 1:35 that Jesus prayed very early in the morning ("while it was still dark") and that he deliberately prayed away from other people ("he went off to a solitary place"). Although he was sought out by his disciples (v. 36) because the people were wanting to see him (v. 37), he carried out his intention to go elsewhere because his calling was to preach in a wider area (vv. 38-39). We are not told that his consciousness of this wider mission came to him during such a time of prayer or that he struggled against a temptation to be a miracle-working evangelist in Capernaum. The fact that other people were looking for him suggests (1) that Jesus had got up earlier than them, (2) that he had slipped quietly out of the house, and (3) that they probably sought him at the end of his prayer time rather than at the beginning.

Prayer in the very early morning hours of the day may have been part of the pattern of Jesus' life — which would suggest that he was more pious than other Jews. And this is probably why such an early time for prayer is mentioned by Mark. Otherwise, no specific motivation for mentioning that it was "while it was still dark" is discernible. The parallel in Luke 4:42 softens the time expression simply to "daybreak" (and omits any mention of prayer), thereby suggesting that the reason for Jesus' solitude was simply to get away from the crowds. In 5:16 and 9:18 Luke also makes generalized references to Jesus' practice of withdrawal when at prayer.

In Mark 6:46 Jesus leaves the crowd after feeding them in order to pray by himself in the mountains. This time his prayer is late at night rather than early in the morning, and, again, no motivation is provided. Here, as before, prayer is a solitary experience, without the distraction of people. Solitary prayer is an important motif in the Gospels, one which is frequently noted. The saying of Jesus in Matt. 6:6 about going into one's private room to pray — which must be a metaphorical statement, since most small houses in Palestine would not have had separate rooms — underlines the point. At the same time, individual, solitary prayer does not exclude corporate prayer, as the saying of Matt. 18:19-20 makes clear: "Again, I tell you that if two of you on earth agree about anything you ask for, it will be done for you by my Father in heaven. For where two or three come together in my name, there am I with them."

The third specific occasion of prayer in Mark's Gospel is in the depiction of Jesus' Gethsemane experience in 14:32-42. Here Jesus is portrayed as being with his eleven remaining disciples, yet as separating himself — along with Peter, James, and John — from the others while he prays. He is still, evidently, somewhat close to the three of the inner circle and the others, but he goes off by himself to pray. This time the content of Jesus' prayer is indicated, thereby raising the question as to how the disciples knew what he was saying — especially since they are said to have been asleep at the time! It is not indicated whether their sleepiness was due simply to the lateness of the hour or to some divinely-caused stupor. But the fact that they were upbraided for not keeping awake suggests not only human weakness but also a lack of sympathy for Jesus, and possibly a lack of realization regarding the significance of what was happening.

The fourth instance of prayer in Mark is in 15:34, which is paralleled in Matt. 27:46. Here is recorded the agonized cry of Jesus to God from the cross, with the actual words taken from Ps. 22:1 spoken in Aramaic: "*Eloi, Eloi, lama sabachthani?* — which means, 'My God, my God, why have you forsaken me?'" (though the wording differs somewhat between the two Gospels). Luke 23:46 omits this cry, but does have the words of Jesus commending himself to God in his dying moments (echoing Ps. 31:5).

117

In Luke's Gospel Jesus is depicted in 3:21 to have prayed at his baptism, in 6:12 to have prayed all night before the choice of his twelve disciples, in 9:18 to have been praying when he asked his disciples "Who do the crowds say I am?" and "Who do you say I am?", and in 9:28 to have been at prayer on a mountain at the time of his transfiguration. Luke also notes in 22:39 that when Jesus went to the Mount of Olives to pray it was what he was accustomed to do — and implies by reference to "the place" in 22:40 that when he was in Jerusalem Jesus frequently went to a particular place on the Mount of Olives to pray. Also suggested in the portrayal of 22:39-46 are the themes of (1) withdrawal in prayer, for Jesus and his disciples are away from the crowds, and (2) intensity in prayer, for Jesus there spends at least one night in prayer.

The prayers of Jesus are highlighted in Luke's Gospel at the crucial events in the story of Jesus. They have, of course, occasioned considerable discussion among Lucan scholars (cf. P. T. O'Brien, "Prayer in Luke-Acts"). The most extensive treatment of them is by David Crump (*Jesus the Intercessor*), who has argued (1) that Jesus as the Son of God in Luke is the interceding mediator who prays for his disciples, and (2) that in Luke there is a self-revelatory function to Jesus' prayers, so that through them the disciples come to a deeper realization of who he is.

3. Thanksgiving and Blessing

In a number of passages in the Synoptic Gospels the verbs "to bless" *(eulogeō* or *kateulogeō)* and "to give thanks" *(eucharisteō)* are used with reference to prayer. The significance of "bless" varies, depending largely on its object. Three categories of such texts are discernible.

In some cases, which we may call category 1, the verb is directed toward God, in which case the thought is clearly that of thanking or praising him. To call God "blessed" *(eulogētos)* is a way of thanking and praising him (Luke 1:68) — with the form of expression always being in the third person. Mary's hymn is one in which she says: "My soul praises God [i.e., 'I praise God'] . . . because he . . ." (Luke 1:47-55). Her hymn is thus more in the nature of a public announcement to other people than a prayer directed to God, and yet it is clearly intended to be a vehicle for praising God. The same applies to the song of Zechariah, which begins similarly (Luke 1:68-75) but then changes halfway through to become an address to the newly-born child and is prophetic in character (Luke 1:76-79). The utterance of Simeon, however, in which he blesses God, is a prayer that, despite its surface syntax, is thanksgiving to God (Luke 2:28-32). And the final words of Luke's Gospel are that the disciples, on their return to Jerusalem after Jesus' ascension, "stayed continually at the temple, praising *(eulogountes)* God" (Luke 24:53).

In category 2, Jesus prays before the two recorded feeding miracles, giving thanks for the food (Mark 6:41 and 8:7, par.). And he does likewise at the Last Supper (Mark 14:22-23, par.). He thus does what might be expected of a pious Jew. To bless food is to give thanks to God for it, as is shown by the parallelism with the verb "to thank" in Mark 8:6-7, 14:22-23 par., and Matt. 26:26-27. This was a normal act by the head of a household at a Jewish meal. There is no ground for supposing that praying or "giving thanks" for one's food somehow makes the food different, whether physically or spiritually. Rather, prayer is nothing more than an expression of thanks to God, which includes a recognition that he is the supplier of the food.

In the case of the feeding miracles a problem arises as to the relation of the act to what follows. On neither occasion does it appear that the prayer was one of asking God to multiply the food, but only an act of blessing God or thanking him for the food. The miracle, it seems, was not specifically connected with the prayer. Rather, when Jesus simply did the normal thing that one did at a meal, the food sufficed for all present.

In category 3, God is petitioned to bless people — that is, to show his favor to them in undefined ways (cf. Luke 2:34; 6:28, parallel to "pray for"; 24:50-51). In Mark 10:16 Jesus lays his hands on children and blesses them *(kateulogeō)*. Matthew understands the meaning to be that Jesus was asked to pray for the children (cf. Matt. 19:13). The prayer of Jesus in both Mark 10:16 and Matt. 19:15 was accompanied by the laying on of hands, which was an outward accompaniment to prayers for divine blessing.

We should perhaps include in this third category Matt. 10:12-13, where Jesus tells his disciples to greet a house (i.e., its residents) when they enter into it and their peace will rest on it. This is, in effect, a prayer for God's blessing to be on the family or household that lives there. And Jesus himself blessed the disciples when he parted from them in Luke 24:50-51 — which reflects, as H.-G. Link has noted ("Blessing," 214), the practice of giving a blessing when someone leaves (cf. Tobit 5:17) and/or at the time of one's approaching death (cf. Gen. 48-49).

People may also be said to be blessed in that they are perceived to be people to whom God has shown his favor in some way, as in Elizabeth's words to Mary of Luke 1:42: "Blessed are you among women, and blessed is the child you will bear!" In some cases it is not clear whether the statement of blessing is an affirmation of the existing blessedness of a person (and hence, indirectly, an expression of thanks to God for it), or a prayer for blessing (cf. Mark 11:9-10 par.), or a thanksgiving to God for the person or thing being blessed. At times the language may well be inclusive of all of these thoughts — as, for example, in Matt. 25:34, where "the blessed of my Father" are those on whom God's favor already rests and who will receive further blessings.

All of the texts cited in this section use the *eulogeo* word-group. But "blessed" also translates *makarios,* a word that conveys more the sense of "happy" or "fortunate" — being used frequently in statements that, in effect, say that "the person who is/does such-and-such is [truly] fortunate." The word is used in this way in the Beatitudes of Matt. 5:3-11 and Luke 6:20-23. In some cases, such a statement may be effectively a prayer for God to act, in that the person who is truly fortunate is so because God shows his favor to him or her (cf. H.-G. Link, "Blessing," 206-15).

4. Prayer as Petition

Prayers for divine blessing (as cited above) are petitions for God to do good to other people. Jesus himself prayed for others — including Peter, who denied him (Luke 22:31-32), and those who crucified him (Luke 23:34, which is textually uncertain but probably Lucan; cf. Marshall, *Luke,* 867-68). And he commanded his disciples to pray for their persecutors (Matt. 5:44). But they were also to pray for themselves and their own needs. This is evident in the so-called "we-petitions" of the Lord's Prayer, as well as in Jesus' commands to pray regarding temptation and the dangers to which they were exposed (cf. Mark 13:18; 14:38; Luke 21:36).

The teaching in Luke 11:5-13 (cf. Matt. 7:7-11) is concerned with what God gives to those who pray to him. The material in 11:9-13 is about requests to God, which are expressed in terms of "asking," "seeking," and "knocking" and responded to in terms of "receiving," "finding," and "opening." The statements convey the certainty that God will respond, and this is stated simply as an assertion.

It has been suggested that Luke 11:9-13 expresses a "beggars' wisdom" and reflects beggars' requests being answered. But it is doubtful that this is the case, for the requests of beggars are not always answered and there are often long periods of disappointment. It is more likely that the basis for the assertion lies in a combination of (1) Jesus' authority (note the "I say to you" of 11:9a), (2) God's promise to respond to prayer (cf. Deut. 4:29; Prov. 8:17; Isa. 55:6; 65:1; Jer. 29:13-14), and (3) the sayings set out in 11:9-13, where the contrast is drawn between human fathers who, though evil by nature, nevertheless show kindness to their children, and God the heavenly Father, who is by nature good and can be depended on all the more to answer their prayers.

There is an important difference in the Gospels regarding what God, the heavenly Father, will give to the disciples when they ask him. Matt. 7:11 has the generalized expression "good things." But Luke 11:13 has the more specific "Holy (or, in some MSS, 'good'] Spirit." How are the disciples to ask?

Mark 11:24 may seem to be a rather depressing injunction: "I tell you, whatever you ask for in prayer, believe that you will receive it, and it will be yours." How does one develop a faith like that? The matter is not helped by the way in which the disciples have just seen Jesus cause a fig tree to wither and been told that faith can move mountains (cf. Mark 11:20-23). How can these things be — even if it be granted that the saying is metaphorical and hyperbolical? Our concern is not usually with moving mountains! Far more often it is about doing things that are a great deal more ordinary by comparison.

The answer is perhaps to be found by taking into consideration other teachings of Jesus on the matter. The sayings about the certainty of being heard in Luke 11:9-13 are preceded by the parable of "the friend at midnight" in Luke 11:5-8. In this parable the person in bed is not moved to helpfulness by the fact of an existing friendship between himself and the neighbor who comes and asks for bread, but, rather, by the *anaideia* of the caller. After much dispute, it now seems most probable that the word *anaideia* refers to the shameless behavior of the man knocking at the door at midnight, despite all social propriety (cf. K. R. Snodgrass, "*Anaideia*").

But the lesson of the parable of the friend at midnight is surely not that disciples must show a similar shamelessness toward God, since God is their friend. How, then, must they pray? The parable does not say. What it does say is that they must not shrink from asking — perhaps from disbelief that God will answer — but must come to God with confidence.

121

There is nothing in Luke 11:5-8 that suggests that importunity, or continued and intense effort, is required for prayers to be heard by God — that is, there is nothing in the parable of the friend at midnight that implies that prayer must go on at great length until God responds or must take unusual measures in order to gain a hearing (like the priests of Baal in 1 Kings 19:26-29). This question, however, does arise with the parable of "the persistent widow" in Luke 18:1-8, which is often paired with the parable of the friend at midnight in Luke 11:5-8. The parable of the unjust judge is an encouragement to pray at all times and not to despair of getting an answer. It relates how a judge eventually responds to a widow's plea for justice — not because he is godly and fair, but because he is being worn out by the woman's constant petitioning and because he will get a bad reputation if he does not respond to her (cf. I. H. Marshall, *Luke*, 673). The lesson of the parable is drawn up in terms of a contrast: if even an unjust judge says this, will not God avenge his elect, his chosen people?

The point of the parable of the unjust judge is the certainty that God — being who he is and having a relationship to his people — will answer their prayers, even if the answer is not immediate. Is the parable, then, an incentive to importunate prayer? But if people need to be importunate, this cancels out the contrast with the unjust judge. The point of the parable is that people should go on praying to God, even if their prayers are not immediately answered — and that they should maintain this attitude. It is not the case that prayer for one specific thing is in mind. Rather, it is that people should pray at all times, for whatever needs, and that, in particular, they should pray for God's final vindication of his people at the end.

The parable of the unjust judge of Luke 18:1-8 is an encouragement to have faith in God. It is an exhortation for people to continue to pray, instead of despairing or believing that God is not there or that he is not good. Here, as in the sayings of Luke 11:9-13 and the parable of Luke 11:5-8 that precedes them, the thought is not of importunity but of faith in God through thick and thin. It may well be that the parable of the unjust judge had originally a more general application to prayer, but that Jesus here related it specifically to the situation of his disciples in tribulation and their longing for the coming of the Son of Man.

All this suggests that the really important factor in prayer is the character of God as the One who wants to do good for his people and to accomplish his own purpose, which will also be for their good. Petitionary prayer depends on the character of the one petitioned rather than on the effort of the petitioner to have the right attitude of faith. Prayer is the expression of a relationship with a God whom we are learning to trust because he is faithful and good.

5. Prayer and Fasting

Max Turner makes the interesting observation that Jesus is not portrayed in the Synoptic Gospels as praying in connection with his healing miracles and exorcisms — probably because victory over Satan had already been won and his prior times of prayer were determinative for his subsequent acts of authority (cf. "Prayer in the Gospels and Acts," 61). There is one story in Mark 9:14-29, however, that relates exorcism to prayer (cf. also Mark 7:34, where Jesus "looked up to heaven" before healing the man who was deaf and mute). Prior to the story of Mark 9:14-29, the disciples had been given authority to cast out demons (Mark 6:7) and had been active in so doing (Mark 6:13). But on the occasion reflected in the story of Mark 9 they were unable to exorcise a very troubling spirit (cf. vv. 17-18) — and the implication is that they were surprised that they couldn't (cf. v. 28).

What had gone wrong? The story does not tell us that Jesus engaged in prayer on this particular occasion; rather, it is related like any other story of an exorcism. Furthermore, nothing suggests that the particular situation of Mark 9:14-29 was a special case that required prayer, whereas "easier" cases did not require prayer — and no indications are given as to how one would recognize that it was a special case, and so in need of special treatment. What did Mark's readers know that we don't know?

The discussion of the theme of prayer and fasting is bedeviled by the continuing folk-memory of Matt. 17:21, which existed in some ancient manuscripts (i.e., in a later "corrected" version of Codex Sinaiticus and in Codices Ephraemi Rescriptus and Bezae Cantabrigiensis) and has been continued in the Authorized or King James Version, where it is declared: "Howbeit this kind [of evil spirit] goeth not out but by prayer and fasting." But Matt. 17:21 does not appear in the better Greek manuscripts (so the NIV and NRSV translations do not include it). And while the verse probably came about because of later scribal assimilation to the reading of Mark 9:29, as contained in some inferior manuscripts, the better manuscripts of Mark 9:29 do not have the words "and by fasting." It is generally agreed, therefore, that both verse 21 of Matthew 17 and the words "and by fasting" of Mark 9:29 were added by later scribes, who — whether consciously or unconsciously — conformed these texts to the practices of their day.

Pursuing first the issue of fasting, the fact that the better manuscripts (e.g., the uncorrected Codex Sinaiticus and Codex Vaticanus) omit "and by fasting" at the end of Mark 9:29 makes it unlikely that fasting should be included in this verse as part of Jesus' instructions to his disciples. Fasting, however, was a recognized accompaniment of prayer in Judaism. In particular, Jews fasted on the Day of Atonement as an indication of penitence for sin. Furthermore, it is mentioned in Luke's nativity narrative as the practice of Anna, who was continually in the temple worshiping God with "fasting and praying" (cf. Luke 2:37). And Jesus himself went without food for forty days in the desert when he was tempted by Satan.

There are two places where the subject of fasting is taken up in the teaching of Jesus. The first is in Mark 2:18-20 par., where Jesus defends his disciples in not fasting while the disciples of John and the Pharisees were fasting. The reply of Jesus to those who questioned him was that fasting was inappropriate at a wedding, which is a joyous occasion, whereas fasting is to be seen as a sign of penitence or mourning. In the presence of the bridegroom one does not fast. But when the bridegroom is taken away — as, for example, at the wedding described in Tobit 6:13-14 — then fasting is appropriate. The presence of Jesus is the presence of the kingdom of God, and fasting as a sign of mourning is replaced by rejoicing.

In what sense, however, is the bridegroom taken away? A reference to the death of Jesus is possible. This would have been a time of sadness (cf. Luke 24:17) — though the resurrection was unequivocally a time of gladness. It hardly seems possible, therefore, that Jesus is saying that his disciples will rejoice while he is alive but will be sad and should fast after he has left them. The saying, therefore, cannot be taken as a justification of fasting as an expression of sadness after the resurrection. Moreover, the sayings immediately following, which draw a sharp contrast between the old and the new (cf. Mark 2:21-22, par.), reinforce the fact that the old way of fasting is inappropriate in the new situation brought about by the presence of the kingdom of God. Similarly, John 16:16-24, which speaks of the disciples' temporary grief being turned into joy, rules out sadness after the resurrection.

The second passage is Matthew 6:16-18, which is part of a threefold set of instructions on not performing religious duties in order to impress other people with one's piety, and so failing to please God through them.

The reference is probably not to communal fasts but to voluntary acts of individual piety that went beyond what was legally required. Those who fast should disguise the fact and practice it secretly to God alone. The saying is directed to those who hear the Sermon on the Mount (Matt. 5:1–8:1) and is cast in terms of their current religious practices — that is, the giving of alms, the saying of prayers, and fasting.

Elsewhere in the Sermon on the Mount the practice of offering sacrifices at the temple is taken for granted. It follows, therefore, that not all of the practices assumed by Jesus in order to communicate with his audience on its own terms necessarily carry forward as things that his followers will do. They would, of course, continue to give alms and to pray; but they would cease to offer sacrifices in the Jerusalem temple. If they do fast in the way described here, the implication is that this should be a private and personal matter rather than a corporate occasion.

There are in the Acts of the Apostles, however, two examples of prayer being accompanied by fasting in a corporate fashion. The first is in 13:1-3, where the worship of God and fasting are conjoined; the second in 14:23, where the appointment of elders in local churches takes place amidst prayer and fasting. There is also some sort of parallel in 1 Cor. 7:5, where husbands and wives may abstain from intercourse in order to pray — though the situations of 2 Cor. 6:5 and 11:27, where going without food is because of adverse circumstances (such as the pressure of work or being robbed), are hardly to be classed as fasting. While prayer and fasting are treated in Matt. 6:16-18 as two separate activities, fasting in Acts 13:1-3 and 14:23 is linked with prayer. It was not a sign of mourning in these two latter cases, but had some other function. Fasting was sometimes an accompaniment of prayer in the Old Testament, and occasions of public penitence may be understood as a form of prayer.

It would not be unfair to say that fasting is marginal to prayer in the Gospels. This is not to say, however, that prayer may not on occasion be intense and difficult, as the records of Jesus' prayers in Gethsemane and on the cross vividly demonstrate (especially if Luke 22:43-44 is an authentic part of the text). The writer to the Hebrews knew that Jesus prayed with "loud cries and tears" (Heb. 5:7). And, whatever our attitude to fasting, the implication of Mark 9:14-29 is surely that whether or not we know how to recognize them, some occasions need special prayer.

6. Wrong Ways of Praying

In the teaching on prayer in Matthew 6, the concern is with voluntary prayers and is of a piece with the rest of the teaching of Jesus directed against religious practices carried on for show — whether done to win a reputation for piety or to deceive other people. Prayer is to be private. Prayer, as Oscar Cullmann notes (*Prayer in the New Testament*, 17), is conversation *with God*. In the litany of cases set out in Matt. 6:1, 2, 5, 7, and 16, the pray-ers are not really talking to God but simply trying to impress other people or talking to themselves.

Long prayers as a sign of piety are condemned in Mark 12:40. By the conjunction of ideas, the long prayers of this verse are probably those meant to deceive people into thinking that the one making the prayer is an honest person, and so fit to be entrusted with the care of widows' affairs. In Matt. 6:7, however, long prayers, like those of the heathen, are intended to impress God — as if he needed to be told at great length and with much eloquence what the petitioner's needs are, which he doesn't! Rather, prayers can be short and to the point, and the Lord's Prayer in Matt. 6:9-13 is contextually introduced as an example of how to pray without excess verbiage. Nevertheless, the fact that Jesus could spend a night in prayer indicates that there can be lengthy periods of prayer which are free from wasted words.

The parable of the Pharisee and the tax collector of Luke 18:9-14 clearly fits in at this point. The main lines of interpretation are clear enough, though, of course, discussion about the parable still continues. The Pharisee's prayer to God is simply a record of his piety, which he sees as distinguishing him from other people, whereas the tax collector's prayer is a record of sins for which he needs forgiveness. Jesus pronounces with absolute certainty that the Pharisee was not justified, but that the tax collector was. The issue in both cases is a request for forgiveness and a right relationship with God, which is granted by God not on the basis of self-congratulation but on the basis of the admission of sin and casting oneself on the mercy of God.

What is perhaps not clear in the parable of Luke 18:9-14 is whether the Pharisee failed to be justified because he relied on his own good deeds to that end or because he compared himself with other people to their detriment. The opening comment by the evangelist in verse 9 is that the basis for condemnation is twofold: (1) trusting in one's own good deeds, and

(2) despising other people because one thinks oneself to be better than them. Luke, however, did not distinguish between the two grounds, and neither should we. It is probably inevitable that people who come to God to remind him of their piety are in fact stating a case for preferential treatment of themselves over against other sinners.

A wrong attitude to prayer is also present when people are not willing to forgive others, even as they pray that God will extend forgiveness to them (cf. Mark 11:25, par.). The rationale for this statement is expressed most clearly in the parable of the unforgiving servant of Matt. 18:21-35. Here Jesus brings out the enormity of the action of a servant who was forgiven his own enormous debt, which he was unable to pay, but who endeavors to exact the full amount of a comparatively trivial debt from another servant, who is equally unable to pay. The force of the parable renders argument superfluous: God will not forgive those whose lives are not changed by the grace that they experience. Casuistic discussions as to whether the forgiveness that we must show to our debtors is a condition or a result of divine forgiveness are pointless.

7. Prayer and the Kingdom

We have seen that in many respects the practice and teaching of Jesus reflect Jewish prayer patterns and beliefs. How then, if at all, is prayer related to his own distinctive mission and message? There are two main considerations.

The first is that it is generally agreed that the distinctiveness of Jesus' understanding of prayer is integrally and vitally related to his relationship to God as his Father, a relationship to which he admitted his disciples. In the Old Testament, which is slightly over three times the length of the New Testament, the word "father" is used just over 1200 times, while in the New Testament "father" is used 415 times. These figures are about what would be expected in view of the relative lengths of the two testaments: the book that is three times the length of the other has about three times as many occurrences of the word. But if we now count the number of times that "Father" is used with reference to God, then we will find that only 40, or 3%, of the occurrences of the word in the Old Testament refer to God, but in the New Testament 260, or 63%, of the occurrences refer to God as Father. There has been, thus, a huge quantitative leap from the Old Testament to the New Testament in speaking of God as Father, whether the word is used as a name for him or as a description of him. This really enormous difference between the two testaments demands an explanation.

While it is the case that the Jews were beginning to make greater use of "Father" with reference to God, it is agreed that the major reason for the shift in the New Testament lies in the teaching of Jesus. Jesus frequently referred to God as Father in the teaching he directed to his disciples — though not, it must be noted, in his teaching to the people at large or to his opponents. Furthermore, and more significantly, Jesus is portrayed as addressing God as "Father" in all of the records of his actual prayers, with the sole exception of his "cry of dereliction" (based on Ps. 22:1) from the cross. Whether or not the wording in all of these cases goes back directly to Jesus himself is immaterial. The point here is that this is the self-image that was created by Jesus for the evangelists.

In particular, in Mark 14:36 God is addressed using the Aramaic word *Abba*. This is an unusual grammatical form of the word, and the evidence shows that it was the term used by a son or daughter for their physical father and was expressive of a close, intimate relationship (though the hypothesis that it was "baby talk" has been shown to be ill-founded). The evidence for individual Jews addressing God as Father in prayer is extremely limited, and the use of the intimate term *Abba* is so far without parallel — despite claims sometimes made to the contrary. Here, then, we have the actual word used by Jesus, and his usage appears to be unique.

But this is not all. The significance of the term *Abba* or "Father" on the lips of Jesus is that Jesus enjoys a unique, personal relationship to God as his Son — a relationship that goes well beyond the idea of God as Father in that he is the Creator or the understanding that he exercises particular care and protection for a person, such as the king of Israel. God is now the loving Father with whom Jesus has a relationship like that of a human son with a father. (If this metaphor does not convey the closeness of relationship to a modern audience, the better analogy may be the close relationship between wife and husband, which in our culture is probably closer than that between son and father.) This relationship comes to expression in the saying in Matthew 11:25-27//Luke 10:22 where Jesus talks about the close relation between father and son and applies it to his own situation.

Jesus' prayers, therefore, reflect a unique, personal relationship with God. And it is on the strength of this relationship that Jesus is able to speak so confidently about God as the one who hears prayer sympathetically.

Furthermore, he confers on his disciples this same intimate relationship with God, encouraging them to pray to God as "Father." The way that Paul preserves the use of *Abba* for Christian use in Gal. 4:6 and Rom. 8:15 confirms that behind the Greek word for "father" in places such as Luke 11:2 there lies, in all probability, the same Aramaic word as Jesus himself used. For when Jesus talked about prayer to his disciples, he referred to God as "Father," as we have already observed.

A second consideration when relating prayer to Jesus' mission and message is that the heart of Jesus' message was the announcement of the coming of the kingdom of God and his teaching about the implications of this for people generally. The Lord's Prayer brings together the two themes of God as Father and the kingdom of God, for it is addressed to God as Father and then immediately proceeds to petition him that his name be reverenced and his kingdom come. The kingdom is the kingdom of the Father (cf. Luke 12:30-31; the parallel in Matt. 6:32-33 reads "the kingdom of God," but some MSS omit "of God"; also Matt. 26:29, though the parallel in Mark 14:25 reads "kingdom of God"). It is the Father who has appointed Jesus to his place in the kingdom (cf. Luke 22:29, though the sentence is missing in Matt. 19:28). Matthew, however, has the saying in which it is those who are blessed by the Father who enter the kingdom that has been prepared for them since the foundation of the world (Matt. 25:34). Whatever be the basis for these texts in the actual words of Jesus, they show that the synoptic evangelists recognized that the kingdom proclaimed by Jesus was the kingdom of the Father, and they thus brought the two concepts together.

One of the novel features in the teaching of Jesus, as A. M. Hunter once noted, is simply that "the King in the Kingdom is a Father" (*Introducing New Testament Theology*, 31-33). Although the setting up of his rule is his action, it is related to the people over whom he rules in that they pray to him for the accomplishment of his will — thereby declaring their loyalty to him and their longing for the defeat of evil. Prayer and the kingdom are thus brought into relationship. Also tied in with this link is the saying in Matt. 9:38//Luke 10:2 in which the disciples are to pray to God as the lord of the harvest to send workers into his field, with the injunction being closely related to the sending out of the Twelve themselves with the task of proclaiming the arrival of the kingdom.

Finally, it is significant that the purpose of the cleansing of the temple by Jesus is that it should be purged in order to be a house of prayer for all nations (Mark 11:17). This most challenging act of Jesus is concerned with what the temple ought to be. It is of lesser moment to decide whether Jesus was attempting to purify an existing institution to fulfill its intended function or declaring God's judgment on it for failing to do so. The message of the kingdom is intended not only to restore Israel to what God intended it to be, but also to renew it. And that divine process culminates in the establishment of a new temple — one in which all people can enjoy the relationship of prayer to their God and Father.

8. Conclusion

Prayer is the medium for expressing praise and thanksgiving to God for his goodness. It is also the medium for asking him to do specific things for the petitioners and for other people. Clearly, its purpose is that petitioners receive what they ask for; the correlative implication is that if prayer does not take place the results will not be achieved. Yet at the same time, not all prayers are answered in the way that the petitioners desire — as is supremely seen in the Gethsemane story, where Jesus had to be content that the Father's will, rather than his own desires, would be fulfilled. The language is paradoxical. The fact that the Father knows what we want even before we ask (cf. Matt. 6:8) is not part of the paradox. Human parents often know what their children are going to ask them for, but it doesn't affect the fact that they respond to the children's desires. Ultimately, however, it is God's will that is carried out rather than ours.

Is prayer, then, something that changes the attitude of the petitioners, so that they put themselves in the position of agreeing with whatever God intends to do? Or is prayer an action that can affect the determination of God's will, so that he responds by doing what he would otherwise not have done? We have to say that both possibilities are found in the Synoptic Gospels.

Prayer would not be prayer, but would be something else, if it were simply a device for enabling petitioners to give up their own desires in favor of God's will. That is not how it is described in the Gospels. Rather, in the example and teaching of Jesus on prayer in the Gospels it is genuinely presented as an expression of what God's people want God to do. At the same time, however, there is the recognition that God's will may not be identical with the petitioner's. We are not, then, to say that prayer is not answered.

Rather, we are to recognize that on some occasions God has to say: "Not your way but mine!" — for reasons that we may well not understand at the time, but which are part of his good purpose in establishing his kingly rule in the face of the opposition of sin and evil. What Jesus has highlighted in his example and emphasized in his teaching about prayer, as Oscar Cullmann has pointed out (*Prayer*, 30-37), is the goodness of the Father.

Selected Bibliography

Crump, David M. *Jesus the Intercessor: Prayer and Christology in Luke-Acts.* Tübingen: Mohr-Siebeck, 1992.

Cullmann, Oscar. *Prayer in the New Testament.* London: SCM; Minneapolis: Fortress, 1995.

Dunn, James D. G. "Prayer." In *Dictionary of Jesus and the Gospels*, ed. J. B. Green, S. McKnight, and I. H. Marshall. Downers Grove: InterVarsity, 1992, 617-25.

Hunter, A. M. *Introducing New Testament Theology.* London: SCM, 1957.

Jeremias, Joachim. *The Prayers of Jesus*, trans. J. Bowden *et al.* London: SCM, 1967.

―――. *New Testament Theology: The Proclamation of Jesus*, trans. J. Bowden. London: SCM; New York: Scribner's, 1971, 178-203.

Liefeld, Walter L. "Parables on Prayer (Luke 11:5-8; 18:1-14)." In *The Challenge of Jesus' Parables*, ed. R. N. Longenecker. Grand Rapids: Eerdmans, 2000, 240-62.

Link, H.-G. "Blessing, Blessed, Happy." *New International Dictionary of New Testament Theology* I:206-15.

Lohmeyer, Ernst. *The Lord's Prayer*, trans. J. Bowden. London: Collins; New York: Harper & Row, 1965.

Marshall, I. Howard. *The Gospel of Luke.* Exeter: Paternoster; Grand Rapids: Eerdmans, 1978.

O'Brien, Peter T. "Prayer in Luke-Acts." *Tyndale Bulletin* 24 (1973): 111-27.

Snodgrass, Klyne R. "*Anaideia* and the Friend at Midnight." *Journal of Biblical Literature* 116 (1997): 505-13.

Turner, Max M. B. "Prayer in the Gospels and Acts." In *Teach Us to Pray: Prayer in the Bible and the World*, ed. D. A. Carson. Exeter: Paternoster; Grand Rapids: Baker, 1990, 58-83.

CHAPTER 7

The Lord's Prayer as a Paradigm
of Christian Prayer

N. T. WRIGHT

"As OUR SAVIOR CHRIST hath commanded and taught us, we are bold
to say: 'Our Father. . . .'" So runs the old liturgical formula, stressing the
Pater Noster as a command and its use as a daring, trembling, holy boldness. At one level, this is entirely appropriate. At another level, however, it
fails to catch the most remarkable thing about the Lord's Prayer — and so
fails to grasp the truly distinctive feature in Christian prayer that this
prayer points us to. For the Lord's Prayer is not so much a command as an
invitation: an invitation to share in the prayer-life of Jesus himself.

Seen with Christian hindsight — more specifically, with trinitarian
perspective — the Lord's Prayer becomes an invitation to share in the *divine* life itself. It becomes one of the high roads into the central mystery of
Christian salvation and Christian existence: that the baptized and believing Christian is (1) incorporated into the inner life of the triune God *and*
(2) intended not just to believe that this is the case, but actually to experience it.

The Lord's Prayer, along with the Eucharist, forms the liturgical
equivalent to what Eastern Orthodox church architecture portrays and
western Gothic architecture depicts — both developing, each in its own
way, the central temple theology of Judaism. The God worshiped here, says
this architecture, is neither a remote dictator nor simply the sum total of
human god-awareness. This God is both intimately present within the

world *and* utterly beyond, other, and different from it. He is present to cel-ebrate with his people and to grieve with them, to give them his rich bless-ings and to rescue them from all ills, because he is also sovereign over heaven and earth, sea and dry land, all the powers of this world, and even over the urgings of the human heart. The Lord's Prayer is an invitation to know this God and to share his innermost life.

All this is so, more particularly, because the Lord's Prayer is the "true Exodus" prayer of God's people. Set originally in a thoroughgoing eschato-logical context, its every clause resonates with Jesus' announcement that God's kingdom is breaking into the story of Israel and the world, opening up God's long-promised new world and summoning people to share it. If this context is marginalized — or regarded as of historical interest only (be-cause, for instance, as some would suggest, the Parousia did not arrive on schedule) — the prayer loses its peculiar force and falls back into a general-ized petition for things to improve, albeit still admittedly to God's glory. In order for it to be prayed with anything approaching full authenticity, there-fore, it is necessary to be grasped afresh by the eschatological vision and message of Jesus himself, who announced the true Exodus, the real return from exile, and all that is implied by these wide-ranging shorthand expres-sions. (On these topics, see my *Jesus and the Victory of God* [1996].)

I begin this article, therefore, with some reflections on the rooted-ness of the Lord's Prayer within the ministry and kingdom announcement of Jesus. This will lead to a fuller exposition of the way in which the Lord's Prayer opens up the heart of Jesus' "New Exodus" project and invites those who so pray to become part of it. And this will then lead to some reflec-tions on the shape and content of Christian liturgical praying and private praying, and, finally, to some concluding remarks moving on from the "Our Father" of Jesus' ministry to the *Abba* cry of which Paul speaks in Galatians 4 and Romans 8.

1. The Lord's Prayer and Jesus' Own Prayer Life

References to Jesus' own practice of private prayer are scattered through-out the Gospels and clearly reflect an awareness on the part of his first fol-lowers that this kind of private prayer — not simply formulaic petitions, but wrestling with God over real issues and questions — formed the un-dercurrent of his life and public work. The prayer that Jesus gave his followers embodies his own prayer life and his wider kingdom ministry in every clause.

Father/Our Father

Jesus' own address to God, it appears, regularly included "Father." Though the Aramaic word *Abba* is only found in the Gospels in the Gethsemane narrative at Mark 14:36, there is a broad consensus (1) that Jesus indeed used this word in prayer, and (2) that the notion of God's fatherhood — though, of course, known also in Judaism — took central place in his own attitude to God in a distinctive way. So when the prayer given to his followers begins with "Father" (Luke 11:2) or "Our Father" (Matt. 6:9; cf. *Didache* 8:2-3, which also begins "Our Father"), we must understand that Jesus wants them to see themselves as sharing his own characteristic spirituality — that is, his own intimate, familial approach to the Creator. The idea of God's fatherhood, and of building this concept into the life of prayer, was not, as must again be stressed, a novelty within Judaism. But the centrality and particular emphasis that Jesus gave it represents a new departure.

Hallowed Be Your Name

The sanctifying of God's name, as in the clause "hallowed be your name" (Luke 11:2//Matt. 6:9), is not a major theme in the Gospels. Where it does occur — as, for example, in Mary's exclamation, "Holy is his name!" (Luke 1:49); or Jesus' prayer, "Father, glorify your name," and the Father's response, "I have glorified it, and will glorify it again" (John 12:28) — it appears as a natural, and typically Jewish, affirmation of God's holiness and majesty. But the hallowing or sanctifying of God's name is thoroughly consistent with the sort of work that Jesus conceived himself to be undertaking.

Your Kingdom Come

The coming of God's kingdom, however, as expressed by the petition "your kingdom come" (Matt. 6:10//Luke 11:2), is a major theme throughout the entire Gospel tradition. And though its interpretation has sometimes been controversial, there is no doubt (1) that Jesus made this the central theme of his proclamation and (2) that he meant by it that the long-awaited kingdom or rule of God, which involved the salvation of Israel, the defeat of evil, and the return of YHWH himself to Zion, was now at last happening (see my *Jesus and the Victory of God*, chs. 6-10).

Inaugurated eschatology, or the presence *and* the future of God's kingdom, was a hallmark of Jesus' public career — as it was, probably, of the Teacher of Righteousness a century or more earlier (see M. O. Wise, *The First Messiah*, which is a stimulating and suggestive book, even if the argument is possibly pressed too far) and of Simeon ben-Kosiba a hundred years later. Where the leader, God's chosen one, was present, the kingdom was already present. But there was, of course, still work to be done, redemption to be won. The present and the future did not cancel one another out, as in some unthinking scholarly constructions. Nor did "present" mean "a private religious experience" and "future" mean "a Star Wars-type apocalyptic scenario."

The presence of the kingdom meant that God's anointed Messiah was here and was at work — that he was, in fact, accomplishing, as events soon to take place would show, the sovereign and saving rule of God. The future of the kingdom was the time when justice and peace would embrace one another and the whole world — the time from which perspective one could look back and see that the work had, indeed, begun with the presence and work of the anointed leader (see *Jesus and the Victory of God*, ch. 10).

To pray "your kingdom come" at Jesus' bidding, therefore, meant to align oneself with his kingdom movement and to seek God's power in furthering its ultimate fulfillment. It meant adding one's own prayer to the total performance of Jesus' agenda. It meant celebrating in the presence of God the fact that the kingdom was already breaking in, and looking eagerly for its consummation. From the centrality of the kingdom in his public proclamation and the centrality of prayer in his private practice, we must conclude that this kingdom prayer grew directly out of and echoed Jesus' own regular praying.

Your Will Be Done

The performance of God's will, as voiced in the entreaty "your will be done on earth as it is in heaven" (Matt. 6:10) — whether one sees that clause as subordinate to the clause "your kingdom come" (Matt. 6:10//Luke 11:2) or as distinct — chimes in with the emphasis of Jesus at several points in his recorded work. This is particularly noticeable in John's Gospel. But it finds many echoes in the Synoptic Gospels, not least in Luke's repetition of how God's will *must* be fulfilled.

Give Us Today Our Daily Bread

The prayer for bread, as in "give us today [or, 'day by day'] our daily bread" (Matt. 6:11//Luke 11:3), awakens echoes that resound throughout Jesus' public ministry. The two evangelists who give us the Lord's Prayer also give us the temptation stories, where Jesus' hunger and his refusal to create bread for himself feature prominently (cf. Matt. 4:2-4; Luke 4:2-3). The wilderness feeding stories suggest both a literal feeding and a symbolic act that demonstrated God's power, operative through Jesus, to provide for the needs of the people (cf. Mark 6:32-44 par.; 8:1-10 par.). Jesus' own prayers of thanks on these occasions (cf. Mark 6:41 par.; 8:6 par.; see also Luke 24:30) are translated by the Lord's Prayer into a trustful prayer for God's regular provision.

One of the most securely established features of Jesus' public ministry in recent discussion, with only an occasional dissenter (e.g., D. C. Allison Jr., *Jesus of Nazareth*), is his frequent participation in the festive meals of his day, where he celebrated the kingdom with all comers. One does not have to go all the way with the members of the Jesus Seminar, who have described Jesus as "the proverbial party animal," in order to appreciate that the sharing of food, both actually and symbolically, was a central feature of his life.

The sequence of meals in the story of Jesus reaches its climax, of course, in the Last Supper. The bread there was — again in the context of prayer — given a special meaning, which echoes back throughout Jesus' lifetime and on to the cross and his resurrection. To pray for bread (whether for "today," as in Matthew, or for "day by day," as in Luke), therefore, is once again to align oneself with one of the most central and practical symbols of Jesus' kingdom work. Bread follows from and symbolizes the kingdom, both in the Lord's Prayer and in Jesus' own career.

Forgive Us Our Debts/Sins

The prayer for forgiveness — "forgive us our debts, as we also have forgiven our debtors" (Matt. 6:12); "forgive us our sins, for we also forgive everyone who sins against us" (Luke 11:4) — is the one instance of a prayer Jesus taught his followers to pray that they did not suppose he needed to pray himself. The well-known scene of John the Baptist's initial objection to baptizing Jesus (Matt. 3:14-15) and the very early tradition of Jesus' personal sinlessness (cf. John 7:18; 8:46; 2 Cor. 5:21; Heb. 4:15; 1 Pet. 2:22) bear witness to the great divide at this point between Jesus and his followers. They needed to repent and seek God's forgiveness, but he did not.

This exception, however, clearly proves the rule that the Lord's Prayer was intended by Jesus to bind his followers closely to the agenda of his whole ministry. Forgiveness, which is offered freely and without recourse to the temple system, was another hallmark of Jesus' work — indeed, so much so that it was the cause of scandal (as, e.g., in Mark 2:5-12). Furthermore, there is good reason to think that Jesus regarded this free offer of forgiveness as a central part of his inauguration of the new covenant, and that he saw the corresponding obligation to mutual forgiveness as a necessary badge of membership (see my *Jesus and the Victory of God*, 268-74). This prayer for forgiveness, therefore, though not aligning itself with anything in Jesus' own spirituality, belongs very closely with the total picture of Jesus' public ministry, as his ministry is set out in the Gospel narratives.

Lead Us Not into Temptation, but Deliver Us from the Evil One

With the prayer about deliverance from temptation *(peirasmos)* and the evil one *(ho ponēros)* of Matt. 6:13, we are back again with Jesus. Again, the temptation narratives of Matt. 4:1-11 and Luke 4:1-13 are close at hand as part of the context; and again, the Gethsemane scene and the complex of "trials" before Caiaphas and Pilate offer themselves as the wider setting.

Jesus' whole public career was marked by "trials" of one sort or another — by what he, and the evangelists, saw as a running battle with the powers of evil, whether in the form of possessed souls shrieking in the synagogues or angry souls challenging in the marketplace. The fact that Jesus was not spared these trials, but had to face them at their fiercest, suggests a clue as to the meaning of this controversial clause, which we will pursue later.

Here in the prayer of deliverance is, once again, one of the clearest overtones in the Lord's Prayer: "Let me be as my Master." "You are those," says Jesus in Luke 22:28, "who have continued with me in my trials *(en tois peirasmois mou)*." So in giving this prayer, Jesus is inviting his followers to share his own struggles and to experience the same spirituality that sustained him.

This brief survey is enough to demonstrate that the Lord's Prayer is by no means simply a collage of vaguely suitable material culled from the liturgical culture of Second Temple Judaism. Its shape and content remind us of the public career of Jesus at every point. And since Jesus' public career was solidly rooted and reflected in his own life of prayer, we must conclude that the Lord's Prayer is an invitation to share Jesus' own prayer life — and with it his agenda, his work, his pattern of life, and his spirituality. The Lord's Prayer marks out Jesus' followers as a distinct group not simply because Jesus gave it to them, but because it encapsulates his own mission and vocation. And it does this in a form appropriate for his followers, which turns them into his co-workers and fellow-laborers in prayer for the kingdom.

Of course, if one thinks of Jesus simply as a great human teacher, then summoning his followers to share his own pattern and style of prayer is a reasonable commonplace. But if we accept the early Christian assessment of Jesus — with its dramatically high, though still Jewish, Christology — what has been said so far strongly implies that here within the Lord's Prayer we are meeting the beginnings of trinitarian soteriology: the Son is inviting his followers to share the intimacy of his own life with the Father.

2. People of the New Exodus

All of what we have set out above, however, leads us to the present, main section of this article. In this section the theses will be proposed (1) that Jesus saw his kingdom work in terms of the much-hoped-for "New Exodus," and (2) that the Lord's Prayer encapsulates this vision.

The Lord's Prayer as Encapsulating and Celebrating a New Exodus Vision

The events of Israel's Exodus from Egypt, the people's wilderness wanderings, and their entry into the promised land were of enormous importance in the self-understanding and symbolism of all subsequent generations of Israelites, including Jews of the Second Temple period. The geographical "return" of the nation from exile, however, had not been matched by the fulfillment of the promises that Israel would be free from pagan domination and free to serve YHWH in her own land. When that happened, it was expected that the Exodus would form the backdrop for that much-longed-for real return from exile (see my *Jesus and the Victory of God*, xvii-xviii and *passim; idem*, "In Grateful Dialogue").

When YHWH restored the fortunes of Israel, it would be like a new Exodus — a new and greater liberation from an enslavement greater than that in Egypt. There are signs of this theme scattered liberally throughout the Gospels. The reported conversation of Moses and Elijah with Jesus on the Mount of Transfiguration in Luke 9:31, where the focus of their discussion is on Jesus' "exodus" that he was about to accomplish at Jerusalem, is one prominent example of this theme. And the Lord's Prayer can best be seen in this light as well — that is, as the prayer of the new wilderness wandering people.

Typological correspondences between the Exodus of Israel's memory and the New Exodus of Christian proclamation are complex, and should not be pressed for exact one-to-one correspondences. That is not how this sort of thing works. Nonetheless, it may be reasonably claimed that for the evangelists — and arguably for Jesus himself — the equivalent of the crossing of the Red Sea is the death and resurrection of Jesus. The Last Supper is the Passover meal that anticipates, and gives meaning to, the great act of liberation. From that point of view, the wilderness wandering, led by the pillar of cloud and fire, does not occur until the post-Easter period — where exactly this theme is picked up, as we will see, by Paul in Romans 8.

There are some signs, indeed, that Jesus saw the period of his ministry as, at least in certain respects, parallel to that of Moses at the court of Pharaoh. Luke 11:20, for example, alluding to Exod. 8:19, portrays Jesus as saying: "If I by the finger of God cast out demons, then the kingdom of God has come upon you." The parallel in Matt. 12:28 has "spirit" for "finger," so it is, of course, possible that Luke deliberately created an Exodus allusion in a Jesus saying where it was not originally present. But even if an accumulation of such points were held to prove that Jesus regarded his followers prior to Calvary and Easter as still "in Egypt," I would still argue that the Lord's Prayer was designed to constitute them as "Exodus People," "Freedom People" — indeed, as "New Covenant People."

The Lord's Prayer, in fact, was designed to encapsulate and celebrate, in the presence of God, the liberation that had already begun to take place and that had yet to be completed. It was designed to enable Jesus' followers to beseech the Father that they would be enabled to remain loyal to his freedom purposes through all the tribulations that lay ahead. This can be seen more particularly as we look again at each of the clauses of the Lord's Prayer from a New Exodus perspective.

Father/Our Father

In highlighting echoes from the Exodus tradition in the Lord's Prayer, we must begin, of course, with "Father": "Israel is my son, my firstborn; let my people go, that they may serve me" (Exod. 4:22-23); "When Israel was a child I loved him, and out of Egypt I called my son" (Hos. 11:1). Calling God "Father" not only evokes all kinds of associations of family life and intimacy; more importantly, it speaks to all subsequent generations of God as the God of the Exodus, the God who rescues Israel precisely because Israel is God's firstborn son. The title Father says as much about Israel, and about the events through which God will liberate Israel, as it does about God.

Jesus' own sense of vocation, that of accomplishing the New Exodus, was marked principally by his awareness of God as Father (cf. my *Jesus and the Victory of God*, ch. 13). Now in the Lord's Prayer he invites his followers to consider themselves Exodus people. Their cry for redemption will be heard and answered.

Hallowed Be Your Name

God revealed himself to Moses in the burning bush, speaking his name and giving it as the main reason why he could be trusted to bring the children of Israel out of captivity (cf. Exod. 3:13-16). And it was the honor and reputation of YHWH's name that Moses would subsequently use as the fulcrum in his great prayer for Israel's forgiveness after the episode of the golden calf — a theme that was also picked up by Joshua after the debacle at Ai (cf. Exod. 32:11-14; Josh. 7–9). The sanctifying of God's name, in other words, has to do once more not merely with God's own reputation in, as it were, a private capacity, but with the fact that he is committed to and in covenant with the people of Israel. To pray that God's name be hallowed, therefore, is to pray that the Exodus may not only happen but be followed through to its proper conclusion — that is, that Israel be redeemed not only from the original slavery of Egypt, but also from the sin and rebellion that keeps her from arriving and safely settling in the promised land.

Your Kingdom Come

The sovereign rule of the one true God is, of course, the main subtext of the battle between Moses and Pharaoh. As with Elijah and the prophets of Baal, the story of the Exodus is a story about which God is the stronger. It is in deliberate evocation of the Exodus theme that Isa. 52:7-10 writes of the great return:

> How beautiful upon the mountains
>> are the feet of the messenger who announces peace;
> who brings good news, who announces salvation,
>> who says to Zion, "Your God reigns."
> Listen! Your sentinels lift up their voices,
>> together they sing for joy;
> for in plain sight they see YHWH returning to Zion. . . .
> YHWH has made bare his holy arm before all the nations;
>> all the ends of the earth shall see the salvation of our God.

The Exodus is the background; the great return the foreground; the kingdom of YHWH the main theme. This is the context of Jesus' own kingdom announcement, the setting that gives meaning to the kingdom clause in the Lord's Prayer.

Your Will Be Done

The doing of YHWH's will on earth as in heaven is, of course, part of the whole apocalyptic theme in which heavenly truths and events become embodied in their earthly counterparts. Part of the point of the whole Sinai theophany — the central part, in fact, of the Exodus story — was the meeting of heaven and earth, with Moses as the intermediary who went to and fro between the two spheres, so that laws and instructions made in heaven could be carried out on earth. This anticipates (or, depending on one's view of Pentateuchal origins, reflects) the temple theology in which the sanctuary was considered to be quite literally the place where heaven and earth met. If Torah was the means by which, within Israel, God's will was to be done on earth as in heaven, and if the temple was the place where this was embodied in cultic celebration and sacrifice, to pray that this might happen anew — within the context of the New Exodus motifs already so strongly present — was to pray not merely that certain things might occur within the earthly realm that would coincide with plans that God had made in the heavenly realm, but that a fresh integration of heaven and earth would take place in which all that temple and Torah had stood for would be realized afresh. It was to pray both that God's saving purpose for Israel and the world would come about through God's personal action, and that God's people would find themselves not merely shaped by a law, however divine, or focused on a building, however God-given, but embraced by a saving personal love.

"Thy will be done on earth as in heaven" can, of course, carry all sorts of further overtones, such as prayers for wise political solutions to world-shaking crises, prayers for bread for the hungry, and prayers for justice for the oppressed. But at its heart lies a prayer for the appropriate integration of heaven and earth that the early Christians came to see already accomplished in Jesus himself — who was like Moses, but so much more so — and came to long for in God's eventual future (cf. Rev. 21; see also Rom. 8:17-30, which we will discuss later).

Give Us Today Our Daily Bread

The prayer for bread has its historical background in the provision of manna in the wilderness. God's daily gift, following the people's grumbling, became the stuff of legend. Jesus' actions in the feeding miracles alluded to the wilderness stories, as the evangelists (especially John) suggest. In the context of the Lord's Prayer, this clause aligns the followers of Jesus with the wilderness generation and their need to know God's daily supply of not only literal bread but also of all that it symbolized.

Manna was not needed in Egypt. Nor would it be needed in the promised land. It is the food of inaugurated eschatology, the food that is needed because the kingdom has already broken in and because it is not yet consummated. The daily provision of manna signals that the Exodus has begun, but also that we are not yet living in the land.

Forgive Us Our Debts/Sins

The story of the manna, however, was also the story of Israel's sin and lack of faith. The prayer for forgiveness, therefore, is quite appropriate in this context, and not merely another item in a shopping-list of spiritual needs and wants. In the light of Jeremiah 31 and Jesus' offer of forgiveness as the central blessing of the new covenant — that is, the great return that was happening through his work — forgiveness is raised to a new height. If the Egypt from which the New Exodus is freeing God's people is the Egypt of sin and all that it produces, then the prayer "forgive us our sins" becomes precisely the prayer of those still in Egypt: "Deliver us from Pharaoh!"

Matthew and the *Didache,* of course, present Jesus as speaking of the forgiveness of debts (as in Matthew) or debt (as in the *Didache*). I have elsewhere agreed with those who see in this a sign of the Jubilee, and of Jesus' intention being that his followers should celebrate it amongst themselves (see my *Jesus and the Victory of God,* 294-95). The Jubilee provisions, of course, look back to the fact that Israel had been enslaved in Egypt and that God had rescued and delivered her (cf. Lev. 25:38, 42, 55). They were part of the Exodus theology. In the same way, Jesus' demand that his followers should forgive one another belongs precisely within the same logic. Redeemed slaves must themselves live as redemption people. The inner connection between forgiving others and being forgiven oneself, which is so strongly emphasized in Matt. 6:14-15 and 18:21-35 (cf. *Sirach* 28:1-7), grows directly out of this Exodus motif.

143

Lead Us Not into Temptation, but Deliver Us from the Evil One

In this wider context the difficulties about the clause "Do not lead us to 'the testing,'" which are reflected in current debates about the wording for liturgical use, may be addressed with some hope of success. Who is testing whom, with what intent, and with what result?

The normal assumption is that the prayer is asking to be spared having one's faith tested by God. But the tradition throughout early Christianity that sees the testing of one's faith as a necessary part of discipleship — indeed, as a following of Jesus — speaks strongly against such an understanding. Is it, then, as Albert Schweitzer thought, the eschatological *peirasmos* — the Great Tribulation, the worst moment in history — that the prayer is asking to be spared from? A strong case for this reading can be made out, and I have myself taken this line in the past (cf. *Jesus and the Victory of God,* esp. 577-79).

On this view, Jesus believed that "Messianic Woes" were coming on Israel, and that it was his particular task and vocation to go out ahead and take the full weight of them on himself, so that the people would not need to undergo them. This would explain the repetition in Gethsemane of his command to his disciples: "Watch and pray, that you may not enter the *peirasmos*" (Matt. 26:41; Mark 14:38; Luke 22:46) — meaning by that command: "Pray that you may be spared this great moment of anguish; it is my task to enter it alone." (We may note, however, that when Jesus himself prayed a somewhat similar prayer the answer was "No."). And such an interpretation fits well with what I have elsewhere argued to be Jesus' perception of the moment of crisis in which he saw himself to have a central role.

But it remains somewhat strange to see this as the complete explanation of "lead us not into temptation." For if the early church came to believe that in some sense the great *peirasmos* had, indeed, happened to Jesus on the cross, why would they have continued to pray this clause in the Lord's Prayer thereafter? Granted, the fall of Jerusalem, which was still in the future for those who handed on the early traditions, had been spoken of by Jesus in similarly dramatic terms, as witness Mark 13 and its parallels. But what about after that, in the period when we must assume the *Didache*, at least, to have been written — and most likely the Gospels of Matthew and Luke as well?

One possible answer, of course, is that in the days following AD 70 the church looked beyond the fall of Jerusalem to the final moment when God would redeem the whole of creation — and that such a futuristic vision included a final, yet-to-occur tribulation. But this possibility, which we can see reflected perhaps in the Book of Revelation, only sharpens the question. For then we must ask: Did the church expect to be in some sense spared the sufferings of this final tribulation? Did not salvation consist, rather, in remaining faithful within it? This, then, leads us to reconsider the Exodus tradition and to search for other possible meanings.

The most probable explanation, I propose, is that the "testing" is not God's testing of his people but the people's testing of God (cf. J. Gibson, "Testing Temptation"). One of the central charges against the wilderness generation was that they, in their unbelief, "put YHWH to the test" by challenging him to produce demonstrations of his presence with them (cf. Exod. 17:7). The particular issue, of course, was YHWH's provision of water from the rock, which followed directly on the people's grumbling about food and YHWH's provision of manna. The deuteronomic memory of the wilderness "testings" echoes on in the prophetic traditions, with Ahaz using the old warning as an excuse not to look for the sign that Isaiah was offering (cf. Isa. 7:12; see also Ps. 78:18, 41, 56; 95:9; 106:14). In one of Paul's alignments of the church with the wilderness generation, he cites this specifically as a central failing that the church must not emulate (cf. 1 Cor. 10:9). This was, more specifically, one of the key failings of the wilderness generation that Jesus specifically avoided during his initial temptations (cf. Matt. 4:7//Luke 4:12, quoting Deut. 6:16).

The passage in Paul's letters in which this theme finds expression — that is, 1 Cor. 10:9: "We must not test the Lord [or, 'the Christ'] as some of them did" — also suggests that the early church had become used to taking "the *peirasmos*" in a wider sense than simply the sharply focused eschatological one. For in 1 Corinthians 10 Paul draws a close parallel between the church and the wilderness generation, speaking of that earlier generation as having been "baptized" into Moses (v. 2) and as having all eaten "spiritual food" and drunk "spiritual drink" (vv. 3-4). Their testing of the Lord — or, as the preferred reading has it, of "the Christ" — was one aspect of their many-sided failure.

Nonetheless, when Paul speaks of *peirasmos* a few verses later, it is clear that he means not the Israelites' testing of God but the "temptations" that come on God's people, not least from the pagan environment in which they live. 1 Cor. 10:13 is the clearest statement of what *peirasmos* had come to mean in the early church and of how, with its Exodus over-tones, it was being reapplied:

> No *peirasmos* has overtaken you but that which is normal to the human race. God is faithful: he will not allow you to be tested beyond your strength. He will make, with the *peirasmos*, also the way out, so that you are able to bear it.

This can only refer to the much more general "temptation," within which the temptation to put God to the test is one, but only one.

What we see here in this reapplication of the Exodus tradition is not so much the downgrading of eschatology into moralism, but the taking up of moral instruction into typological eschatology. Paul will not rest content with simply telling the Corinthians how to behave and chiding them if they go wrong. He will teach them to think of themselves as the people of the true Exodus, and within that framework show them how the moral struggles they face — including the temptation to devise tests to see how strong their Lord is — are the equivalent of the temptations which brought the wilderness generation to ruin. They must now succeed where their typological predecessors failed.

Who, then, is the author of this "temptation" of 1 Cor. 10:13? Paul does not say directly, but the context strongly implies that it is the evil one. Despite the apostle's firm conviction regarding the sovereignty of God, such "testings" come from "the Satan" (cf. 1 Cor. 7:5; the word *peirasmos* occurs in the Pauline corpus only in 1 Cor. 10:13; Gal. 4:14; and 1 Tim. 6:9). 1 Corinthians 10, therefore, might be seen as a practical commentary on the Lord's Prayer, particularly on its concluding clauses. What Paul, in effect, is saying is: You are the Exodus generation; therefore trust God to lead you out of your moment of testing without succumbing to it — that is, to deliver you from the evil one.

If this is accepted, then we may understand the last part of the Lord's Prayer (i.e., the last two clauses in Matthew's version and the *Didache*) as follows: Jesus' followers are instructed to pray that they may be spared the great *peirasmos* that is coming on Jesus himself *and* the cognate tribulation that is coming on Jerusalem and the whole world. To this extent, the petition is similar to what Jesus urges in Matt. 24:20//Mark 13:18: "Pray that your flight may not be in winter."

But the petition also broadens out to include all of what Paul speaks about — that is, the variegated temptations, which, coming from "the Satan," include the temptation to put God to the test, but also include such other sins as idolatry and grumbling. Thus "Lead us not into temptation" would then mean, in that broader context, "Do not let us be led into temptation [from which we cannot escape]." The fact that God has promised to be faithful and to provide the way of escape does not mean, in the logic of New Testament prayer, that one should not pray for it, but rather the reverse. Those who pray the Lord's Prayer are designed by Jesus to be those who remain faithful to the God who intends to remain faithful to them — and who thereby constitute the true eschatological Israel, the people of the New Exodus.

The Lord's Prayer as the Heart of the New Covenant Charter

We may now stand back briefly from this Exodus-based exposition of the Lord's Prayer and examine the results. Certain features from our investigation can be highlighted. The prayer is given by Jesus to constitute his followers as the true Exodus people. They are to succeed, not least by prayer, where the original wilderness generation failed. The prayer moves from the disciples' relation to God, through the honoring of God's name and the doing of his will, to provisions for bodily needs and dealing with evil. Furthermore, the prayer has something of the same shape — and, within the new eschatological moment, something of the same role — as the Decalogue within the Exodus narrative. Thus the Lord's Prayer may be seen as being to the church as the Ten Commandments were to Israel: not just something to do, a comparatively arbitrary rule of life, but the heart of the new covenant charter.

Of course, it is not quite as easy as that. Matthew, who one might have expected to make this point, may be thought to have hinted at it by his placing of the Lord's Prayer within the Sermon on the Mount, redolent as it is of Exodus typology. And it would be sheer folly to think that the Decalogue has no abiding significance within the church, albeit reinterpreted in various ways — just as it would be folly to suppose that Israel bc was not also commanded and invited to pray the intimate covenantal prayer, the Shema, that Jesus himself reaffirmed (though, interestingly, as ethic rather than prayer, as in Judaism; cf. Matt. 22:34-40; Mark 12:28-31; Luke 10:25-28). Nevertheless, there is an important point here, which is at the very heart of our investigation: If we are looking for characteristic marks of the church, the Lord's Prayer offers itself more readily than the Ten Commandments, despite the parallel use of them in some systems of Christian education, as though they were, respectively, simply a timeless prayer and a timeless moral code.

The Lord's Prayer takes its place, rather, alongside baptism and the Eucharist. Both are thought of in Exodus terms in the New Testament, not least in 1 Corinthians 10. It is, therefore, appropriate that praying the Lord's Prayer should take place corporately and publicly within the liturgies for both baptism and the Eucharist. But it is also the case that the Lord's Prayer will be most fully understood and most fully "meant" within those Exodus-based narratives, which are symbolically and dramatically acted out in their new Christ-centered form. These sacraments are precisely among those moments when — within the inaugurated eschatology through which alone Christianity makes sense — both past and future, heaven and earth, are brought together in one dramatic action.

The Lord's Prayer is the means by which the church celebrates what has been accomplished already in Christ and strains forward for what lies ahead. And in the course of living between the present and the future, the church prays in the Lord's Prayer for grace and strength to remain faithful to its Lord and not to fall away from the bracing agenda of his kingdom announcement.

3. Prayers and Paradigms

The church that prays the Lord's Prayer claims, thereby, the status of the eschatological people of God. In so praying, it locates itself between Calvary, Easter, and Pentecost, on the one hand, and the great consummation (sometimes, by metonymy, called "the Parousia"), on the other hand. The Lord's Prayer is thus a marker, a reminder, to the church of who it is and why.

To locate oneself on this historical scale is, of course, to look with dismay at the many times when the church, like the wilderness generation, has betrayed its Lord, put its God to the test, and committed various idolatries and immoralities. But it is, at the same time, also to claim that, with the cross and resurrection of Jesus behind it, forgiveness and restoration are ever-present realities as well.

A Paradigm for the Church's Liturgy

The shape of the church's regular worship, therefore, ought to be ordered, I suggest, in ways that highlight this identity. All sorts of Christian traditions have been tempted in various ways to de-eschatologize themselves, and so to settle down into being simply a religion, with or without an accompanying moralism. It is this, perhaps, that has allowed so much contemporary thought to assume, without more ado, that Christianity is simply one "religion" among many — a view that the New Testament's characteristic eschatology would never permit.

One obvious way of keeping the church's eschatological focus would be to allow the shape as well as the content of the Lord's Prayer to inform its liturgy more strongly, not just in that part of the worship service labeled "prayer" but also in the structure of the whole. Invocation of God as Father, worship and prayer that sanctifies God's name, prayer for Jesus' kingdom work to find its complete fulfillment on earth as in heaven — all of these might come first. Intercession for particular blessings, of which bread is among the most basic and hence symbolic of the rest, would occur within this larger context.

Furthermore, we should note that, against the grain of some post-Augustinian liturgies, the church is not instructed by its Lord to approach its Father with "Sorry" as its first word. Even the Prodigal Son began his speech with "Father." There is, to be sure, an appropriate place for penitence, both for communities and individuals. But the normal Christian approach to the Creator God is the unfettered and delighted "Father." There is a time for penitence, but its location within the Lord's Prayer suggests that it should not take pride of place in regular liturgical worship.

There are, of course, some theologies still current in which all penitence is pushed to one side as gloomy or doleful. That this is a gross caricature should not need to be said. The Lord's Prayer indicates both that penitence is a regular necessity and that it is not the most important element. Pride and paranoia are alike to be avoided.

If the Lord's Prayer is correctly understood in its New Exodus eschatological context, a liturgy that grows up on this basis is likely to choose Scripture readings in such a way as both to celebrate God's deliverance of his people and to remind the congregation that they belong within this overarching story. This does not mean the avoidance of the non-narrative parts of Scripture, such as the Book of Proverbs. But it does mean that the sequence from the Old Testament to the New has some importance, and that at some point that sequence, which gave birth to the church, should be brought into explicit focus, whether by prayer or song.

The church's task in using the Lord's Prayer as a paradigm for liturgy, therefore, is (1) to thank God for its identity as the people of the New Exodus, (2) to pray that God's achievement in Jesus Christ may reach its complete fruition for both the church and the entire creation, and (3) to pray for grace and strength to remain faithful to God's calling in the present. In so doing, the church is explicitly identifying with Jesus himself in his own prayer and work (as we have highlighted in the first section of this article) — a stance that can only be taken without gross arrogance when it is remembered that the prayer, as given by Jesus, is not simply a command but an invitation. Like a good deal in the Gospel accounts, it requires a belief in the Holy Spirit to make full sense of this picture (which is what John and Paul, in particular, supply, as we will note later in this article).

A Paradigm for Christian Living

The Christian is also called to make the Lord's Prayer paradigmatic in his or her own personal life. The context in Matthew 6 includes Jesus' command to go into one's own room, shut the door, and pray to the Father who sees in secret (6:6). (We might want to ask, how many of Jesus' original hearers had private rooms into which they could retreat, with doors by which they could shut out all others?) The life of the individual Christian is lived out between baptism and bodily death and resurrection on the same principle as the life of the corporate church. It is true, of course, that the story of Israel's wilderness wanderings has been more regularly applied to the Christian life than to church history, and the symbolism is well enough known: the crossing of the Jordan symbolizing death, and so forth — or, as in some "second blessing" traditions, altered so that the crossing of the Jordan signals an entry into a "higher life" of full sanctification. Nonetheless, the Exodus story is still a fruitful source of imagery for reconstructing a genuinely Christian spirituality.

The Lord's Prayer, as used by a Christian who is conscious of his or her pilgrimage to the eventual promised land, celebrates the great beginning of that pilgrimage when, in baptism, that individual is united with Christ in his death and resurrection. Calling God "Father" says and celebrates all of that. The early petitions of the prayer, with their focus on God's name, God's kingdom, and God's will, can all be used in this context as the framework for focusing in one's private prayer on God himself, and for claiming already in the present — as, indeed, is done in the sacraments — the blessings of the future that are already secured in Christ. And within private prayer, as with public prayer, all of the other elements take their place: intercession, the prayer for forgiveness, and the clear-eyed plea against *peirasmos* and against the *poneros*. These all find their appropriate, though still subordinate, home. The individual Christian is called to be a man, woman, or child of prayer as a New Exodus person.

But that cannot be the whole story. For, as I said in the first section of this article, at its heart the Lord's Prayer is an invitation to each Christian to share in the praying life of Jesus himself. The early Christians were very conscious of Jesus' exalted presence before God's throne, where his constant task is to intercede on behalf of his people (cf. Rom. 8:34; Heb. 7:25; 9:24). The Lord's Prayer, therefore, by uniting Jesus' people with their Lord in the prayer that formed the inner core of his own life, brings about the situation where those who pray it are even now, whether they realize it or not, "seated in the heavenly places in Christ Jesus" (Eph. 2:6; cf. Col. 3:1, 3).

There are different ways of appropriately embodying this reality. Precisely because we are to pray God's kingdom into existence "on earth as it is in heaven," it is always worthwhile exploring and reflecting on those ways — including matters of place, posture, timing, musical accompaniment, and so on. These are not mere incidentals. They will, of course, vary quite widely with culture, personality, and opportunity. Such variations, however, do not suggest that there are not some more and some less appropriate outward forms and fashions. Rather, the reverse is true. Each individual Christian and every church community is responsible, under God, for not just maintaining a human tradition — or, for that matter, demolishing one — but for discovering the forms that the Lord's Prayer itself prompts and suggests within a particular culture and for the particular people who are going to be using it.

4. Abba, Father: Conformed to the Pattern of Christ

It is striking that at the two places where Paul quotes Jesus' use of *Abba,* the Aramaic word for "father," he also speaks in dramatic language of the two things that have formed the underlying structure of this article: (1) the New Exodus in Christ, and (2) the incorporation of the worshiping Christian into the inner trinitarian life of God. I conclude this article, therefore, with a brief look at these two passages and some suggestions as to what they mean for our regarding the Lord's Prayer as a paradigm of Christian praying.

In Gal. 4:1-11, as is fairly obvious though not always fully drawn out, Paul tells the story of the Exodus again. Only it is not now the Exodus from Egypt, when God sent Moses and gave the Law, but the Exodus of God's people in Christ, both Jews and Gentiles, in long-term and complete fulfillment of the promise to Abraham. Thus in verses 4-7 he says:

> When the time had fully come, God sent forth his Son . . . to redeem . . . and because you are children, God has sent the Spirit of his Son into our hearts, crying "*Abba,* Father." So you are no longer a slave, but a son; and, if a son, then an heir, through God.

As a result, as he emphasizes in verse 8-11, there can be no "going back to Egypt." God has now been revealed, not in a burning bush but in the Son and the Spirit — or, rather, as the One who sent the Son and now sends the Spirit of the Son.

The God of the New Exodus is the God revealed as Father, Son, and Spirit. The only alternative is some kind of paganism, even if, paradoxically, it is hiding underneath the Jewish Torah. And the revelation of God as Trinity is completed in the experience of Christian prayer — that is, in the *Abba,* which certainly refers to Jesus' own usage and may well refer to the practice of saying the Lord's Prayer in the early Aramaic-speaking church.

Two reflections on the use of this *Abba* prayer by Christians may be of note. First, just as the Lord's Prayer is still known as the "Pater Noster" by many Roman Catholics who actually now say it in English, so perhaps — though it can only ever be a guess — the same prayer may have continued to be known as the "Abba" by those who said it in Greek. Second, it may be asked: Is it simply a coincidence that the key prayer word of the early Christians, like some of the key prayer words of their pagan counterparts, was a palindrome (that is, a word or number that reads the same backward or forward) — indeed, one of the simplest possible palindromes?

The point, anyway, is that the Lord's Prayer — by (1) reflecting the prayer of Jesus and inviting his followers to share it, and (2) embodying

the New Exodus stance that summed up so much of Jesus' whole agenda
— is now the appropriate vehicle of a specific type of prayer. This prayer is
not shouting across a void to a distant and perhaps unknown God. Nor is
it simply getting in touch with one's own deepest feelings and self-
awareness. Nor is it getting in tune with the wider spirit of the whole cosmos. It is prayer that grows directly out of the Jewish experience and
knowledge of the one creator God, but that finds, without leaving that
Jewish base behind, that the knowledge of this one God has three intertwined aspects — not least of all because Jesus himself, as a human being,
remains at the heart of it.

Rom. 8:12-30 completes the circle (see my "New Exodus, New Inheritance"). Here we find the fully inaugurated, but not yet consummated, eschatology that so perfectly reflects Jesus' own kingdom announcement, albeit seen now from the post-Easter perspective. We are saved in hope; but
hope that is seen is not hope. And this salvation is precisely the New Exodus. Led by the Spirit, who here takes on the role of the pillar of cloud by
day and of fire by night, we are called the children of God. We are no longer slaves, and must not dream of going back to Egypt. Rather, because we
are those who cry "*Abba*, Father!" we are not only children but heirs, heirs
of the true promised land.

The true promised land is not a strip of territory in the Middle East
or elsewhere, nor yet "heaven" as a far-off and basically disembodied final
resting place. Rather, it is the renewed creation itself. It is God's world restored, healed, and flooded with the Spirit, sharing in the freedom that
goes with the glorification of God's children. Creation itself, in other
words, will have its own Exodus. Our Exodus experience in the death and
resurrection of Jesus Christ is both the key starting point of that long project and the guarantee that God will complete what he has started.

In the midst of all of this, the characteristic Christian prayer is that
which, inspired by the Spirit, catches the Christian up in the mysterious,
and even painful, dialogue of the Father and the Spirit (cf. 8:26-27). It is
this that forms the Christian according to the pattern of the crucified and
risen Son (cf. 8:17, 29). And it is this that constitutes Christians as "those
who love God" (cf. 8.28) — in other words, those who fulfill, at last, the
great Exodus prayer-command of Deut. 6:4: "Hear, O Israel, YHWH our
God, YHWH is one; and you shall love YHWH your God with all your
heart, and with all your soul, and with all your might."

The Lord's Prayer, then, though not explicitly referred to by Paul, points on to what in many ways must be seen as the crown of early Christian theology and practice. For the *Abba* prayer, inspired by the Spirit of Jesus, is the characteristic Christian prayer. It encompasses within itself that celebration of God's goodness and kingdom, that intercession for and grief over the world in pain and need, and that anguish over trials and temptations that still beset and besiege what is the normal state of Christian existence. More than all that, however, as an invitation to share in Jesus' own prayer life and as the New Exodus prayer, it enables the baptized and believing Christian to share — humbly, wonderingly, painfully, joyfully — in the life of God himself, Father, Son, and Spirit.

Selected Bibliography

Allison, Dale C., Jr. *Jesus of Nazareth: Millenarian Prophet.* Minneapolis: Fortress, 1998.

Gibson, Jeffrey. "Testing Temptation: The Meaning of Q 11:4b" (unpublished paper given at the 1998 meeting of the Society of Biblical Literature in Orlando, Florida).

Keesmaat, Sylvia C. *Paul and His Story: (Re)Interpreting the Exodus Tradition.* Sheffield: Sheffield Academic Press, 1999.

Koenig, John. *Rediscovering New Testament Prayer: Boldness and Blessing in the Name of Jesus.* San Francisco: Harper, 1992; repr. Harrisburg: Morehouse, 1998.

Wise, Michael O. *The First Messiah: Investigating the Savior Before Christ.* San Francisco: Harper, 1999.

Wright, N. T. *Jesus and the Victory of God.* Minneapolis: Fortress, 1996.

———. *The Lord and His Prayer.* Grand Rapids: Eerdmans, 1996.

———. "New Exodus, New Inheritance: The Narrative Structure of Romans 3–8." In *Romans and the People of God: Essays in Honor of Gordon D. Fee on the Occasion of his 65th Birthday,* ed. S. K. Soderlund and N. T. Wright. Grand Rapids: Eerdmans, 1999, 26-35.

———. "In Grateful Dialogue." In *Jesus and the Restoration of Israel,* ed. C. C. Newman. Downers Grove: InterVarsity, 1999.

CHAPTER 8

God's Name, Jesus' Name, and Prayer in the Fourth Gospel

ANDREW T. LINCOLN

THE DISTINCTIVENESS OF the Fourth Gospel, in comparison with the Synoptic Gospels, extends even to its perspective on such a basic matter as humanity's relationship to God in prayer. The Greek verb "to pray" *(proseuchomai)*, which is used eleven times in Mark, fifteen times in Matthew, and nineteen times in Luke, does not occur at all in John. More significantly, however, what sets John's Gospel apart is that its portrayals of Jesus' prayer life are extensively affected by its understanding of Jesus' unique relationship as Son to the divine Father — and its teachings about prayer in the lives of Jesus' followers are also heavily colored by this relationship.

In this article we will deal first with the portrayals of Jesus at prayer in John's Gospel, considering the references to his praying in the earlier narrative of his public ministry and then focusing our attention on the prayer of 17:1-26 that concludes his Farewell Discourse. Inevitably, given its prominence and placement in the narrative, an investigation of Jesus' prayer in John 17 will take up the largest part of our discussion. We will then discuss more briefly what Jesus says to his disciples about prayer in that Farewell Discourse of 13:31–16:33. Finally, we will highlight the significance of the themes of God's name and Jesus' name in the Fourth Gospel for the praying and living of those who believe in Jesus.

ANDREW T. LINCOLN

1. Jesus at Prayer in His Public Ministry

After a reading of the Synoptic Gospels, what is most striking about John's portrayal of Jesus' public ministry is that it contains so little about Jesus praying. And what little it does contain raises some major questions. It is worth here briefly rehearsing the evidence.

The Strange Case of John's Jesus

What the Synoptics and John have in common is that, as we might expect, both traditions depict Jesus as a typical Jewish male who engaged in ritual prayer at meals and who gave thanks for, or blest, the bread and fish in their feeding stories (cf. Mark 6:41//Matt. 14:19//Luke 9:16; and Mark 8:6//Matt. 15:36; with John 6:11, 23). Although in their accounts a specific prayer to God does not precede any of Jesus' miraculous deeds — these miraculous deeds simply being carried out as authoritative acts — the Synoptic Gospels make it clear that Jesus' entire ministry was undergirded by prayer. Mark and Matthew record specific instances when Jesus either prays in a deserted place (Mark 1:35) or goes up a mountain to pray (Mark 6:46; Matt. 14:23). Luke, as is well known, develops this characterization of Jesus and relates a number of other occasions of him at prayer (cf. 3:21; 6:12; 9:18, 28-29; 11:1; 22:32) — and in one place implies that such activity was, indeed, characteristic of his life: "But he would withdraw to deserted places and pray" (5:16).

Not only does John fail to mention any of these occasions or to characterize Jesus' ministry in this way, but other significant references in the Synoptic Gospels to prayer in Jesus' life are also absent. In John 2:13-22, for example, there is no reference by Jesus to the Jerusalem temple as a house of prayer (contrast Mark 11:17//Matt. 21:13//Luke 19:45). Furthermore, there is no "Lord's Prayer" in John's Gospel (cf. Matt. 6:9-13//Luke 11:2-4), no prayer in Gethsemane (cf. Mark 14:32-42//Matt. 26:36-46//Luke 22:39-46), and no prayer from the cross (cf. Mark 15:34//Matt. 27:46//Luke 23:46).

Only two prayers of Jesus during the period of his public ministry are recorded in John's Gospel, and both have rather strange features. The first is at the tomb of Lazarus in John 11, where Jesus utters a prayer that is not a prayer of petition but of thanksgiving — a prayer that echoes the

156

psalmist who, after experiencing God's victorious deliverance in the face of death, says, "I thank you that you have answered me" (Ps. 118:21; cf. vv. 15-18). Before he calls Lazarus from the tomb, and without mention of any preceding prayer request, Jesus, we are told, "looked upward" and said: "Father, I thank you for having heard me. I knew that you always hear me" (vv. 41-42a).

The portrayal of Jesus in John 11 is of One who presupposes a relationship with the Father that makes it a matter of course that any prayer of his will be heard — so much so, that he does not need to articulate any individual request. This inference is reinforced by the words that follow: "But I have said this for the sake of the crowd standing here, so that they may believe that you sent me" (v. 42b). Explicit prayer, even of thanksgiving, was not strictly necessary for Jesus — even when raising someone from the dead. Nonetheless, he accommodates to the needs of those who require insight into the nature of his relationship with God.

The second prayer of Jesus in John's Gospel occurs in chapter 12 — at the point to which John has moved Jesus' Gethsemane experience as recorded in the Synoptic Gospels. In John's Gospel this experience is found toward the end of Jesus' public ministry and *before*, rather than after, the last meal with his disciples. Here Jesus concedes "Now my heart is troubled!" at the prospect of what lies ahead (v. 27), and he prays: "Father, glorify your name" (v. 28a). Yet his distress immediately recedes into the background and his prayer distances him from the very human figure with whom we can identify in the Gethsemane accounts of the Synoptic Gospels. For in John's portrayal, Jesus explicitly rejects the sort of prayer with which the Jesus of the synoptic portrayals began his agonizing struggle in the garden to conform his will to that of his Father.

In the Synoptic Gospels Jesus could request, "Remove this cup from me" (Mark 14:36//Matt. 26:39//Luke 22:42). But John's Jesus reasons: "And what should I say — 'Father, save me from this hour'? No, it is for this reason that I have come to this hour" (v. 27). In John's Gospel, Jesus is portrayed as being conscious from the very start of his ministry that everything is moving toward his "hour" — the supreme point of fulfillment — and that that climactic hour entails both his death and his glory. Now in John 12, at this stage in his public ministry, he is conscious that the hour has arrived. He has, in fact, just stated this in conversation with Andrew and Philip: "The hour has come for the Son of Man to be glorified" (v. 23). And he has gone on to tell them about the necessity of his dying (v. 24).

Because of his unique relationship with God, for Jesus to be glorified is at the same time for God to be glorified (cf. 13:31, "Now is the Son of Man glorified and God is glorified in him"). For this reason, the only appropriate prayer is that which Jesus utters in chapter 12: "Father, glorify your name" (v. 28a). This appeal to God's name and glory is typical of Israel's prayer, where it frequently functioned as the motive for an appeal for God's help (cf. Ps. 25:11; 31:3; 79:9; 109:21; 143:11; Jer. 14:7, 21). But Jesus refuses any appeal for deliverance. Instead, his sole concern is with his Father's reputation, which is, paradoxically, to be established through both non-deliverance and what appears to be the very opposite of glory by human standards — that is, Jesus' death by crucifixion.

If prayer presupposes a two-sided relationship in which there is both a petitioning and a response — both an asking and an answering — what now ensues again raises the question whether Jesus' praying is normal praying. For whereas in the Lazarus episode of John 11 Jesus' prayer was not really necessary for him, here in John 12 an answer to his prayer is not really required for One who is aligned to the will of his Father. Nonetheless, an answer does come in the form of a voice from heaven and with the words: "I have glorified it, and I will glorify it again" (v. 28b). But Jesus' explanation of this phenomenon is: "This voice has come for your sake, not for mine" (v. 30). Again, this is an accommodation for the crowd, signaling that the crucial moment of the cosmic trial is at hand (cf. v. 31, "Now is the judgment of this world") and attesting to them the relationship of Jesus to God — which is the issue at stake in this trial. Jesus' awareness of his relationship with God in John's Gospel is so assured that he knows, without the help of external reinforcement, that God will be glorified in his actions.

Understanding Jesus' Own Prayer Life

What little is said about Jesus' prayers and prayer life during the course of his ministry in John's Gospel, other than his prayers over food, makes it problematic whether we should consider his prayers as normal prayers. But before we conclude that the Jesus of the Fourth Gospel is totally beyond our human experience of prayer, it is important to note some tantalizing hints that something more was going on in Jesus' prayer life than the evangelist has explicitly said. In 9:31, when the man born blind responds to his interrogators' questions about whether Jesus was responsible for his being now able to see, the man says, "We know that God does not listen to sinners, but he does listen to one who worships him and obeys his will." There is no prayer on the part of Jesus recorded in the account of the man receiving his sight. Yet the man's statement seems to presuppose that God has listened to a request from Jesus.

Similarly, after Martha reproached Jesus for not being on the scene earlier to prevent Lazarus's death, she adds, "But even now I know that God will give you whatever you ask of him" (11:22). Again, this presupposes that Jesus engaged in petitionary prayer and that his prayers were effective. And Jesus' words directed to the Father, "I knew that you always hear me" (11:42), suggest that in his relationship with God there was a continual speaking and hearing — even if Jesus was not in need of that relationship coming to expression in words.

The narrative as a whole, then, suggests that there was an asking and receiving taking place between Jesus and God that did not always need to come to verbal expression, but was nevertheless the backdrop to Jesus' entire ministry. This perspective is reinforced when we note the language of listening and seeing that characterizes Jesus' relationship as Son to the Father. For, with regard to listening, Jesus repeatedly claims he can do nothing on his own, but that he only declares what he has heard from his Father (5:30; 8:26, 28; 12:49-50; 14:10; 15:15; cf. 10:18). Similarly with regard to seeing, Jesus asserts: "The Son can do nothing on his own, but only what he sees the Father doing. . . . The Father loves the Son and shows him all that he himself is doing" (5:19-20), and "I declare what I have seen in the Father's presence" (8:38).

When did this listening and observing in the presence of the Father occur? The formulations suggest that these activities are not to be seen as those having taken place in Jesus' preexistence with God, but were part of his continuing relationship with his Father during his public ministry — a relationship in which he saw visions and heard auditions, and for which prayer would not be an inappropriate description.

There are two ways of thinking about the phenomena we have noted, and each of them contains a significant amount of truth. The first is to insist that the strangeness of Jesus' prayers in John's Gospel is related to the evangelist's distinctive portrayal of Jesus' divine identity. The fact that Jesus is not seen as struggling in prayer — or even as taking specific times to engage in prayer, whether on his own behalf or that of others — is part of the overall Johannine interpretation of Jesus. In John's Gospel Jesus' unique relationship with God is so stressed that, if this Gospel were all we had, it might lead in the direction of a docetic Christ — perhaps even provoking the question whether the Jesus of John's Gospel is fully credible as a human being (for the classic overstatement of this view, see E. Käsemann, *Testament of Jesus*, 4-26, who claims that the Fourth Gospel presents a naive docetism).

The second response is to ask — rather than claiming that John's Jesus does not really pray — whether our own conception of prayer may be too limited. For prayer is not simply speaking and interceding. Prayer is also being silent and listening. The narrative of the Fourth Gospel makes it clear that Jesus' relationship to God is one of constant listening to and seeing the Father, so that he can carry out the Father's will. Prayer for Jesus in John's Gospel, therefore, is a sustained spiritual communion with God in which he asks for and receives what is needed for his ministry, but without needing to express his concerns in actual uttered words.

Perhaps these two reflections can be brought together by saying that what is distinctive about the Fourth Gospel's portrayal of Jesus at prayer is (1) that it assumes the intimate relationship narrated in the synoptic Gospels as being one of prayer, but (2) that it heightens the Synoptic portrayals by depicting Jesus as so much at one with the will of the Father that he really does not need to petition on his own account. What C. K. Barrett says about John 17:24 is true of Jesus' prayer life as a whole: "The ordinary language of prayer breaks down because Jesus is speaking, as it were, within the Godhead. He expresses his *will*, but his *will* is identical with the Father's" (*Gospel according to St. John*, 514).

For One whose will is already in alignment with the Father's will, prayer takes the form of an attentiveness to God that hears and sees God's will in such a way that this becomes totally determinative for what he says and does. It takes the form of a loving relationship in which each partner is attentive to the desires of the other. The only prayer that matters for a person in such a relationship is that God's reputation be seen for what it is — that is, "glorify your name," which is equivalent to "hallowed be your name," the first petition of the Lord's Prayer.

2. Jesus' Prayer to the Father in John 17

If there is a sense in which Jesus does not need to pray, the question may legitimately be asked: Why, then, does the fourth evangelist highlight Jesus'

160

long prayer of petition in 17:1-26? An answer to that question demands a close and careful investigation of the prayer itself.

The One Who Prays

Both strands of the data noted above are also present in Jesus' prayer of John 17: the full humanity of Jesus, which is presupposed, and Jesus' unique relationship with the Father, which the evangelist wants to highlight. So Jesus is portrayed, like other humans, as One whose relationship to God at a time of crisis — here, in particular, the crisis of an impending death — is expressed in prayer. But the content of Jesus' prayer, with its divine perspective on the world, makes it quite unlike that of any other human.

Jesus begins by praying for himself. He prays for his glorification, which in the discourse of the Fourth Gospel turns out to have the same force as the earlier prayer that God be glorified (cf. 13:31-32). His prayer, however, quickly becomes a prayer on behalf of his disciples. In fact, it becomes a prayer that is ultimately not for his own sake, but for the sake of his followers — including the Gospel's implied readers, who are enabled to listen in on Jesus' relationship to the Father and his perspective on God's purposes for the continuation of his ministry in their mission. John's Jesus is already assured of the outcome as far as his own destiny is concerned. What is more, the Jesus who prays in John 17 is the Jesus who has just proclaimed: "I have overcome the world" (16:33).

The voice of Jesus in the prayer of John 17 is the voice of the risen and exalted Jesus, who speaks of himself in the third person as "the Son" and "Jesus Christ" (vv. 1, 3), sees his work on earth as already completed (vv. 4, 6-8), says he is no longer in the world (v. 11a), asks that his followers be where he already is (v. 24), and thinks of himself as being "in them" (vv. 23, 26). Yet here, as elsewhere in the evangelist's narrative, pre-resurrection and post-resurrection perspectives are combined. So Jesus can, at one and the same time, view his departure and glorification as being imminent (vv. 1, 5), see himself as in the process of returning to the Father (vv. 11b, 13a), and consider himself still in the world (v. 13b). In this way the different facets of the eschatological hour of exaltation, which include Jesus' death and return to the Father, are in play in the temporal perspective that informs the prayer.

When compared with the Synoptic Gospels, it can be seen that Jesus' prayer of John 17 replaces their Gethsemane prayer. The difference in its content, together with its presupposition of Jesus' sovereign awareness of the outcome of his mission, highlight the distinctiveness of John's portrayal of Jesus. For this Jesus, who already has his will completely aligned to that of the Father, is the Logos who has become flesh, but who at the same time is the Son who remains in the bosom of the Father.

If Jesus is, then, to be conceived of in this way, how might we imagine his ongoing relationship with God? The prayer of chapter 17 constitutes the Fourth Gospel's most extensive depiction of what is entailed in the intimate union of the Son and the Father — a union that was experienced in this world, yet one that transcends this world's categories of time and space.

Genre and Structure

The material of John 13–17, as a whole, comprises the recognizable genre of a "farewell setting and address," which is familiar from both Jewish and Greco-Roman literature. In such scenes, the main character announces his impending death, gathers his children or successors around him, reviews the past, and prepares them for the future beyond his death. Praying for those who remain was also a feature of a hero's farewell — as, for example, Moses in Deuteronomy 33, where some of his blessings of the tribes take the form of prayers (cf. vv. 7, 8, 11), and Paul in his farewell to the Ephesian elders (cf. Acts 20:36).

Here in John 17, however, the prayer element is significantly expanded and becomes the climactic feature at the end of the farewell. But the prayer does not only elaborate on themes appearing earlier in the narrative. It also picks up themes from the immediately preceding Farewell Discourse regarding Jesus' relationship with his Father and his departure as "glory," as well as various aspects of Jesus' instructions to the disciples about their mission in the world.

The overlapping of themes and their repetitions mean that the moves in the prayer's progression of thought are not always clearly signaled. Our discussion of John 17, however, will treat the actual petitions as providing the main structural markers of the prayer and will follow those who see three major units in the prayer, with a widening scope of reference in those three units: (1) Jesus' prayer for his own glorification in verses 1-8; (2) Jesus' prayer for the disciples in verses 9-19; and (3) Jesus' prayer for both present and future believers in verses 20-26. In line with the evangelist's fondness for structuring episodes in seven parts, the prayer contains seven specific petitions, with the first and last sections having two each and the longer middle section three. And in the case of each petition, the grounds on which the request is made are also set out — with those grounds sometimes preceding, sometimes following, and sometimes both preceding and following the request.

Jesus' Prayer for His Own Glorification (17:1-8)

The first part of the prayer contains two petitions about Jesus' glory, with each petition being introduced by a direct address to the Father: "Father, the hour has come. Glorify your Son, that your Son may glorify you" (v. 1); and, "Father, glorify me in your presence with the glory I had with you before the world began" (v. 5). Jesus' address to God as Father — which occurs six times in the prayer (vv. 1, 5, 11, 21, 24, and 25), with the addition of the adjectives "holy" in verse 11 and "righteous" in verse 25 — sets the tone of intimacy for the whole prayer. The glorification of Jesus in John's Gospel is his exaltation, which means his departure from this world and his return to the Father who sent him. And the two petitions of this first part of Jesus' prayer take up these two features of his glorification.

In the first petition of verse 1, with its statement "the hour has come," the focus is on Jesus' glorification in history — that is, his departure by means of the cross. Jesus' own talk about the arrival of "the hour" picks up from the narrator's reference to the coming of "the hour" at the beginning of the farewell scene in 13:1. Jesus prays that he will be glorified in that hour. The following purpose clause, "that your Son may glorify you," highlights the fact that the petition includes the glorification of the Father. Throughout the narrative, Jesus' cause and God's cause have been intertwined (cf. esp. 13:31-32). So here Jesus' hour of exaltation through death will be the paradoxical establishment of the reputation of both God and Jesus.

The ground for the petition is the authority delegated to Jesus by God to give eternal life: "You granted him authority over all people that he might give eternal life to all those you have given him" (v. 2). Earlier mention of the authority given to Jesus in the Fourth Gospel was in terms of his authority to judge (5:22, 27), with that judging including the giving of "life to whom he is pleased to give it" (5:21). Here the purpose of Jesus' "authority over all flesh" is also tied to the salvific aspect of his role as judge — that is, his giving of a positive verdict of eternal life in the cosmic trial. What is entailed in receiving eternal life is knowing "the only true God, and Jesus Christ, whom you have sent" (v. 3) — that is, the one true God and this God's uniquely authorized representative.

Yet, although Jesus as God's unique agent is one with God, it need be noted that this relationship in John's Gospel does not entail any abrogation of monotheism. The formulation "the only true God" of verse 3 is reminiscent of the exclusive claims for Israel's God found in the Jewish Scriptures. Among those claims is God's own assertion, "I am the Lord, that is my name; my glory I give to no other" (Isa. 42:8). So if there is one God, how can this God share the divine name and glory with Jesus without Jesus being seen as a second god?

For the fourth evangelist, as the second petition of this first part of Jesus' prayer will make clear, Jesus' relationship as Son to the Father is intrinsic to this one God's identity, for he was always included in the identity and glory of the one true God even before the foundation of the world. It is not the case, then, that in glorifying Jesus God shares the divine glory with some lesser being. Rather, the exaltation and glorification of Jesus display the glory of the one God.

In the second petition of verse 5, "Father, glorify me in your presence with the glory I had with you before the world began," the reference is to the completion of Jesus' exaltation — that is, his return to God, via the cross, which entails the resumption of the experience of glory that he enjoyed in the divine presence before the foundation of the world. Statements as to the grounds for this second petition both precede and follow the request: (1) the Son's "completing the work" that the Father gave him to do (v. 4), and (2) the Son's having "made known" God's name to the disciples, who belong to God and have been given by God to Jesus from out of the world (v. 6). The first is in line with Jesus' final words on the cross: "It is finished!" (19:30). The second highlights the importance of revealing God's name in Jesus' ministry.

In the ancient world, a person's name stood for who the person was and what the person represented — that is, the person's identity and reputation. Jesus has, therefore, made known who God is and what God's reputation entails. In the process, he used a particular name of God. For in Isa. 52:6 (LXX) God says: "Therefore my people shall know my name; therefore in that day they shall know that it is 'I Am' who speaks." One of the distinctives of Jesus' witness in John's Gospel is his use of this divine self-identification "I Am" in relation to himself (cf., e.g., 8:28, 58; 13:12; 18:5, 6).

In Jesus' accomplishment of making God's name known to the disciples, both God's sovereign initiative and the disciples' human response were involved: "You gave them to me and they have kept your word" (v. 6). In the perspective of this prayer, disciples are to see themselves as part of that intimate relationship between the Father and the Son — that is, as the gift of the Father to the Son (cf. also 6:37, 39, 44). The Father who gave the only Son to enable life, rather than to bring about perishing or death (3:16), has also given to the Son those to whom the gift of life has been granted. Jesus' mission, therefore, was successful because (1) the Father has given to the Son those who have been granted eternal life, and (2) those to whom life has been given have kept God's word.

From a post-resurrection perspective, the disciples are seen as having received and remained faithful to the divine message spoken and embodied by Jesus, his witness to the truth. In receiving "the word" (v. 6, *ton logon*), they have also received "the words" (v. 8, *ta rhēmata*) — that is, particular words or sayings. They know that Jesus' work and words, as well as Jesus himself, are from God. In short, they have believed that God sent Jesus (vv. 7-8).

Jesus' Prayer for His Disciples (17:9-19)

In what follows in Jesus' prayer of John 17, attention turns explicitly to those who are the fruit of Jesus' completed work. For them Jesus makes three specific requests: that they be kept in the divine name (v. 11); that they be protected from the evil one (v. 15); and that they be sanctified in the truth (v. 17). These three petitions are preceded by a general statement of intercession: "I am asking on their behalf" (v. 9a) — which is grounded by the statements that follow in verses 9b and 10. Here Jesus intercedes for his disciples and not for the world. This is because in John's Gospel the term "world" *(kosmos)* stands generally for human society in its hostility to God. Jesus' prayer is concerned with the mission of his disciples in this world (cf. vv. 18, 20-23). The hope for this world is that it ceases to be "the world in hostility to God" by receiving the witness of Jesus' followers. Hence Jesus' focus in his prayer is on his disciples, with that focus spelled out in the following three petitions.

The first of Jesus' petitions for his disciples, "Holy Father, protect them in your name that you have given me, so that they may be one, as we are one" (v. 11b), asks that they be kept or preserved as a community by the revelation of who God is, as that revelation has been embodied in Jesus. The purpose clause indicates that in this way they will also be protected against divisions. Since for John there is a unity between God's name and Jesus' name, it is not surprising that those who are kept in God's name, as given to Jesus, are expected to display this unity.

The grounds for the petition are stated both before it in verse 11a, "Now I am no longer in the world, but they are in the world, and I am coming to you," and after it in verses 12-13, "While I was with them, I protected them in your name that you have given me. I guarded them, and not one of them was lost except the son of perdition, so that the Scripture might be fulfilled." The first of these grounds highlights the fact that in Jesus' absence the disciples need the Father's protection — especially protection of their unity. The second makes it clear that Jesus had been doing what he now asks the Father to do. And with the statement "not one of them was lost" (cf. 6:39) it becomes evident that the keeping or protection being requested entails the disciples' salvation.

There is a rich scriptural background of "keeping" language for God's relation with Israel — as expressed, for example, in Jer. 31:10: God "will keep Israel, as a shepherd keeps his flock" (cf. also Gen. 28:15; Ps. 121:7-8; Isa. 42:6; 49:8). Here in the expressions "protected them," "guarded them," and "not one of them was lost" of 17:12b are echoes also of the language in John's Gospel about Jesus as the Good Shepherd in 10:28: "They will never perish. No one will snatch them out of my hand." But it is also in 17:12b immediately noted that in the case of the one obvious exception — that is, Judas — it was not because of Jesus' deficiency in keeping but rather because of his own destiny, for he was "the son of perdition" and his actions were done in order that Scripture might be fulfilled (cf. 13:18 with its citation of Ps. 41:9).

"I speak these things in the world" (v. 13) indicates that Jesus' words of prayer were intended to be overheard by the disciples for their encouragement — "so that they may have my joy made complete in themselves" (cf. also 15:11; 16:24). Just as Jesus' joy stems from his unbroken intimate relationship with God, so the disciples will participate fully in the same joy by being kept in the name that represents that relationship. The disciples' unity, their future destiny, and their joy are all viewed, therefore, as dependent on their being kept in God's name.

The second of Jesus' petitions for his disciples in John 17 is "Protect them from the evil one" (v. 15b). The reference in this one substantival use of "the evil" *(tou ponērou)* in John's Gospel is likely to be "the evil one" — that is, the personification of cosmic evil, who is portrayed earlier in the Fourth Gospel as "the ruler of this world" (cf. 12:31; 14:30; 16:11). The juxtaposition between the language of being kept in the Father's name and that of being kept from the evil one indicates the two antithetical spheres of power operative in the world. The grounds for this petition are found in its surrounding framework. While they are in the world, the disciples will need protection against "the ruler of this world" — since, as the recipients of God's word through Jesus, they experience the hatred of the world against them (v. 14a).

Neither the disciples nor Jesus, however, are "of the world" (vv. 14b, 16, cf. also 15:19). They do not have this world in its hostility to God as the determinative source of their lives. Yet, even though they are not of this world, Jesus does not ask that his disciples be taken out of the world (v. 15a). They still have a mission within the world. But they need protection from its evil ruler while they are engaged in that mission.

In Jesus' third petition for his disciples, "Sanctify them in the truth" (v. 17a), the request is grounded in the assertion that follows in the next verse about the continuity that exists between the mission of Jesus and the mission of the disciples: "As you have sent me into the world, so I have sent them into the world" (v. 18; cf. 20:21b). The disciples had been told that their mission in the world is to be one of witness (15:27), and Jesus will later sum up his mission in the world as being "to bear witness to the truth" (18:37). So if his followers are to continue such a mission of witness to the truth, they will need to be set apart in the truth.

"Truth" in John's Gospel is the revelation of God in Jesus. The Prologue portrayed Jesus as God's word, the Logos (cf. 1:1, 2, 14); Jesus proclaims himself in the Farewell Discourse to be the truth (14:6); and here in his prayer to "sanctify them [the disciples] in the truth," the explanatory statement is given: "Your word is truth" (v. 17). More specifically, in light of the Gospel's dominant lawsuit motif, truth is the issue that is at stake in the overall trial of Jesus. And this truth has to do with the identity of Jesus as one with God.

The disciples, then, are to be set apart for witnessing to the verdict established in the trial — that is, that Jesus is the One in whom God uniquely displays the divine glory. This, too, is in continuity with Jesus who sanctifies himself for his task, as depicted in 17:19: "For their sake I sanctify myself, that they also may be sanctified in truth." In 10:36, where Jesus is depicted as the fulfillment of the Feast of Hanukkah that celebrated the rededication of the temple altar, he talks of himself as "the one whom the Father has sanctified and sent into the world." Here in 17:19, therefore, when Jesus speaks of sanctifying himself, this is in line with the way John's Gospel portrays Jesus as (1) sharing what would normally be considered divine prerogatives and (2) being in control of his own life and mission (cf. 10:17-18).

Jesus' Prayer for Present and Future Believers (17:20-26)

As a result of the disciples' mission in the world, others will become believers (v. 20b). The scope of Jesus' prayer in John 17, therefore, expands to include two petitions for this whole company of believers, both present and future.

Jesus' first petition for all believers, "that they may all be one" (v. 21), is a request for unity — both for the disciples and for those who will come to believe through their witness. It is clear that what is envisioned is a unity that results from believers participating in the foundational unity that already exists between the Father and the Son. Again, the grounds for the petition follow. In verses 22-23 Jesus states that he has already laid the basis for the unity requested in the petition by giving to the disciples the glory that the Father has given him. God's glory — that is, the honor and reputation of the divine name — has been bestowed on Jesus. Jesus, therefore, has granted to his followers a share in that glory by making known to them the divine name (v. 6) and by enabling them to share in his own reputation and honor (v. 10b).

This complete unity between Father, Son, *and* believers ("As you, Father, are in me and I am in you, may they also be in us," v. 21a) has as its goal the world's coming to know the truth about Jesus' mission: "so that the world may believe that you have sent me" (v. 21b). Its purpose, however, is not only knowledge about Jesus. It is also that the world might know the truth about believers' relationship to God — a relationship in which they, as well as Jesus, are loved by God: "so that the world may know that you have sent me and have loved them even as you have loved me" (v. 23; cf. 14:21-23).

The community in which the believers' witness is embodied is to be a united one, and the issues at stake in Jesus' mission hinge on the reality "that they may become completely one, so that the world may know that you have sent me" (v. 23b). Since the truth established in the cosmic trial has to do with the unity that exists between the One who is sent and the One who has sent him, it is not surprising that the testimony to that truth is to be displayed by the oneness of the witnesses.

It is not simply that the unity of the witnesses mirrors the unity that exists between the Father and the Son. Rather, the unity of the believing community actually participates in the unity that defines the relation between Jesus and God (cf. v. 21). For the goal of its mission is not only that the world comes to know Jesus' identity as the One sent by God, but also that it comes to know that his followers are loved by God just as Jesus is loved by God (v. 23c). How does the world come to know God as love? Not only through hearing the witness that Jesus' death was God's loving gift to the world, but also through seeing and experiencing the enacted witness of a community that is united in loving acceptance of one another.

Jesus' second petition for the whole company of believers is "Father, I desire that these also . . . may be with me where I am, to see my glory" (v. 24). Whereas Jesus' requests for his disciples and all believers in verses 9-23 had in view the mission of his followers in the world, this second petition for all believers — and the final request of Jesus' prayer — turns to their future destiny. The change of verb from "ask" (*erōtō*, cf. vv. 9, 15, 20) to "desire" *(thelō)* serves as a reminder that Jesus' will is one with that of the Father, and so underscores the efficacy of his prayer. At the beginning of the prayer Jesus had prayed for his own glorification. Now at its conclusion this glorification features in his desire for his followers.

Those who have struggled and suffered over the issue of Jesus' glory are to experience it fully for themselves, for they will be with him in the Father's presence and see for themselves the divine glory that he has shared from before the foundation of the world. When, exactly, this will occur is not specified. The referent may include what will happen to individual believers at death. Yet the prayer is for Jesus' followers as a whole. So it gives a vision of the eschatological destiny of the entire new community, which results from Jesus' mission in this world and shares at the end in the glory that Jesus enjoyed in the beginning (cf. 1:1-3; 17:5; see also 1 John 3:2).

The grounds for this final petition are given in verses 25-26. Since believers are those who know that God has sent Jesus *and* those to whom Jesus has made known God's name and will make it known, it is appropriate that their destiny is to be with Jesus and see his glory. The address here to God as "righteous Father" *(patēr dikaie)* is significant. The adjective "righteous" *(dikaios)* and the noun "righteousness" *(dikaiosunē)* have occurred earlier in forensic contexts in 5:30, 7:24, and 16:8, 10. The Father, then, is also the righteous judge of the cosmic trial. So the end of Jesus' prayer puts believers into the hands of this judge and sees them as those who can be confident of God's loving judgment — which is their destiny because they (1) have aligned themselves with the divine verdict on Jesus and (2) know that God has sent him and revealed through him the divine name and reputation.

The statement "I made your name known to them" of verse 26 picks up on "I have made your name known to those whom you gave me from the world" of verse 6 in summarizing the mission of Jesus in the trial. At the same time the next clause of verse 26, "and I will make it known," points to the ongoing trial that is carried forward through the witness of the Paraclete and the community of Jesus' followers (cf. 15:26-27). God's name is made known in the relationship of love between God and Jesus. Just as important in Jesus' prayer for believers is the reality that it continues to be made known as this relationship of love shapes the life of the community of Jesus' followers — and as, through that relationship, Jesus, who embodies God's name, is present in that community.

The Function and Impact of the Prayer

Jesus' prayer in John 17 provides a replay of what the Gospel in general and the preceding Farewell Discourse in particular say about the mission of Christ and the situation of his followers in the world after his departure and return to the Father. But the reformulation of such themes as a prayer gives them an intensified emotional force. Through this means, the readers of John's Gospel are let in at last on that which the narrative has hinted at earlier — that is, Jesus' intimate relationship as Son with the Father. As his death approaches, Jesus is presented as baring his heart to his Father about the future of his cause in the world. He has already given instructions about the future to his disciples. But now he turns that future over to God.

Since the Jesus who prays in John 17 is also the exalted Christ, the prayer has an additional force. For it reflects the belief that even after his departure Christ's advocacy in prayer supports the mission of his followers. Everything they have been told about their future role now has Jesus' prayer backing. He gives the Spirit as the advocate who is present on earth. But he himself also remains an advocate with the Father (cf. also 1 John 2:1, 2).

Although Jesus' prayer is addressed to God, it is also the disciples in the narrative — and, in particular, the implied readers — who are being indirectly addressed. Given what the Fourth Gospel has already indicated about the efficacy of Jesus' prayers, to know that the risen and exalted Christ prays for those readers who believe is a major factor in shaping their identity and providing reassurance. The situations in which believers will find themselves have not only been foreseen and prayed for by Jesus, but they are also part of the outworking of God's purposes for this world.

Believers in Jesus, of course, have a significant role to play in the ongoing divine lawsuit. But the ultimate source of their confidence is that their mission remains God's cause and God can be entrusted with it. For just as God has given Jesus what it took to accomplish his role, so now Jesus summons God to give what it will take for his followers to complete theirs. Despite the opposition they will face, believers can be encouraged because they are in an intimate relationship with the Father and the Son — whose love and protection provide full support in the mission for which they have been set apart.

At the same time, Jesus' prayer reminds his followers that unity and love are essential for their mission. They are to make God's name known to the world, just as Jesus made it known to them. And it is through their unity and love that this making known will take place. This is only to be expected if the God who is to be made known is the Father who has a relationship of unity and love with the Son. To believe in Jesus, therefore, means being incorporated into this relationship of oneness and love that exists between Christ and God — that is, to experience the reality of Jesus' prayer: "May they also be in us!" (v. 21). And that relationship implies that believers in Jesus are part of the unique prayer experience between Christ and God, and so are caught up in his intercessory praying and share in it themselves when they pray in Jesus' name.

But this immense privilege cannot be divorced from the context of Jesus' prayer in John 17, which is anticipated throughout the Fourth Gospel and signaled in the opening words of the prayer itself: "Father, the hour has come" (v. 1). This is a reminder that the intimacy between the Father and the Son — particularly the glorifying of each of their names — is costly and will take place through Jesus' death. And as long as they are in this world, the followers of Jesus, while sharing this intimacy, can expect it will also be costly for them. Protection from the evil one and being kept in God's name will not necessarily mean protection from hostility, persecution, or even violent death for the sake of Jesus' name. Jesus' route to the glorification of his own name and God's name remains the route for his followers' participation in such glory (cf. 12:24-26; 15:18-21; 16:2-3).

3. Jesus' Teaching about Prayer to His Disciples

It is hermeneutically advantageous, we believe, to reflect first on Jesus' prayer in John 17 (as above) before examining Jesus' teaching about prayer to his disciples, as given in the Farewell Discourse of John 13–16. For, while this is not the place to develop it, a convincing case can be made for the thesis that John 17 takes up and reworks major motifs from the Lord's Prayer, particularly as it appears in Matt. 6:9-13 (see, e.g., the articles by W. Schenk and W. O. Walker listed in the bibliography). Jesus' prayer of John 17 can be seen as the Lord's Prayer transposed into its Johannine key. And as it can be said of the Lord's Prayer that Jesus "gave it to his disciples as a summary of what he stood for . . . [and that] in a very real sense, the Lord's Prayer is the first ever in Jesus' name, even though we do not explicitly speak his name when we offer it up" (J. Koenig, *Rediscovering New Testament Prayer*, 46), so the prayer of John 17 summarizes what the Johannine Jesus stands for and shows what it means to pray in Jesus' name.

No instruction about prayer is given to the disciples during Jesus' public ministry in the Fourth Gospel. All of the teaching about prayer is clustered in the Farewell Discourse. But in that teaching, the variety of form and content found in the Synoptic Gospels is missing. There are no parables about prayer; no contrasts with the praying of the scribes or Pharisees; and no associations of prayer with the notions of forgiveness, vigilance, perseverance, or the need for laborers in the harvest. Instead, there is a relentless focus on Jesus' promise that whatever the disciples ask in his name they will receive — which, by the fact that the promise is in the Farewell Discourse, serves to underline the reality that prayer will be especially important for Jesus' disciples during the time of his physical absence from them.

Understanding the Farewell Discourse of John's Gospel to be structured along the lines of three major units — that is, 13:31–14:31; 15:1–16:4a; and 16:4b-33 — it should be observed that each unit contains two sayings about prayer. Furthermore, it needs to be noted that the teaching about prayer in these Johannine sayings can be seen as an elaboration and intensification of two somewhat similar sayings in the Synoptic Gospels: (1) in Mark 11:24, "Whatever you ask for in prayer, believe that you have received it, and it will be yours" (cf. Matt. 21:22); and (2) in Luke 11:9-10, "Ask, and it will be given you; seek, and you will find; knock, and it will be opened to you. For every one who asks receives, and he who seeks finds, and to him who knocks it will be opened" (cf. Matt. 7:7-8).

The first two Johannine prayer sayings in the first unit of the Farewell Discourse (i.e., 13:31–14:31) come in a context that emphasizes the relationship of mutual indwelling between the Father and the Son (14:11) and speaks of believers doing Jesus' works — even greater works than Jesus did — after his departure to the Father (14:12). In these two sayings Jesus promises that "I will do whatever you ask in my name, so that the Father may be glorified in the Son" (14:13); *and,* "If in my name you ask me for anything, I will do it" (14:14). That the works of believers are to be a continuation of Jesus' works is underlined in these verses in two different ways, each of which is mentioned twice — that is, by the repeated assertion "I will do ['whatever you ask'/'it']," which makes it clear that it is Jesus who is at work in the mission of his followers, and by the repeated phrase "in my name," which indicates that the praying that results in the works is carried out by believers as the authorized representatives of Jesus. The continuity between the believers' activity in prayer and the mission of Jesus is further seen in that the purpose of Jesus' response to such praying — "so that the Father may be glorified in the Son" (14:13b) — is the same as was the goal of his whole ministry (cf. 7:18; 11:4; 12:28; 13:31-32; 17:1). So the continuation and heightening of Jesus' mission through the works of believers will be made possible through their prayer.

The next two promises about prayer in the second unit of the discourse (i.e., 15:1–16:4a) are part of Jesus' teaching about himself as the true vine and the disciples as branches who need to abide in him in order to bear fruit: "If you abide in me, and my words abide in you, ask for whatever you wish, and it will be done for you. My Father is glorified by this, that you bear much fruit and become my disciples" (15:7-8); *and,* "I appointed you to go and bear fruit, fruit that will last, so that the Father will give you whatever you ask him in my name" (15:16b). In the former saying, the condition specified for answered prayer is the mutual abiding of Jesus and the disciples in each other. Just as abiding in Jesus is synonymous with abiding in Jesus' word (cf. 8:31), so here Jesus' words abiding in the disciples is synonymous with Jesus abiding in them (cf. 15:5). Abiding, then, involves conformity to Jesus' revelation and is functionally equivalent to the notion of "in Jesus' name" — with the enhancement of God's reputation and cause being, once again, what is at stake in the prayer of a believer and God's answer. In the latter saying, the condition explicitly specified for answered prayer is that it be made in Jesus' name.

In both of the prayer sayings of 15:7-8 and 15:16b, the result of answered prayer is described in terms of bearing fruit — thereby linking these sayings to the vine imagery of the first part of chapter 15. Interpreters differ as to what is entailed in the expressions "bear much fruit" (15:8) or "bear fruit that will last" (15:16). For some, the key lies in the mention of love and keeping Jesus' commandments, which follows both sayings and speaks of the commandments as being reducible to one, namely, loving one another (cf. 15:9-14, 17). For others, the talk of *going* and bearing fruit in the second reference suggests that mission and its results are involved. The two ideas, of course, are not incompatible, since it has already been suggested that believers' love for one another will be their most effective means of witness in the world (cf. 13:34-35).

The third pair of sayings about prayer in the final unit of the Farewell Discourse (i.e., 16:4b-33) is to be found near the end of the discourse. Jesus asserts: "On that day you will no longer ask me anything. Very truly, I tell you, if you ask anything of the Father in my name, he will give it to you. Until now you have not asked for anything in my name. Ask and you will receive, so that your joy may be complete" (16:23-24). He then elaborates: "On that day you will ask in my name. I do not say to you that I will ask the Father on your behalf; for the Father himself loves you . . ." (16:26-27a). The prediction in the first saying — that the disciples will no longer ask Jesus anything — is best interpreted in the light of the confused questioning of the disciples in the previous verses. So here Jesus promises that the time is coming when their need to ask such questions will cease.

Both sayings are introduced by the phrase "on that day," which refers to a time after Jesus' death and resurrection when he will see the disciples again and when their sorrow will be turned to joy (16:22) — a time when he will no longer use figures of speech, but will be able to speak plainly to the disciples about the Father (16:25). Both sayings make it clear that in the time after Jesus' exaltation, the disciples in their prayers will be in direct communication with God the Father. And the second saying stresses that at that time they will not need Jesus to request the Father on their behalf.

This second prayer saying, however, raises the following question: Do Jesus' words, "I do not say to you that I will ask the Father on your behalf," of 16:26b, which are given from the perspective of the exalted Christ, mean that Jesus in his exalted state will not continue to offer intercessory prayer on behalf of his followers? In the light of 14:16 and 17:1-26, it is unlikely that the force of 16:26b should be read as a renunciation of any intercessory role on Jesus' part. Its main point appears to be to assure Jesus' followers (1) that their relationship of love and trust in him puts them in an intimate relationship to the God who loves them, and (2) that they can speak directly to this God as Father and can make claims on him in prayer.

Jesus has mediated his followers' relationship with God — that is, it is because he as the Son invokes God as Father that his disciples can now do the same. And this truth is preserved in the repeated formulation that believers' prayers to God are to be in Jesus' name. Jesus' departure, therefore, will be advantageous, since his followers' praying as representatives of all that he stands for means that this new stage of their relationship with the Father will exceed anything that they have experienced before. The joy inaugurated by their having seen the risen and glorified Jesus (cf. 16:20-22) will be completed by their experience — even though in his absence — of sharing in Jesus' relationship to God as Father, and thereby receiving whatever they ask for in prayer. In short, as Raymond Brown has aptly expressed it, "Jesus will not have to ask the Father on behalf of the Christian, for the Christian's prayer will be Jesus' prayer" (*Gospel According to John*, 2:735).

That Jesus' teaching on prayer in the Fourth Gospel occurs in the Farewell Discourse, where Jesus is portrayed as preparing his disciples for the period after his departure, means that to the main characteristics of that period — that is, the witness of Jesus' followers, their need to love one another, the hostility and persecution of the world, and the presence of the

175

Paraclete — should be added this further most important characteristic: God's answering of prayer in Jesus' name. One of the major reasons why Jesus' departure will be advantageous for his disciples is that they will be able to engage in this sort of prayer. In addition, just as the narrative is constructed so that having been told ahead of time about their need to witness, the disciples are then able to see Jesus as the paradigm for that witness in his own witness in his trial and death, so it is also arranged in such a way that, having been told about their need to pray in Jesus' name, they are then given a model for such prayer in Jesus' own prayer that follows. For in the prayer recorded in John 17 the Son enacts what is entailed in a confident asking of the Father, which the disciples have been told will be their privilege after his glorification.

It is striking that the magnificent promises about the efficacy of prayer in the Farewell Discourse mention six times that the presupposition or condition of such prayer is that it is in Jesus' name (cf. "in my name" in 14:13, 14; 15:16; 16:23, 24, 26; see also "abide in me" in 15:7). Just as Jesus has come and has done his works in the Father's name, acting as the Father's fully authorized representative (cf., e.g., 5:43; 10:25), so the praying of believers is in Jesus' name and to be carried out by his fully authorized human representatives (cf. 17:18; 20:21b: "As the Father has sent me, so I send you"). Since after his departure Jesus himself will not be present to pray, his followers will pray on Jesus' authority. One could say that they are given his "power of attorney" so that their praying will be the equivalent to Jesus himself praying.

Therefore an unconditional response can be linked to such prayer. It will be answered because, as we have already seen, Jesus' praying is so in line with God's purpose that it is automatically answered — without his really needing to pray. "Whatever you ask" does not mean whatever is on your wish list, but, in effect, whatever you ask in line with Jesus' prayer — because what is in line with Jesus' prayer represents his name, what he stands for, and what his mission in the world entails. This explanatory qualification is not intended to rationalize unanswered prayer but to encourage prayer that is in line with the will of God, as revealed in Christ, and that can therefore confidently expect to be answered (cf. 1 John 3:21-22).

There should be no doubt about what is involved in such prayer, for Jesus' own prayer is then immediately given in John 17. Its concerns for the Father's name to be glorified, for believers being kept in that name, for the protection of Jesus' followers from the evil one, for their being set apart in the truth, and for their mission of love and unity in the world, become the topics and scope of believers' prayers. In this way believers become partners in Jesus' praying that the world may come to know the nature of his mission (17:21, 23) and his identity — that is, that God's name has been given to him (17:11). Prayer, then, is one of the primary means for cooperation in God's mission in the world. And requests supporting the essentials of Jesus' prayer will be answered because they conform to God's purposes for this world in the making known of the divine name through Jesus.

One might have thought that the Fourth Gospel's portrait of Jesus as being completely at one with the will of God the Father would have introduced a major discontinuity between Jesus and his followers in terms of prayer. But, on the contrary, John's Gospel claims that those who pray in Jesus' name become part of the incredibly intimate relationship with the Father that Jesus himself had. In fact, the same sort of language that was used of Jesus is now used in connection with his followers. Just as it could be expected of Jesus that "God will give you whatever you ask of him" (11:22), so Jesus expects of his followers that "if you ask anything of the Father in my name, he will give it to you" (16:23).

This confident intimacy of relationship — a relationship in which our wills are aligned with those of Jesus and God — might still appear to remove the evangelist's notion of Christian prayer from our grasp when we struggle to formulate even our most basic requests. Yet it provides both a vision of what is possible and an invitation to appropriate a relationship of which we already know just a little. The invitation is to see ourselves as those who by God's gracious initiative have been caught up in God's cosmic purposes, so that, through Jesus' prayer — as we open our hearts to God and pray in Jesus' name as his representatives — (1) we know what we must pray, (2) we lose preoccupation with ourselves, and (3) our wills become fused with his will in desiring supremely God's name, glory, and reputation to be promoted in our world.

4. God's Name, Jesus' Name, and Prayer

In the Old Testament both God's name and God's glory are viewed as God's immanent presence and are particularly associated with the Jerusalem temple. The account of the dedication of the temple and Solomon's prayer in 1 Kings 8 makes this clear. Not only has "the glory of the Lord filled the house of the Lord" (v. 11), but the temple is also described as "this house, the place of which you said, 'My name shall be there'" (v. 16). The temple was to be "a house for the name of the Lord, the God of Israel" (vv. 17, 20), "the house for my name" (v. 19), and "the house that I [Solomon] have built for your name" (vv. 44, 48). What is more, "because of your name" foreigners — that is, Gentiles — are to participate in the prayers that ascend from this temple, "so that all the peoples of the earth may know your name" and "know that your name has been invoked on this house" (vv. 41-43).

In John's Gospel Jesus is portrayed as the true place of worship. Already in the Prologue we read that the Logos "pitched his tent ['tabernacled'] among us, and we have seen his glory" (1:14). Jesus promises Nathanael that he "will see heaven opened and the angels of God ascending and descending upon the Son of Man" (1:51) — which language takes up the language used of Jacob's vision in Gen. 28:12, and so portrays Jesus, the Son of Man, as the new Bethel or house of God. Later, when asked for a legitimating sign for his action in the temple, Jesus says: "Destroy this temple and in three days I will raise it up" (2:19). This saying is then explained from a post-resurrection perspective to mean that Jesus was speaking of his crucified and risen body as the temple, the locus of God's presence and glory (2:21-22).

This perspective is reinforced in Jesus' conversation with the Samaritan woman when the topic turns to worship in 4:19-26. In speaking with the Samaritan woman, Jesus claims that the hour is coming and is now here when for true worshipers Mount Gerizim and Jerusalem, with their respective temple worship, will no longer be important, because they will worship the Father in Spirit and in truth (vv. 21-24). Indeed, as Jesus goes on to insist, the Father is actively seeking just such worshipers and does so through Jesus, who reveals himself to the woman through the divine name as "I Am" (vv. 23b, 26). Furthermore, the Spirit will be sent in Jesus' name as his fully authorized representative (14:26; 16:17), and the truth — that is, that God is known in him and that he is one with God — is disclosed in Jesus' person and mission. It is, in fact, Jesus' making known the divine name in the time of eschatological fulfillment that enables the encounter with God that produces the worship of the Father in Spirit and in truth.

What was central to temple worship — that is, experiencing and promoting the glory of God's name — remains the goal of prayer and worship that is in Spirit and in truth. It is simply that in the Fourth Gospel that goal has been transformed christologically, for Jesus has been given the divine name and shares in the divine glory. To be part of the believing community is to participate in the worship made possible by Jesus, who is the new temple, and so to experience the presence of God's name made known in Jesus' name.

God's name and Jesus' name are inextricably linked in unity and love. As such, they decisively shape believers' praying and living. Petition usually presupposes a gap between the human will and the divine will. Yet prayer where there is no such gap — as in the case of Jesus, and as is assumed will be the case for disciples who pray in his name — becomes a relationship of loving intimacy. This sort of praying, which consists of breathing out one's deepest desires in the confidence of their acceptance, does not need fixed places, set times, or a regular pattern of words. The ultimate desire of those who pray in Jesus' name will be, as it was for Jesus, that the intimate Other in their relationship of love receives due recognition — that is, that God's name and identity, as it is revealed in Jesus, be glorified. If this is to happen and if this God is to be made known in the world, those who in their passion for God's honor experience the conjunction of the names of Jesus and God in their praying also understand that the unity and love that exists between those two names, and in which they too participate, is to be lived out in their own unity and love in the mission entrusted to them and for which they pray.

Selected Bibliography

Barrett, C. K. *The Gospel according to St. John,* 2nd ed. Philadelphia: Westminster, 1978.

Barth, Karl. *The Christian Life.* Grand Rapids: Eerdmans, 1981, esp. 111-204.

Beasley-Murray, George R. *John.* Waco: Word, 1987.

Brown, Raymond E. *The Gospel according to John.* 2 vols. New York: Doubleday, 1966, 1970.

Bultmann, Rudolf. *The Gospel of John.* Philadelphia: Westminster, 1971.

Carson, Donald A. *The Farewell Discourse and Final Prayer of Jesus.* Grand Rapids: Baker, 1980.

179

Cullmann, Oscar. *Prayer in the New Testament*. London: SCM; Minneapolis: Fortress, 1995, esp. 89-111.

Käsemann, Ernst. *The Testament of Jesus. A Study of the Gospel of John in the Light of Chapter 17*, trans. G. Krodel. London: SCM; Philadelphia: Fortress, 1968.

Koenig, John. *Rediscovering New Testament Prayer: Boldness and Blessing in the Name of Jesus*. San Francisco: Harper, 1992; repr. Harrisburg: Morehouse, 1998.

Lincoln, Andrew T. *Truth on Trial: The Lawsuit Motif in the Fourth Gospel*. Peabody, Mass.: Hendrickson, 2000.

Moloney, Francis J. *Glory Not Dishonor: Reading John 13–21*. Minneapolis: Fortress, 1998.

O'Day, Gail R. "John." In *New Interpreter's Bible*, vol. 9. Nashville: Abingdon, 1995, 491-865.

Schenk, Wolfgang. "Die Umcodierungen der Matthäischen Unser-Vater-Redaktion in Joh 17." In *John and the Synoptics*, ed. A. Denaux. Leuven: University Press, 1992, 587-607.

Schnackenburg, Rudolf. *The Gospel according to St. John*, vol. 3. New York: Crossroad, 1982.

Segovia, Fernando F. "Inclusion and Exclusion in John 17: An Intercultural Reading." In *"What Is John?" Readers and Readings in the Fourth Gospel*, vol. 2, ed. F. F. Segovia. Atlanta: Scholars, 1998, 183-210.

Walker, William O., Jr. "The Lord's Prayer in Matthew and John." *New Testament Studies* 28 (1982): 237-56.

PART III

Acts through the Apocalypse

CHAPTER 9

Persevering Together in Prayer: The Significance of Prayer in the Acts of the Apostles

JOEL B. GREEN

LUKE'S PORTRAYAL OF Jesus' followers at prayer in the Acts of the Apostles presents the early church as a collective poster child and exemplar of the theological formation expected of those who embrace the gospel. By "theological formation" I mean that having been shaped in relationship with Jesus — either in the context of his earthly ministry or subsequently by means of the mediating presence of the Holy Spirit, or both — his disciples experienced a deep-seated conversion in their conception of God, and therefore a radical conversion in their commitments, attitudes, and everyday practices. This transformation comes into sharp focus in Luke's portrayal of their practices of prayer. Throughout Luke's narrative in Acts we see — though, admittedly, at one or two key points the comparison somewhat fails — the perspectives articulated and modeled by Jesus in the Third Gospel coming to life in the experience of Jesus' followers.

Put sharply, Jesus' followers in Acts are people of prayer. The adjective "prayerful" functions as a descriptive character quality, a behavior common to all those of the Christian movement. This assessment is not based on the use of terminological preferences alone — as though Luke's interest in prayer could be limited to the appearance of the noun "prayer" (*proseuchē*) or the verb "to pray" (*proseuchomai*), though such terms are plentiful. Luke, in fact, uses more than a dozen expressions to draw attention to the prayer practices of the early Christians. More important are the strategic ways in which prayer is introduced into the narrative, and especially the ways in which prayer texts in Acts cohere with and build upon Jesus' perspective on prayer as displayed in the Third Gospel.

In this article I want to demonstrate the centrality of prayer in Luke's presentation of faithful discipleship in Acts. First, I want to highlight certain key features in Luke's portrayal of the early church as a people of prayer. Second, I want to explore particular moments of prayer in the life of the early church, dealing with these episodes under a few major categories. Third, I want to sketch the relationship between the picture of prayer in Acts and the material on prayer in the Third Gospel — asking, in essence, what the disciples learned from Jesus regarding the character and practice of prayer. All of this will lead, finally, to an epilogue in which I set out some conclusions and questions on the nature of prayer as a "practice" that embodies the church's deepest convictions, its essential commitments, and, in fact, even identifies the church as the church.

1. The Early Church as a People of Prayer

Over thirty times in the Acts of the Apostles, Luke characterizes Jesus' followers as being at prayer or narrates episodes of prayer. These scenes are most prevalent in the first half of the book, as though, having established a pattern of pervasive prayer, Luke has no need to repeat himself again and again. This strategy is consistent with the character of narrative generally, since narratives (including historical narratives like Acts) seek to establish what is typical — in this case, a devotion to prayer — and treat it subsequently as a presupposition. This means that we can assume from the early chapters of Acts not only the pervasiveness of prayer within the early church, but also that the general patterns of prayer established there pertain for the whole of the Acts narrative. What patterns of prayer, then, does Luke develop?

Prayerfulness: A Character Quality of Disciples

On a number of occasions, instances of the disciples praying are reported by Luke without any reference to the content of their prayers. More often than not, these reports serve to portray the disciples as people who habitually engage in prayer. Prayerfulness, thus, is presented in the Acts of the Apostles as a distinguishing mark of their character.

The first reference to prayer in Acts comes in the summary statement of 1:12-14 and is expressed as follows: "These all with one accord devoted themselves to prayer" (v. 14). The appearance of these words in a summary statement is significant because it is the nature of summaries to indicate what is typical and emblematic. In the opening verses of Acts, the disciples are portrayed as those whom Jesus had commissioned and taught, who witnessed his resurrected life and his departure, and who obeyed his instructions to wait in Jerusalem. All of this, Acts 1:14 tells us, was in the context of "persevering prayer."

The disciples are thus defined in verse 14 by their tenacious orientation toward a common aim — that is, they were single-minded in giving themselves to prayer. The verb Luke uses to depict this tenaciousness is *proskatereō* ("continue," "persevere in"), which appears in the New Testament only ten times, with six being in Acts (1:14; 2:42, 46; 6:4; 8:13; 10:7). A second important term in this verse is *homothumadon* ("with one mind, purpose, or impulse"), an adverb that appears in Acts ten times and otherwise in the New Testament only in Rom. 15:6. In Acts it characterizes the single-minded unity either of the company of believers (1:14; 2:46; 4:24; 5:12; 8:6; 15:25) or those who opposed them (7:57; 12:20; 18:12; 19:29).

Although taught to pray (cf. Luke 11:1-13) and instructed to pray (cf. Luke 22:40, 46), heretofore in the narrative of Luke-Acts the disciples have not been depicted as persons who engaged in prayer. On the other hand, one of the characteristic activities of Jesus was prayer, and throughout the Third Gospel prayer had been the means by which Jesus' identity was manifested, God's plans were revealed, and people aligned themselves with God's plans. Prayer on the part of Jesus' followers — especially the habitual prayer reported in this text as characterizing the disciples — is, therefore, clearly of consequence. Though Luke does not sketch the content of this ceaseless prayer, the close ties of this summary statement to the opening of the Pentecost account in 2:1 suggest that this is prayer in anticipation of the promised Spirit. There may also be here an echo of Jesus' earlier instruction regarding faithfulness in prayer to a God who is ready to give graciously and quickly, even the gift of the Holy Spirit to those who ask (cf. Luke 11:1-13).

The second summary in Acts, that of 2:42-47, also lists prayer as a characteristic activity of the early church, for here the growing company of believers is said to have "held diligently to the teaching of the apostles and to the fellowship, to the breaking of bread and to the prayers" (v. 42). "Diligence" is developed with reference to four distinctive activities, the last being "the prayers" (cf. also "praising God" in v. 47). Luke does not state where the disciples engaged in prayer, though the mention of the temple in verse 46 is suggestive in this regard (cf. Luke 24:53). At the same time, there is no reason to limit prayer to the temple, especially given the explicit mention of homes as centers of Christian activity in this same verse (cf. also 4:24-31).

Since these first believers are depicted by Luke as Jewish, we may justifiably assume that "the prayers" refers to the patterns of prayer associated with Jews during this period. Unfortunately, however, we know little of the specifics of those patterns, though we may imagine the daily recitation of the Shema and participation in prayers of petition along with other Jews in the temple (see D. K. Falk, "Jewish Prayer Literature"; J. H. Charlesworth, "Prolegomena"). One innovation may already be recognized — namely, the probability that prayers were offered to the Lord Jesus, since his is the name on which persons are to call for salvation. At this juncture, however, more important for our purposes than specifying the exact *content* of their prayers is this affirmation that the believers were devoted to prayer.

Elsewhere in Acts a similar perspective is maintained — not least on account of the sheer quantity of references to prayer in the narrative. Nowhere is the disciples' devotion to prayer more clearly set forth, however, than in texts such as these two summary statements (1:12-14; 2:42-47), where it seems important to Luke simply to highlight the fact that the disciples of Jesus devoted themselves to prayer without even mentioning the content of those prayers (see also 3:1; 10:9; cf. 10:2). Furthermore, their devotion to prayer is evident in such expected contexts as scenes of farewell (cf. 20:36; 21:5-6) and at meals (cf. 27:35).

Continuity and Discontinuity with Judaism

As we have already begun to see, Luke portrays the early church as being in continuity with Judaism on the matter of prayer. One prominent example of this continuity has to do with the Jerusalem temple. The Third Gospel emphasizes the function of the temple as a house of prayer (cf. Luke 1:8-

23; 2:27-32, 36-38; 18:10-14; 19:46; 24:53), and the temple continues to serve this role in the Book of Acts (cf. Acts 2:47; 3:1; 21:20-26; 22:17-21). Nevertheless, as will become increasingly obvious in our study of the prayer texts of Acts, the practice of prayer in the early church also signals a discontinuity with Judaism.

In his speech of defense in Acts 22:1-21, for example, having recounted his experience on the Damascus road, Paul reports:

> After returning to Jerusalem, while praying in the temple, I fell into a trance. I saw him saying to me, "Hurry, leave Jerusalem quickly, for they will not accept your witness concerning me." And I replied, "Lord, they themselves know that in every synagogue I imprisoned and beat those who believed in you. They know that, while the blood of Stephen your witness was shed, I was standing by, approving, and watching the coats of those who killed him." But he said to me, "Go, for I will send you far away to the Gentiles." (vv. 17-21)

Here is a fail-proof apologetic for Paul's mission. It was in the Jerusalem temple, while praying, that Paul received the divine mandate to take the gospel to the Gentile world. What is equally clear, though, is that this experience of prayer in the temple served to undermine for Paul the centrality of the temple for faith and life. Thus a form of continuity with Judaism — that is, prayer to God in the temple in Jerusalem — has resulted in a divine mandate that subverts the central role of the temple for Jewish life.

Discontinuity with Judaism is clear at another key point: that prayers were offered by the early church to Jesus. "God" is the object of prayer in a number of the reports of the church at prayer in Acts (e.g., 4:24-31; 10:2, 4; 12:5; 16:25), though more often the narrative does not specify to whom prayers were offered (e.g., 1:14; 2:42; 3:1; 6:4, 6; 9:11; 10:9). On several occasions, however, Luke specifically notes that prayers were offered *to Jesus* — beginning with the prayer regarding Matthias's replacement in 1:24-25.

Some interpreters have argued that Yahweh is the object of the apostles' prayer in 1:24-25, for *God* is the "knower of hearts" in 15:8 and so should be seen as the referent of "Lord" in 1:24 ("Lord, you know everyone's heart"). Other factors in the immediate context, however, are more pressing, and encourage an identification of Jesus as the one addressed in this prayer. One factor is that Luke 6:12-13 and Acts 1:2 present Jesus as the one who chose the apostles, so it would follow that he would choose this latest apostle as well. Another is that Jesus has just been addressed as "Lord" in verses 6 and 21, and the title "Lord" is used of Jesus throughout Acts (cf. esp. 2:21, 36).

Similarly, although the identity of "the Lord" to whom Peter advises that prayer be made in 8:22 ("Pray to the Lord"), and the identity of "the Lord" in Simon's reply in 8:24 ("Pray for me to the Lord"), may be seen as somewhat ambiguous, the fact that elsewhere in this scene "the Lord" is explicitly identified by Luke as "the Lord Jesus" (8:16) means that we may assume in the exchange between Simon and Peter throughout 8:14-25 that Jesus is in view. Furthermore, Stephen offers prayer to Jesus (7:59-60), as does Ananias (9:10-17; see esp. v. 17, where "the Lord" is directly specified as "Jesus"). So routine, in fact, is christocentric prayer to the identity of the early Christians that they can be known as "those who call upon the name" of Jesus (cf. 2:21; 7:59; 9:14, 21; 22:16).

The prayer practices of the early church, therefore, highlight important christological affirmations that move beyond what was characteristic of Judaism. According to Peter's sermon at Pentecost, Jesus is God's co-regent who dispenses the blessings of salvation to all who "call on the name of the Lord" (2:14-41). In this capacity, he has become an object of devotion and a source of salvation — roles reserved only for God within Jewish tradition. The patterns of prayer in Luke's narrative that came to characterize Jesus' early followers, though similar in many ways to Jewish patterns of the day, also distinguished those followers of Jesus from their contemporaries within Judaism.

Continuity with Jesus

The Lucan picture of the early disciples as people of prayer serves to demarcate the church's relationship to Judaism as one of both continuity and discontinuity. Within the Lucan narrative, however, it is also clear — particularly with regard to the practice of prayer — that the early disciples are to be seen as in continuity with Jesus. Some parallels seem quite deliberate: (1) prayer in anticipation of the outpouring of the Spirit (cf. Luke 3:21; Acts 1:14; 2:1-4; 8:15-17); (2) prayer in relation to the selection of apostles (cf. Luke 6:12; Acts 1:24); and (3) prayer in the face of death for forgiveness of one's persecutors (cf. Luke 23:34; Acts 7:60). A close reading of the Gospel of Luke (not least in comparison to the other canonical Gospels) provides a portrait of Jesus as a person of prayer, who was regularly in deep communion with God. In Acts this portrait is expanded into a mural that includes the disciples similarly in prayer (cf. Stephen C. Barton, *Spirituality of the Gospels*, 87-91; P. T. O'Brien, "Prayer in Luke-Acts," 121-23).

From early on in his second volume, then, Luke establishes Jesus' followers as persons who continue to model the piety of Jesus. Even when the content of prayer is unspecified or undeveloped, the devotion of these disciples to prayer speaks volumes about their fundamental orientation to the purpose of God, their alignment with the will of God, and their conviction that God will hear and respond to their prayers. Prayer thus serves for Luke as a means of legitimating these early believers — that is, affirming their role as heirs of the power and ministry of Jesus and sanctioning their role as his faithful witnesses. As people of prayer, they serve an agenda that is not their own but God's, act as instruments of God who exercise God-given authority, and minister with the confidence of those who have learned from their leader the boundless graciousness and faithfulness of God.

2. Major Categories of Prayer in the Early Church

As we move from the more general characterization of the disciples as a people of prayer to explore particular moments of prayer in the early church, a number of episodes in Acts come immediately to mind. These can be grouped into a small number of categories.

Prayer at the Selection and Commissioning of Leadership

One such category of prayer is where prayer is intimately associated with the selection and/or commissioning of leadership, as in 1:24-25; 6:6; 13:3; and 14:23. The first of these episodes, which has to do with Matthias's replacement of Judas in 1:15-26, is of special interest, since it suggests an important relationship between the purpose of God and human participation in that purpose. Judas's own defection from his appointed place among the original disciples of Jesus demonstrates that God's aim can be opposed — that the divine will is not simply a *fait accompli*, but invites and needs human partnership. Prayer is put forward as one of the ways in

189

which God's will becomes manifest, both in the sense that in prayer the divine will is disclosed and in the sense that in prayer humans align themselves with God's will. Verses 23 and 24 narrate parallel actions on the part of the early church: "they put forward" and "they prayed." This is significant for two reasons. First, it follows an emphasis that Luke has already established regarding the unity of the community (see esp. vv. 14-15), which is now shown to act as a collective body. Second, it demonstrates the partnership of believers with God, for "they put forward" and "they prayed, 'Lord, . . . show us clearly.'"

The Lord is addressed as "the one who knows the heart" (kardiognōsta). This is an expression used only twice in the New Testament (here and in Acts 15:8), but one that points to a concept almost proverbial in biblical literature — that is, that God is omniscient, who knows the innermost being of humans and foreordains human destiny. In this prayer, there is the consciousness that the Lord is all-knowing and has already chosen Judas's replacement. This understanding is closely bound up thematically with the prior choosing of the apostles by Jesus (cf. Luke 6:12-16; Acts 1:2) and the prescience of God involving these events, as represented in the interpretation of the Old Testament Psalms in Acts 1:16, 20.

By way of categorically dismissing any possibility for the intrusion of human volition in the process of selection, the prayer of the apostles is followed by the casting of lots. "The lot" had come to serve as a metaphor for divine decision in Jewish thought, and earlier in his Gospel Luke recorded Zechariah's having received by lot the unsurpassed honor for priests of offering incense in the Holy Place (Luke 1:8-9). The selection of Zechariah was not an arbitrary decision nor a matter of chance. Neither was the choice of Matthias. As a consequence, Matthias was counted together with the other eleven apostles, and, in preparation for the outpouring of the Spirit, the apostolic circle was again complete.

This first recorded prayer of Acts in 1:24-25, therefore, functions at multiple levels. Within the narrative, this collective prayer acknowledges God's continuing control of the progress of history. More specifically, it works together with other indications of the divine will at work in these events to certify that the choice of Matthias was the outworking of God's purpose. Furthermore, it demonstrates the early church's commitment to discerning and putting into action God's will.

Prayer in the Face of Persecution and Hardship

Jesus in the Third Gospel had predicted that his followers would encounter hostility (cf., e.g., Luke 6:22-23; 10:1-16; 12:4-10; 21:12-19; 22:35-38). At the same time, he insisted that nothing — not even life-threatening opposition — could happen to them that was outside of God's attentiveness and compassion. In one scene, he urged his disciples, "Are not five sparrows sold for two pennies? Yet not one of them is forgotten in God's sight. But even the hairs of your head are all counted. Do not be afraid; you are of more value than many sparrows" (Luke 12:6-7).

That sparrows are not forgotten by God does not keep them from being sold in the marketplace. Likewise, God's knowledge of the number of hairs on "your head" is not a pronouncement of divine protection from harm. But such statements do indicate the presence and unsurpassed knowledge and care of God in all of life. Given this perspective on God and his working, we should not be surprised to discover that prayers related to persecution and hardship in Luke's second volume, the Acts of the Apostles, are not necessarily for divine rescue (see 4:24-31; 7:59-60; 12:5, 12; 16:25).

One important episode of prayer in the face of persecution in Acts is in 4:24-30, which takes place on the occasion of Peter and John's release from trial before the Jewish authorities. This episode brings to closure a narrative section in Acts that began in 3:1 with a healing in the vicinity of the Jerusalem temple of a man crippled from birth. The healing scene gives way to Peter's address to the gathered crowds, which itself becomes the occasion for Peter and John to be arrested, called before the Jerusalem authorities, and threatened against speaking further in the name of Jesus. "After they had been released," Luke records, Peter and John "went to the other believers and reported what the chief priests and the elders had said to them." And when the believers in Jerusalem heard it, Luke goes on to say, "they raised their voices together to God and said":

> Master, who made the heaven and the earth, the sea, and everything in them, it is you who said by the Holy Spirit through our ancestor David, your servant, "Why did the Gentiles rage, and the peoples imagine vain things? The kings of the earth took their stand, and the rulers have gathered together against the Lord and against his Messiah." For indeed in this city both Herod and Pontius Pilate, with the Gentiles and the peo-

ples of Israel, gathered together against your holy servant Jesus, whom you anointed, to do whatever your hand and your plan had predestined to take place. And now, Lord, look upon their threats, and grant to your servants to speak your word with all boldness, as you stretch out your hand to heal, and signs and wonders are performed through the name of your holy servant Jesus. (4:24-30)

The structure of this prayer is suggested by the dual address to God — first as "Master" (*despota*, v. 24) and then as "Lord" (*kyrie*, v. 29). The first half of the prayer affirms God as Creator and Lord of history, whose purpose was not thwarted but actualized in the opposition encountered by his Messiah. The power and authority of God revealed in all of history, but especially and most recently in the events related to the death of Jesus, serve thus as the warrant for the request addressed to him. The second half of the prayer requests divine intervention for the purpose of the continuation of the church's mission.

This prayer demonstrates, first, how the church read its own experience of opposition against the backdrop of the hostility that Jesus had encountered — and, indeed, within the ongoing revelation of God's redemption. Persecution is hardly a sign of God's disfavor. This truth is underscored by the divine portents that follow the prayer: "When they had prayed, the place in which they were gathered was shaken; and they were all filled with the Holy Spirit and spoke the word of God with boldness" (4:31). This perspective on persecution is developed further in 7:54-60, where Stephen, in the face of enraged opposition, visualizes the glory of God and sees Jesus standing at the place of honor with God. Jesus appears as Stephen's intercessor or advocate, and as his intercessor he stands ready to receive Stephen (cf. D. M. Crump, *Jesus the Intercessor*, 176-203, on Jesus as "the heavenly intercessor"). Opposition, therefore, is not a contradiction, but is to be taken into account within the redemptive plan of God (cf. 14:22).

Second, this prayer suggests that the disciples have learned from Jesus the importance of prayer in the midst of trials. On the Mount of Olives, when urged to pray lest they fail in the time of testing, they had slept (cf. Luke 22:39-46). Now, however, in the context of opposition, they pray, with the result that they are emboldened for mission. It is crucial to observe that prayer was offered not for the cessation of threats but to ask God not to allow his redemptive aim to be thwarted.

Prayer in Moments of Missional Innovation

Throughout Acts, prayer provides an opportunity for the disclosure of God's purpose. Given Luke's overall focus on the progress of "the word" in his Gospel and his Acts, however, the presence of divine revelation at pivotal points in the mission receives heightened attention. Of course, God has a variety of ways for communicating his will — as, for example, angelic visitation, interpretation of Scripture, and the intervention of the Holy Spirit. Within such a list, however, prayer figures prominently. This is especially true at those points at which Luke correlates prayer with visions (e.g., 9:10-12; 10:3-4, 9-16, 30-31; 11:5; 22:17-21).

In his account of the encounter of Philip with the Ethiopian eunuch in 8:26-40, Luke goes to great lengths to show that Philip's evangelistic activity was simply a manifestation of God's purpose: "An angel of the Lord said to Philip . . . ," "the Spirit said to Philip . . . ," "the Spirit of the Lord snatched Philip away . . ." (vv. 26, 29, 39). The inclusion of the Ethiopian within the people of God constituted a theological and missional departure of such magnitude that it was important to stress that this innovation bore the divine imprimatur.

The same can be said of Peter's encounter with Cornelius in 10:1–11:18. Indeed, Luke's narration of the Cornelius episode virtually brims with confirmation of the divine hand at work. This can be seen not only in the intervention of divine messengers (as in the episode with the eunuch) but more especially in the strategic role that prayer plays in the story. Cornelius, though a Gentile, was a man of prayer (10:2); and on a certain day he had a vision at three o'clock in the afternoon, which Luke has already identified as a time for prayer at the Jerusalem temple (3:1). That the vision took place in the context of prayer is suggested by the angel's words to Cornelius, "Your prayers . . . have ascended as a memorial before God" (10:4). It is also confirmed in Cornelius's report to Peter of this episode in 10:30-31. Furthermore, what occurred with Cornelius was paralleled by the experience of Peter, who also had a vision while praying (10:9) and later had opportunity to speak of his prayer and vision (11:5). In both cases, the will of God was revealed — both with regard to those individuals who were praying and, more significantly, with regard to the make-up of the people of God.

At stake in the Cornelius episode of 10:1–11:18 was not the legitimization of the communication of the gospel to Gentiles. That had already been mandated by the risen Lord in 1:8 and performed by Philip in ministering to the Ethiopian eunuch in 8:26-40. Instead, full and open hospitality was at stake (cf. the protestations of the Jewish believers at Jerusalem in 11:2-3 [cf. 10:28]). In this case, then, prayer was the means by which God's will for full fellowship between Jewish and Gentile believers was revealed and enacted — just as the actualization of God's purpose among Jesus' followers and in the Christian mission had been earlier demonstrated in 2:1-13 by an expression of prayer, namely, the doxological speaking in tongues.

This does not mean that the purposes of God are somehow set loose by prayer, or otherwise placed in motion. Rather, these episodes reveal that God is already at work redemptively. The question is whether people will recognize and, having recognized, embrace and serve God's purpose. In Acts, prayer is (1) a means by which God's aim is disclosed and discerned, and (2) the means by which people get in sync with and participate in what God is doing.

Prayer for Salvation

Other aspects of prayer are developed in Acts, including, for example, those texts where prayer is bundled together with kneeling (7:60; 9:40; 20:36; 21:5-6) and fasting (13:3; 14:27) — that is, where prayer is related to dispositions of humility and dependence before God. The final category I want to develop here, however, has to do with that roster of texts in Acts where prayer is related to salvation.

Salvation comprises, above all, a person's incorporation into and participation in the community of God's people, whose life is drawn from and focused on Christ. Salvation includes the forgiveness of sins and the gift of the Holy Spirit, but it must also be understood holistically to include other blessings as well — as, for example, physical healing and divine rescue (cf. J. B. Green, "'Salvation to the End of the Earth'"). In a sense, salvation is always related to prayer, since salvation comes to all "who call on the name of the Lord."

One of the names given to Jesus' disciples in Acts, as we noted above, is "those who call on the name" (9:14, 21). Rooted exegetically in the citation of Joel 2:32 in Acts 2:21, this descriptive label identifies those who believe in the name of Jesus and have identified with his name in baptism (cf. 2:38; 3:16; 8:12, 16; 9:48; 19:5; 22:16). At its most basic level, "to call on" refers in biblical language to prayer in times of need. By using this designation for followers of Jesus, Luke thus indicates how fundamental prayer is to Christian experience, for it marks the beginning of one's incorporation into the messianic community and designates one of the practices that speak of faithfulness within that community.

Additionally, in a handful of scenes in Acts we read of specific petitions being made on behalf of others for salvation and its blessings. Peter, for example, prays for the resuscitation of Tabitha (9:40), and Paul prays for the physical healing of Publius's father (28:8). In these episodes we have reminders that the power to heal does not reside with men and women — not even with heroes of faith like Peter and Paul — but that healing is from the Lord (cf. 3:12-16; 14:8-15).

In one text, but only one, prayers are made that others might receive the Holy Spirit (8:15). This is unusual in the Book of Acts, for the Spirit's outpouring is not dispensed by human hands but through the agency of the exalted Jesus (cf. 2:33). Likewise, before Festus, Agrippa II, and Bernice, Paul uses the language of prayer to express his desire that Agrippa — and, indeed, all who had gathered to hear Paul's testimony — might become Christians (26:29). Paul thus expresses a hope reminiscent of the words of Jesus (cf. Luke 23:43) and of Stephen (cf. Acts 7:59-60), who responded to persecution by intercession on behalf of their persecutors. And in other scenes in Acts, even when the content of the prayers is not given, prayer is nonetheless intimately associated with manifestations of the saving activity of God (cf., e.g., 2:1-4; 16:25-34).

Conclusion

Because of the importance of prayer at the most fundamental levels of Christian experience in the Lucan narrative, it is difficult to summarize the significance and features of prayer as these are developed in the Acts of the Apostles. Prayer is a practice that brings to expression a renewed understanding of God, together with a belief in the exalted lordship of Jesus. It is also a practice that reveals one's confidence in a God who is graciously present and who will act to bring to fruition his redemptive purpose. Episodes of prayer comprise some, though not all, of the contexts in which God chooses to reveal his purpose and to invite human participation in it. And it follows that prayer is a practice through which Jesus' disciples seek to know the aim of God and to commit themselves to its service. With his emphasis on prayer in Acts, Luke establishes Jesus' followers as persons (1) who continue to model the piety of Jesus, and (2) who bear the power and ministry of Jesus.

3. Jesus on Prayer — The Disciples at Prayer

Having highlighted a number of central features of the experience of prayer in the early church as presented by Luke in Acts, I now take up the third part of my agenda. Here I will deal with the relationship between the depictions of the disciples at prayer in Acts and the portrayals of Jesus regarding prayer in the Third Gospel. My concern here is the theological unity of Luke's two volumes. Given that Jesus modeled prayer for his disciples and that he repeatedly instructed them regarding prayer, we may now ask: How have the practices of the disciples been shaped under Jesus' tutelage?

The Prayer Practices and Instructions of Jesus in the Third Gospel

Risking oversimplification, we begin this discussion with a few summary remarks about the contours of Luke's presentation of prayer in the Third Gospel. Because I am interested in possible points of coherence between Jesus and his disciples, my focus will be on what we learn from Jesus' instructions about prayer. These can be reviewed under four headings.

First, Luke's presentation of Jesus at prayer is noteworthy not only for the way he stresses the centrality of prayer to Jesus' life, but also, and especially, for the *revelatory function of prayer* (cf. D. M. Crump, *Jesus the Intercessor*). This emphasis begins as early as Jesus' baptism (3:21-22), where Jesus' prayer provides the immediate context for God's disclosure of Jesus' identity: "You are my son" (cf. also 2:36-38; 9:18-27, 28-36; 10:21-22; 23:34, 46; 24:30-31).

Second, and of equal significance, Jesus' teaching is oriented fundamentally around the "fatherhood" of God. In Luke 10:21-22, Jesus speaks of his unique capacity to reveal the Father to those whom he chose, and this is exactly what he seeks to do in his teaching on prayer. This is most evident in 11:1-13, where Jesus teaches his disciples to address God as "Father" and then undertakes to teach them in what sense God is "Father." Jesus' instruction on prayer, however, does not emphasize a certain technique. His concern is much more basic: that those who pray know the One to whom they are praying.

The disciples' request, "Lord, teach us to pray" (11:1), is in Luke's Gospel not an invitation for Jesus to provide a kind of "technology of prayer" — that is, to teach them to pray like this, in this manner, on this timetable, following these steps, or whatever. Rather, it is an opportunity to identify God as the Father whose graciousness is realized in his provision of what is needed — indeed, far beyond what might be expected — to those who join him in relationship. Because the disciples have to do with such a God, Jesus insists, they are liberated to ask, to search, to knock, knowing that God will answer prayer in accordance with his graciousness and goodness (cf. 11:9-10).

Third, prayer in Jesus' teaching is always more than an isolated "act of piety." It is a practice that grows out of one's dispositions — that is, one's attitudes, convictions, and commitments — indeed, one's innermost beliefs. This is the essence of Jesus' instruction on prayer in 18:1-8 and 18:9-14, which comprise two back-to-back instances of Jesus' parabolic teaching in Luke's Gospel. In these scenes, prayer is metonymic for one's character, for Jesus here uses prayer to speak to the issue of what sort of people, with what sort of commitments and character as well as behaviors, are fit for the kingdom of God.

In the "Parable of Faithfulness in Anticipation" (also known as the "Parable of the Unjust Judge" or "Parable of the Persistent Widow") of 18:1-8, Jesus observes, first, that God is not like some unjust judge who must be badgered into assisting those in great need, like the widow who had been denied justice; and, second, that praying and crying out to God are exemplified in the whole life of believers engaged in the active quest for justice under the reign of God. In the "Parable of the Pharisee and the Toll Collector" of 18:9-14, how one prays is inseparably wrapped up with one's comportment before God and others, in light of the inbreaking kingdom of God. Praying, fasting, tithing — these pious acts performed by the Pharisee were all admirable. In his case they were unacceptable, however, for they flowed out of a heart filled with self-aggrandizement, self-justification, and self-reliance. The toll collector's prayer, however, in which he recognized his state of unworthiness before God, bespeaks the humility that God desires and that attracts God's compassion and restoration.

Fourth, in anticipation of times of hostility, Jesus urges his disciples in the Third Gospel "to be alert at all times, praying that you may have the strength to escape all these things that will take place, and to stand before the Son of Man" (21:36). In the face of diabolic opposition, faithful perseverance comes through prayer (22:40, 46). Jesus not only instructed his disciples concerning this reality, but he also demonstrated it on the Mount of Olives — where his faithfulness in a crucial time of testing was paralleled by their failure (22:39-46).

The Prayer Practices of the Disciples in Acts

When the prayer practices of the disciples in Acts are read against the backdrop of the Third Gospel, three points of interest emerge. First, and perhaps most obviously, the disciples seem to have taken to heart the message of Jesus concerning prayer in the face of trials. Their failure on the Mount of Olives contrasts sharply with their faithfulness in Acts — both with regard to the fact of their praying in the face of opposition and with regard to the substance of their prayers. Even if Jesus' prayer on the eve of his execution raised the possibility of rescue from death, it was more focused on his discerning, and submitting to, the will of his Father. The "time of testing," as Jesus' encounter with the devil in Luke 4:1-13 plainly shows, was not about survival but about faithfulness to God's purpose. And this concern about being faithful to God's purpose is clearly in evidence in the scenes of persecution in Acts.

Second, however, although Jesus' example and instruction on prayer are centered on the fatherhood of God, the prayers of his followers in Acts do not provide even one instance in which God is addressed as "Father." Indeed, God is referred to as "Father" only three times in Acts — twice with reference to the promised Holy Spirit (1:4; 2:33) and once in reference to God's sovereignty with regard to the consummation of history (1:7). And neither is Jesus identified as the Son of God, apart from 9:20; 13:33. Prayers in Acts are addressed to God as "Master," "Lord," or simply as "God," but never to God as "Father." As we have already noted, prayer is also addressed to the Lord Jesus.

Why is it that Jesus made so much of God's character as Father in the Gospel of Luke, only for this emphasis to disappear in Acts? Three related answers may be proposed. One is that, more important than identifying

God as Father is the recognition of what the ascription "Father" suggests about his identity. In the Gospel there is a marked contrast between notions of "fatherhood" that were current in Roman antiquity, which conjured up authoritarian images practically devoid of compassion, and Jesus' portrait of God as the Father who both cares for his children and is Lord of history, so that he can act compassionately and redemptively on their behalf. In this respect, it is perhaps of interest that God is sometimes represented in Acts as Creator (cf. 4:24; 14:15; 17:24-28), which is a depiction that underscores in a related way God's sovereignty over the cosmos and over history. A second answer that may be given as to why Jesus' followers in Acts do not address God as "Father" in their prayers has to do with a christological point to which we have already alluded: on account of his resurrection and ascension Jesus is coregent with God, so the blessings of salvation are available through him.

A third reason for the lack of the address "Father" in their prayers, however, is that most of the prayers in Acts have "the Lord" as their object. Luke's readers today are fond of finding in this term a reference to Yahweh in the Greek Old Testament. In the world of the early church, however, the title "lord" would have had wider connotations related to benefaction. Roman political economy consisted of stair-stepped levels of dependents and obligations. At the top were "the gods," from whom Caesar himself had received benefaction. As such, Caesar was the benefactor of "the whole world," the father of the Roman "household," the "lord" of the empire. To refer to Jesus as "Lord," then, was also a political and soteriological statement — one that underscored one's ultimate loyalty not to Caesar but to the Lord Jesus. Addressing Jesus as "Lord" signified the early believers' expectation that *as Lord* Jesus would provide for his people the gracious benefaction of God.

In short, though the term "Father" is missing in the prayers of Acts, the vision of God presented by Jesus in Luke's Gospel is pervasive in Acts. The disciples, unable at first to see beyond their own preconceptions of the nature of God, had their minds opened after the resurrection of Jesus (cf. Luke 24:44-49). Consequently, they were able to relate to God in fresh ways that were consistent with God's own character, and to grasp the significance of Jesus' status as the unique agent of divine beneficence. This transformation of relationship and thought is manifest in their prayers.

When assessing the portraits of prayer in Acts vis-à-vis the prayer practices and teaching of Jesus in Luke's Gospel, it is important to observe, third, how prayer as an expression of the character of the church comes into sharp focus in Acts. In order to appreciate this aspect of Luke's presentation, it is necessary to see how prayer serves in Acts as much more than just a characteristic quality or distinguishing mark of the disciples, as important as this is. It also serves as a boundary marker in community formation. It was used in this way by the Pharisees to identify themselves over against others. But prayer also came to identify the early church and to express the church's essential commitments.

The practice of prayer is a catalyst for many types of community formation. The question always to be asked, however, is, what sort of community? As depicted in Luke 5:27-39 and 18:9-14, prayer functioned among certain Pharisees as an identity marker, the purpose of which was to maintain clear boundaries between groups — in these instances, as behaviors that separated Pharisees from toll collectors and sinners. Jesus' response to that use of prayer is reminiscent of the Old Testament prophets' criticism of pious acts when those acts are segregated from acts of justice and mercy: "I tell you, this man went to his home justified before God, rather than the other; for all who exalt themselves will be humbled, but all who humble themselves will be exalted" (18:14; cf. Isa. 58:3-9; Jer. 14:12; Zech. 7:5-6). In this context acts of piety and mercy included the humility necessary to extend hospitality and other signs of God's care to those who are marginalized in society.

What is fascinating, then, is that the Book of Acts portrays prayer as a community-defining practice that invariably leads to the expansion of the community — that is, to the possibility of boundary dissolution rather than to boundary maintenance. Prayer among the disciples, as Acts presents it, leads to the inclusion of both Samaritans and Gentiles among the Spirit-anointed followers of Jesus. This is because the habits of prayer, as counseled by Jesus in the Third Gospel, serve as an ongoing catalyst for the conformation of the community around the unlimited mercy of God (cf. Luke 6:35-36). And prayer of this sort allows for the infusion of a worldview that is centered on (1) the graciousness of God, (2) dependence on God, (3) the imitation of God, and (4) God's purpose for humanity — with all of these emphases understood against an eschatological horizon in which the coming of God in sovereignty and redemption figures prominently.

What have the disciples learned from Jesus about prayer? According to the narrative of Acts, apparently a great deal. Most importantly, they seem to have recognized that prayer grows out of a recognition of God's character, as his character is manifest in history and especially in the person and ministry of Jesus. That is, prayer is fundamentally a matter of recognizing to whom one is praying. Furthermore, they seem to have been aware that prayer has as a consequence the transformation of a community's moral and theological imagination, as well as a greatly expanded understanding of God's sovereignty and character, which has significant repercussions for the lives and practices of the people of God. Prayers for God's purpose not to be thwarted, for strength in the midst of testing, for discernment in the church's mission, for the healing and redemption of others, and for the commissioning of leadership in the church and its mission — coupled with confidence that God will act in these ways — have at their root a radical commitment to the gracious God who is Lord of history.

Epilogue: The Practice of Prayer and the Church

There are, undoubtedly, a number of ways by which one could assess the validity and strength of the church. For the Book of Acts, however, chief among all the canons that might be championed is the nature of the church's prayer life. It is here that the church's deepest convictions and commitments about God come most fully to expression. It is here that the church's own proclamation of Jesus as Lord and Messiah is manifest within the community of believers. It is here that the church locates its rallying point. It is here that we are able to take the measure of its orientation to the purposes of God. And it is here that a number of evaluative questions begin to emerge.

Primary among such questions for the church and for Christians today are these: To what extent is the church operating along the lines reflected by some Pharisees in the Gospel of Luke, whose understanding of God and of faithfulness before God was so anemic that prayer functioned only to separate them from those for whom God's graciousness is especially oriented? To what extent is the church allowing its own moral and theological imagination to be challenged and transformed in prayer, so that its understanding of mission is constantly renewed? To what extent is the church devoting itself to prayer on behalf of those who are in the midst of trial and persecution, in order that God's purpose will not be thwarted and the witness of Christ will move forward? To what extent can it be said that Jesus' followers model the piety of Jesus, thereby proving themselves to be his faithful witnesses and heirs of his ministry?

Selected Bibliography

Barton, Stephen C. *The Spirituality of the Gospels*. London: SPCK, 1992.

Blue, Brad. "The Influence of Jewish Worship on Luke's Presentation of the Early Church." In *Witness to the Gospel: The Theology of Acts*, ed. I. H. Marshall and D. Peterson. Grand Rapids: Eerdmans, 1998, 473-97.

Charlesworth, James H. "A Prolegomena to a New Study of the Jewish Background of the Hymns and Prayers in the New Testament." *Journal of Jewish Studies* 33 (1982): 265-85.

Crump, David M. *Jesus the Intercessor: Prayer and Christology in Luke-Acts*. Tübingen: Mohr-Siebeck, 1992.

Falk, Daniel K. "Jewish Prayer Literature and the Jerusalem Church in Acts." In *The Book of Acts in Its Palestinian Setting*, ed. R. Bauckham [*The Book of Acts in Its First Century Setting* 4]. Grand Rapids: Eerdmans, 1995, 267-301.

Green, Joel B. "'Salvation to the End of the Earth' (Acts 13:47): God as Saviour in the Acts of the Apostles." In *Witness to the Gospel: The Theology of Acts*, ed. I. H. Marshall and D. Peterson. Grand Rapids: Eerdmans, 1998, 83-106.

O'Brien, Peter T. "Prayer in Luke-Acts." *Tyndale Bulletin* 24 (1973): 111-27.

Peterson, David. "The Worship of the New Community." In *Witness to the Gospel: The Theology of Acts*, ed. I. H. Marshall and D. Peterson. Grand Rapids: Eerdmans, 1998, 373-95.

Plymale, Steven F. *The Prayer Texts of Luke-Acts*. New York: Peter Lang, 1991.

Smalley, Stephen S. "Spirit, Kingdom and Prayer in Luke-Acts." *Novum Testamentum* 15 (1973): 59-71.

Trites, Allison A. "The Prayer Motif in Luke-Acts." In *Perspectives on Luke-Acts*, ed. C. H. Talbert. Edinburgh: T. & T. Clark, 1978, 168-86.

CHAPTER 10

Prayer in the Pauline Letters

RICHARD N. LONGENECKER

THE ACTS OF THE APOSTLES portrays Paul as a man of prayer. As Paul's story in Acts begins, Ananias is told by God to go into Damascus and search out a man from Tarsus named Saul, "for he is praying" (9:11). Throughout his ministry as a Christian apostle, Paul is represented as praying frequently: when called by God at Syrian Antioch to begin his missionary journeys (13:2-3); when appointing elders in the newly established churches of Asia Minor (14:23); when thrown into a Roman dungeon at Philippi because of his Christian witness (16:25); when leaving Ephesus on his final journey to Jerusalem (20:36); and when healing Publius's father on the island of Malta (28:8). Furthermore, when speaking to a rioting crowd from the steps of the Antonian fortress in Jerusalem, Paul is depicted as saying that it was while he was "praying at the temple" that God told him to leave Jerusalem and go to the Gentiles (22:17). Indeed, throughout Luke's Gospel and Acts, to be an apostle of Jesus, as was Paul — or, to be a follower of Jesus, as are all those who claim Christ's name — is to be a person of prayer, as was Jesus himself.

All the reports of Paul praying in Acts, however, are second-hand reports, whatever might be thought about their accuracy. What is needed is an investigation of the Pauline letters themselves for reflections of the apostle's prayer life and the nature and content of his prayers. This is what we will endeavor to do in what follows, focusing on (1) the Pauline prayer vocabulary, (2) major methodological issues in dealing with the Pauline references to prayer, (3) the background of Paul's prayers, (4) the structure of Paul's prayers, (5) Paul's prayers of adoration, (6) Paul's prayers of thanksgiving, (7) Paul's prayers of petition, and (8) some significant features of Paul's prayers, with a concluding epilogue.

1. The Pauline Prayer Vocabulary

Terms having to do with prayer appear more frequently in Paul's letters than in the writings of any other New Testament author. Robert Morgenthaler's *Statistik des neutestamentlichen Wortschatzes* (Zürich-Frankfurt: Gotthelf, 1958) lists 16 words for prayer (see those cited in the following paragraphs), which occur some 133 times in the thirteen canonical Pauline letters. In comparison, Matthew has 8 of these prayer words, which occur 60 times; Mark has 8 prayer words, which are used 32 times; Luke has 10 used 57 times; John has 3 used 15 times; Acts has 10 used 80 times; Hebrews has 7 used 18 times; while in the rest of the New Testament these prayer terms appear 59 times. The place to begin any study of prayer in Paul, therefore, is with a scanning of the apostle's prayer vocabulary.

Primary expressions for the adoration of God in the Pauline letters are "to bless" or "blessed" (*eulogein, eulogia, eulogētos;* cf. Rom. 1:25; 9:5; 1 Cor. 14:16; 2 Cor. 1:3; 11:31; Eph. 1:3), "to praise" or "praise" (*ainein, exomologein, epainos;* cf. Rom. 14:11; 15:9-11; Eph. 1:6, 12, 14; Phil. 1:11; 2:11), and "to worship" (*proskunein;* 1 Cor. 14:25). They occur in quotations of Scripture and in citations of early Christian hymns and confessions. More commonly, however, they appear in Paul's own statements with reference to prayers of adoration to God.

Paul's use of thanksgiving terminology in prayer contexts is also noteworthy. The verb "to give thanks" (*eucharistein*) appears twenty-four times (Rom. 1:8, 21; 14:6 [twice]; 16:4; 1 Cor. 1:4, 14; 10:30; 11:24; 14:17, 18; 2 Cor. 1:11; Eph. 1:6; 5:20; Phil. 1:3; Col. 1:3, 12; 3:17; 1 Thess. 1:2; 2:13; 5:18; 2 Thess. 1:3; 2:13; Philem. 4), the noun "thanksgiving" (*eucharistia*) appears twelve times (1 Cor. 14:16; 2 Cor. 4:15; 9:11, 12; Eph. 5:4; Phil. 4:6; Col. 2:7; 4:2; 1 Thess. 3:9; 1 Tim. 2:1; 4:3, 4), and the adjective "thankful" (*eucharistos*) used substantively appears once (Col. 3:15). Furthermore, when one takes into consideration the nine times that the noun "thanks" (*charis*) is used to signify gratitude to God (Rom. 6:17; 7:25; 1 Cor. 15:57; 2 Cor. 2:14; 8:16; 9:15; Col. 3:16; 1 Tim. 1:12; 2 Tim. 1:3), the total instances of thanksgiving vocabulary in the Pauline prayer materials comes to forty-six — with those instances being distributed fairly evenly throughout the Pauline corpus, except for Galatians and Titus.

Paul's usual terms for intercessory prayer are the verb "to pray" *(proseuchesthai)*, which appears seventeen times (Rom. 8:26; 1 Cor. 11:4, 5, 13; 14:14 [twice], 15 [twice]; Eph. 6:18; Phil. 1:9; Col. 1:3, 9; 4:3; 1 Thess. 5:17, 25; 2 Thess. 1:11; 3:1); the noun "prayer" *(proseuchē)*, which appears fourteen times (Rom. 1:10; 12:12; 15:30; 1 Cor. 7:5; Eph. 1:16; 6:18; Phil. 4:6; Col. 4:2, 12; 1 Thess. 1:2; 1 Tim. 2:1; 5:5; Philem. 4, 22; the noun "entreaty" or "request" *(deēsis)*, which appears ten times (Rom. 10:1; 2 Cor. 1:11; 9:14; Eph. 6:18; Phil. 1:4, 19; 4:6; 1 Tim. 2:1; 5:5; 2 Tim. 1:3); and the verb "to call upon" *(epikalein* or *parakalein)*, which appears in prayer contexts seven times (Rom. 10:12, 13, 14; 1 Cor. 1:2; 2 Cor. 1:23 [probably]; 12:8; 2 Tim. 2:22). In several places non-prayer terms are also used in connection with prayers of petition — for example, the noun "mention" or "remembrance" *(mneia;* cf. Rom. 1:9; Eph. 1:16; Phil. 1:3; 1 Thess. 1:2; Philem. 4), the verb "to assist" *(sunagōnizesthai,* Rom. 15:30), the verb "to help" *(sunupourgein,* 2 Cor. 1:11), and the verb "to mention" or "remember" *(mnēmoneuein,* 1 Thess. 1:3; perhaps also Col. 4:18).

The greeting "grace and peace to you" *(charis humin kai eirēnē)*, which appears in the salutation of every Pauline letter, and a peace benediction (e.g., "The God of peace be with you all. Amen"), which often begins the concluding section of a Pauline letter, may also reflect the language of Jewish prayers generally and Paul's prayers in particular. In the Pauline corpus, however, such a greeting and benediction function primarily as an epistolary *inclusio* to bracket or enclose the contents of the respective letters, and so — even though echoing the language of prayer — they will not be treated here as prayers. Likewise, the evocative expression "By no means!" *(mē genoito;* "Far from it!," "Never!," "Absolutely not!," or the KJV's "God forbid!") is an emotionally-charged exclamation, which usually appears in Paul's letters after a rhetorical question (cf. Rom. 3:4, 6, 31; 6:2, 15; 7:7, 13; 9:14; 11:1, 11; 1 Cor. 6:15; Gal. 2:17; 3:21; the only exception being Gal. 6:14), and so will not be treated as a prayer. Nor will the cursing statement, "Let that one be eternally accursed by God!" *(anathema estō* of Gal. 1:8, 9; or, *ētō anathema* of 1 Cor. 16:22), for similar reasons. While future indicative verbs are often to be taken as equivalent to optative verbs, the statements of Rom. 16:20a ("The God of peace will soon crush Satan under your feet"); 1 Cor. 1:8 ("He will keep you strong to the end so that you will be blameless on the day of our Lord Jesus Christ"); 2 Cor.

13:11b ("The God of love and peace will be with you"); Phil. 4:7 ("The peace of God, which transcends all understanding, will guard your hearts and minds in Christ Jesus"); 4:9b ("The God of peace will be with you"); 4:19 ("My God will meet all your needs according to his glorious riches in Christ Jesus"); 1 Thess. 5:24b ("The one who calls you is faithful and he will do it"); and 2 Thess. 3:3 ("The Lord is faithful, and he will strengthen and protect you from the evil one") should probably be viewed more as declarations than as prayers.

2. Major Methodological Issues

Any study of prayer in the Pauline letters is immediately faced with a number of major issues regarding the identification, classification, and interpretation of the above references to prayer. Most obvious is the delineation of the Pauline corpus. The safest way, of course, is to consider only the prayer materials of the seven letters most assuredly attested critically and most commonly accepted as authentic — that is, Romans, 1 & 2 Corinthians, Galatians, Philippians, 1 Thessalonians, and Philemon (to list them in their canonical order). But prayers are traditional in nature. So the prayer materials found throughout the Pauline corpus might reasonably be expected to contain many similar features, whether expressed directly by Paul, mediated through an amanuensis or secretary, or reflected by his followers. And, as a matter of fact, though questions about Paul's authorship, his use of amanuenses, and/or the composition of one or more letters by a later Paulinist will certainly affect how one understands many matters within the Pauline corpus, the prayer materials in the thirteen canonical letters have a consistency of pattern and content (as we will see as we proceed) that permits them to be treated together — even while procedurally one must always begin with those materials that are most assuredly authentic before turning to those more problematic.

More serious, however, is the fact that in treating the prayer materials of the Pauline letters we are dealing not with liturgical texts (though such a text may be reflected in 1 Cor. 16:22: *Marana tha*, "O Lord, Come!") but with letters — that is, not with prayers addressed to God but with reports about prayers addressed to the letters' readers. In liturgical texts, God is addressed in the second person and people are spoken about in the third person, whereas in letters the readers are addressed in the second person and

God is spoken about in the third person. Thus prayers of adoration and prayers of thanksgiving have been recast in the Pauline letters to provide a précis of what has been prayed, but they do not address God directly or provide the readers with the prayers themselves. Likewise, prayers of petition have been recast so that, while they express the central concerns of the writer in his praying, they refer to God in the third person and only set out the essence of what has been prayed for.

Furthermore, it often becomes difficult to delineate the exact boundaries of the prayer materials in Paul's letters. Reports about what Paul has prayed for are often merged with descriptions about his readers' situations, and prayer wishes expressed on behalf of the addressees are often combined with exhortations to work out in their lives what has been prayed for. This is particularly true in the opening thanksgiving sections of the letters, where praise, prayer reports, prayer wishes, references to particular situations, and exhortations are frequently intermingled.

Other questions regarding method also arise when we try to interpret the Pauline prayer materials. Chief among such questions are these: What criteria of form, content, or function are to be used in classifying the prayer materials of the Pauline letters? How should the similarities and differences in the Pauline prayer vocabulary be evaluated? What features from his background and experience has Paul incorporated — whether consciously or unconsciously — into his prayers, and how have these features been blended in his praying? And to what extent have Paul's convictions regarding Jesus affected his use of traditional prayer materials?

3. The Background of Paul's Prayers

Jews have always been a people of prayer. It is therefore to the Jewish practice of prayer, particularly Jewish prayer practices of the first century CE, that we must first turn in order to understand Paul's prayers as reflected in his extant letters. For Paul was probably nowhere more traditional than in his prayer life.

Judaism gives high priority to prayer. The Jewish Scriptures contain many prayers, as do also the Jewish apocryphal and pseudepigraphical writings and the Dead Sea Scrolls. The rabbinic tractate *Berakoth* ("Benedictions") — which is the first tractate of the Mishnah, and therefore also the first tractate of the Talmud — is devoted to the subject of prayer. The

Jerusalem temple was called a "house of prayer" (cf. Isa. 56:7; Mark 11:17 par.) because the sacrifices were accompanied by prayers (cf. Sirach 50:19; Josephus, Contra Apion 2.196; Luke 1:10), and so the times of the evening and morning sacrifices were called simply "the hour of prayer" (cf. Acts 3:1). The Jewish synagogue was also called a "house of prayer" (cf. Josephus, Contra Apion 2.10; Life 277) — as well as, of course, "house of study," "assembly house," "little sanctuary," and "schul" (school) — because there prayers were voiced by one appointed by the ruler of the synagogue and the people responded with "Amen" after each benediction or blessing (cf. Neh. 8:6; 1 Chron. 16:36; Tobit 8:8; 1QSerek 1.20; Mishnah Berakoth 8:8; Mishnah Ta'anith 2:5; 1 Cor. 14:16).

Jews also gave thanks to God before their meals, and frequently after them as well (cf. Deut. 8:10; 1QSerek 6.4-5; Josephus, War 2.131; Mishnah Berakoth 6:1–8:8). The Kiddush ("sanctification" or ceremonial blessing) was recited over each of the different kinds of food in a Jewish home. And since in olden times strangers were often fed in the synagogue, the custom arose of also reciting the Kiddush as part of the evening service on Sabbath and festival days in the synagogue (except on the first night of Pesah, when strangers were to be given hospitality in private homes). A typical blessing over the bread would be: "Blessed art thou, O Lord, who brings forth bread from the earth"; a typical blessing over the wine: "Blessed art thou, O Lord, who has created the fruit of the vine" (cf. Mishnah Berakoth 6:1-8). Furthermore, short prayers were to be directed to God in every situation of life that a Jew encountered — as, for example, when a rabbi entered and left a synagogue or "house of study" (cf. Mishnah Berakoth 4:2), or when a traveler faced some danger on the way (cf. Mishnah Berakoth 4:4).

There is no commandment in the Jewish Scriptures that says simply "Thou shalt pray!" Rather, what one finds is a verse like Deut. 11:13, which calls on Israel "to love the Lord your God and to serve him with all your heart and with all your soul." The rabbis of the Talmud asked about this verse: "What kind of service is it that takes place in the heart?" And they answered their own question: "It is prayer!" (b. Ta'anith 2a). Therefore as "the service that takes place in the heart," Jewish teachers concluded that prayer is to be understood as "the free outpouring" of a person's heart before God, "the spontaneous expression" of a person's "deepest concerns" and "highest aspirations" — not just something that one is commanded to do, but something that a person feels like doing or is moved to do from the heart (cf. J. J. Petuchowski, Understanding Jewish Prayer, 3, 17).

Nonetheless, though prayer is to be freely given and voluntarily expressed, it is also regarded by Jews as a divine commandment, an obligation or *mitzvah,* since God commands his people to serve him with all their heart. This dual understanding of the nature of prayer means that in Judaism prayer is viewed as both an inward response of devotion *and* an outward act of obedience — that is, a reflection of individual spontaneity *and* an ordinance of community tradition; a voluntary outpouring of human emotion *and* an obligatory expression of a statutory rite (cf. *ibid.,* 3-25).

Many Jews have assumed that all the prayers in the *Siddur* or Jewish prayer book were not only condoned by the ancient rabbis but also commanded by Scripture. Prominent among them is the Shema, which is the subject of the first two chapters of the tractate *Berakoth,* the first tractate (as noted above) of the Mishnah and Talmud. The Shema begins with the words "Hear, O Israel (שְׁמַע יִשְׂרָאֵל): The Lord our God, the Lord is one." It consists of Deut. 6:4-9, Deut. 11:13-21, and Num. 15:37-41, with these passages then followed by benedictions that enunciate the great Jewish affirmations of God's creation, revelation, and redemption (cf. *Daily Prayer Book* [Orthodox], ed. P. Birnbaum [New York: Hebrew Publishing Company, 1949], 191-97 [Evening Service] and 71-81 [Morning Service]; *Sabbath and Festival Prayer Book* [Conservative], [The Rabbinical Assembly of America and the United Synagogue of America, 1946], 15-19 [Evening Service] and 87-95 [Morning Service]; *Union Prayer Book, Revised* [Reform], [Cincinnati: The Central Conference of American Rabbis, 1940], 13-17 [Evening Service] and 125-41 [Morning Service]). The obligation to recite the Shema twice a day, both evening and morning, was derived from the first paragraph of the Shema itself: "Impress them [these commandments] on your children. Talk about them when you sit at home and when you walk along the road, *when you lie down and when you get up*" (Deut. 6:7). Midday prayer, which also includes the Shema, has some biblical precedent (cf. Ps. 55:17; Dan. 6:10), but as Jakob Petuchowski points out, the reciting of the Shema, with its attendant benedictions, was to the ancient rabbis "not a matter of 'prayer,' but of 'declaration' or 'proclamation,'" with these affirmations or confessions of faith only later turned into statutory prayers (*ibid.,* 20). Originally the Shema was not meant so much to be prayed as to be affirmed or confessed as a declaration or proclamation of Israel's faith.

The only prayer commanded to be prayed in ancient rabbinic lore is the *Shemoneh Esreh,* or "Eighteen Benedictions." It is designated in the Talmud as *Tefillah*, which means "intercession" and signifies "the Prayer" *par excellence*. It functions as the central feature in the daily services of the synagogue and the basic prayer for every Jew (cf. *Daily Prayer Book*, 81-97 [Weekday], 265-73, 349-59, 391-405, 449-59 [Sabbath], 585-97, 609-25 [Festival]; *Sabbath and Festival Prayer Book*, 230-37 [Weekday], 21-25, 96-101, 137-45, 169-76 [Sabbath], 29-33, 146-56 [Festival]; *Union Prayer Book, Revised*, 320-26 [Weekday], 19-25, 125-41 [Sabbath], 193-201, 225-43 [Festival]).

The *Shemoneh Esreh* or "Eighteen Benedictions" is commonly known as the *Amidah* ("standing"), since it is to be recited while standing. Jewish tradition has it that it was composed by Ezra in the fifth century BCE (cf. *b. Megillah* 18a; *Sifre on Deuteronomy* 343). Modern Jewish scholars, however, dispute such an early date and have demonstrated various stages in its development (cf. K. Kohler, "The Origin and Composition of the Eighteen Benedictions," in *Contributions to the Scientific Study of Jewish Liturgy*, ed. J. J. Petuchowski, 52-90; L. Finkelstein, "The Development of the Amidah," in *ibid.*, 91-133; J. Heinemann, *Prayer in the Talmud*, 13-76). All that can be said with confidence is that the formulation of the *Shemoneh Esreh* began sometime before the first century CE and that its inclusion of eighteen benedictions antedates the destruction of the Jerusalem temple.

The first three benedictions of the *Shemoneh Esreh* have to do with the adoration of God; its intermediate twelve comprise petitions to God concerning the community's circumstances and the people's needs; its last three constitute prayers of thanksgiving. A number of reasons are given in the Talmud for the fact that the *Shemoneh Esreh* has eighteen benedictions: that God's name is mentioned eighteen times in Psalm 29 and eighteen times in the Shema; that the three patriarchs of the Jewish people, Abraham, Isaac, and Jacob, are mentioned together eighteen times in the Bible; and that the number eighteen corresponds to the eighteen main vertebrae in the human spinal column (cf. *b. Berakoth* 28b). The prayer for the restoration of the Davidic monarchy ("and speedily establish in [Jerusalem] the throne of David"), which was evidently first voiced in Babylon and known in Palestine during the first century CE, did not, however, become a nineteenth benediction, but was combined with the fourteenth, which is a prayer for the rebuilding of Jerusalem (cf. J. Heinemann, *Prayer in the Talmud*, 22, 67, 225). Similarly, the *birkhat ha-minim*, or prayer against "apostates" and "betrayers," which was composed under the direction of Rabbi

Gamaliel II at Jamnia about 80 CE, did not become an additional benediction, but was combined with the twelfth and then later revised to speak more generally against "slanderers" and the "arrogant" (cf. R. A. Pritz, *Nazarene Jewish Christianity* [Jerusalem: Magnes; Leiden: Brill, 1988], 102-7). A number of other developments in the wording of the *Shemoneh Esreh* — particularly in the petitions of its central section — have been identified as well.

Whenever it was first formulated and however it developed over the course of history, the *Shemoneh Esreh* seems to have been the basic statutory prayer of Judaism in the first century CE. Yet while it was the prescribed prayer of Paul's day, it was never viewed by Jews to be without flexibility or spontaneity. It may be that its first three benedictions of adoration and its final three benedictions of thanksgiving were always considered rather fixed. But its intermediate twelve intercessory benedictions seem to have changed and developed over the years — depending, always, on the circumstances of the nation and the needs of the people. The great medieval Jewish scholar Maimonides (1135-1204 CE, in Jewish writings generally called "Rambam" from the initials of his name, Rabbi Mosheh ben Maimon) — commenting on prayer generally ("the service that takes place in the heart"), but particularly on the *Shemoneh Esreh* — encapsulated the Jewish attitude when he said:

> A man should entreat God and pray every day, and proclaim the praise of the Holy One, praised be He [i.e., the first three benedictions]. Afterwards he should voice his needs in petitionary prayer [i.e., the next twelve benedictions, expressed in terms of the community's circumstances and the people's needs]. And, after that, give praise and thanksgiving to God for the goodness which He has abundantly bestowed upon him [i.e., the last three benedictions]. Everybody does so in accordance with his own ability. If, however, he was inhibited in speech, he would merely speak according to his ability and whenever he desired to do so. Similarly, the number of prayers would depend upon the ability of every individual. Some would pray once every day, while others would pray many times. (quotation from J. J. Petuchowski, *Understanding Jewish Prayer*, 19)

Paul's background of prayer in Judaism, therefore, had within it large elements of inwardness, spontaneity, and voluntarism, as well as features

211

of obligation, statutory ritual, and community tradition. Furthermore, Paul's Jewish background provided him with an understanding that in responding to God's mercy and grace, one was both (1) to affirm one's faith in God's creation, revelation, and redemption (as in the Shema), and (2) to pray to God in adoration, petition, and thanksgiving (as in the *Shemoneh Esreh*). All of these matters seem to have been intertwined in Paul's Jewish prayer experience. And, as will be highlighted in what follows, they are features that resonate throughout the references and allusions to prayer in the extant Pauline letters as well.

The phenomenon of prayer in Paul, however, is not to be understood only in terms of his Jewish practice of prayer, important as that background is. Paul's prayer life was also rooted in the piety of the Jewish Scriptures, the traditions of the emerging Christian church, and his own personal relationship with the risen Christ. Thus, though he claimed a large measure of independence as an apostle of Christ in his mission to Gentiles (cf. Gal. 1:16b-2:14), Paul also acknowledged his indebtedness to (1) the Scriptures of the Old Testament, which he quoted extensively and whose language he used in his prayers (cf. my *Biblical Exegesis in the Apostolic Period*, 2nd ed. [Grand Rapids: Eerdmans, 1999], 88-116), and (2) an existing body of early Christian confessional material, which he incorporated at various places into his letters and whose theological perspectives influenced his praying (cf. my *New Wine into Fresh Wineskins: Contextualizing the Early Christian Confessions* [Peabody: Hendrickson, 1999], 9-106). Furthermore, his commitment to Jesus as Israel's Messiah and humanity's Lord had a profound impact on the nature and content of his prayers, as will be evident in our analysis of the Pauline prayer materials below.

4. The Structure of Paul's Prayers

We do not, as noted earlier, have any verbatim reproductions of Paul's prayers, for the Pauline corpus does not include liturgical texts addressed to God but only letters addressed to the apostle's readers. Commentators, therefore, have tried to classify Paul's prayers either according to content or according to form.

Attempting to classify the Pauline prayer materials in terms of content, some have based their analyses on comparative studies of prayer in the human experience and proposed such categories for prayer as (1) "primitive," (2) "ritual," (3) "cultural," (4) "philosophical," (5) "mystical," and (6) "prophetic" — with Paul's prayers, seen as more private, spontaneous, and emotional, being classed as "personal," "mystical" and/or "prophetic" (e.g., F. Heiler, *Prayer: A Study in the History and Psychology of Religion*, trans. S. McComb and J. E. Park [London: Oxford University Press, 1938]). Others have drawn from the Old Testament Psalms such prayer categories as (1) "petitions of the people," (2) "petitions of an individual," (3) "declarative praise of the people," (4) "declarative praise of an individual," (5) "descriptive praise of the people," (6) "descriptive praise of an individual," and (7) "enthronement prayers" (cf. C. Westermann, *The Praise of God in the Psalms*, trans. K. R. Crim [Richmond: John Knox, 1965]), with Paul's prayers, when correlated with these categories, declared to be either "prayers of praise" or "prayers of petition."

More common today is the classification of the Pauline prayer materials according to their form: (1) "prayer reports," which address readers in the second person and tell them what Paul has prayed for them — or, at times, what he has prayed for others (cf. Rom. 10:1) or what others have prayed for his readers (cf. 2 Cor. 9:14), and (2) "wish prayers," which refer to God in the third person and address readers using the optative "may" when speaking about what is desired for them (e.g., G. Harder, *Paulus und das Gebet* [Gütersloh: Bertelsmann, 1936]; P. Schubert, *Form and Function of the Pauline Thanksgivings* [Berlin: Töpelmann, 1939]).

Each of these methods of cataloguing has some descriptive merit. Yet little is achieved by classifying Paul's prayers as "personal," "mystical," or "prophetic," and probably less by speaking of them as simply "prayers of praise" and "prayers of petition," for praise and petition are features that run concurrently throughout many of them. Nor is it sufficient to classify them as either "prayer reports" or "wish prayers," though that terminology may often be appropriate as a subcategory.

A better way of understanding the structure of Paul's prayers, we propose, using the method of what may be called "phenomenological historiography," is first to situate the prayer materials of the apostle's letters in the context of the Jewish pattern of prayer of his day — that is, to seek to understand the structure of Paul's prayers vis-à-vis that of the Jewish *Shemoneh Esreh*, which has prayers of adoration (#1-3), prayers of petition (#4-15), and prayers of thanksgiving (#16-18). We have, of course, no one liturgical text from Paul to support such a proposal. But all of the features of the *Shemoneh Esreh* appear in the prayer materials of the Pauline letters.

And it is highly likely that their presence reflects a basic structuring of Paul's prayer life, which had been conditioned by his Jewish experience.

The closest one gets to a single Pauline passage exhibiting all of these features is Ephesians 1, which, after the salutation, (1) expresses adoration of God *(eulogētos ho theos)* in verses 3-12 (or, possibly, through verse 14), (2) offers thanksgiving for the addressees *(eucharistōn huper humōn)* in verses 15-16, and (3) sets out in the optative mood and second person plural *(hina . . . dōē humin)* prayers for the readers in verses 17-23 (possibly also verses 13-14, which use the second person plural in direct address as well). In the long adoration section of verses 3-12, God is extolled for his blessings of salvation "in Christ" (v. 3), with affirmations made about his election (v. 4), adoption (v. 5), predestination (v. 6), redemption (v. 7), wisdom (v. 8), the mystery of his will (v. 9), and the consummation of all things "under the one head, even Christ" (v. 10). Furthermore, believers are reminded of their status as chosen and predestined by God "in Christ" (v. 11) in order that they "might be for the praise of his glory" (v. 12). In the thanksgiving section of verses 15-16 the writer assures his readers of his prayers for them, highlighting the fact that he prays for them continually. And in the petition section of verses 17-23 the details of what the writer prays for his readers come tumbling out in terms of their growth in wisdom, insight, understanding, and power — with, then, closing statements about how God will bring about the final culmination of their salvation. Intertwined throughout 1:3-23, in fact, are most (if not all) of the distinctive features of the *Shemoneh Esreh* — though, of course, with all of what is presented set in a matrix of commitment to Jesus as Christ (Messiah) and Lord.

The language of Ephesians 1 reflects the theology and piety of the Jewish/Old Testament Scriptures. It also reflects the christological confessions of the early church. And it expresses personal commitment to Jesus as Christ and Lord, as well as direct involvement with God's Spirit. The structure of the passage, however, suggests that its author was conditioned by patterns established by praying the *Shemoneh Esreh*. It is probably best, therefore, to understand Eph. 1:3-23 in the following manner: first, in terms of its structure, which seems to have been inherited (whether consciously or unconsciously) from the writer's Jewish background (whether directly or indirectly); then, in terms of its basic Jewish theology and piety, its distinctive early Christian confessions, and its personal commitment to Jesus and direct involvement with God's Spirit.

It may be, of course, that Ephesians was written by a Pauline follower. Or it may be that Paul, through an amanuensis or secretary, wrote what we know as "Ephesians" as something of a circular letter (however defined) to believers in Christ who lived in certain cities and towns of western Asia Minor. Either hypothesis would account for many of the features that distinguish this letter from the other letters of Paul. But whatever is thought about provenance, canonical Ephesians must be viewed in some manner as "Pauline." And since the same features of the prayer materials found in Ephesians 1 appear in various places and contexts in the other Pauline letters, we may assume that the same explanation given for their appearance in Ephesians is also to be proposed for their appearance elsewhere in the Pauline corpus. In what follows, therefore, the prayer materials of the Pauline letters will be discussed in terms of the structure provided by the *Shemoneh Esreh*, "the Prayer" *par excellence* of Paul's Jewish background.

5. Paul's Prayers of Adoration

The Hebrew noun ברכה means "blessing" or "praise." It appears in every prayer of the *Siddur*, the Jewish prayer book — usually at the beginning of a prayer in praise to God, but also at the end of long prayers as a eulogy extolling God. Two types of adoration prayers, therefore, can be identified in the Jewish prayer materials. The first is the "*berakah*-formula prayer," wherein (1) praise to God is declared in the opening address ("Blessed art Thou, O Lord" or "Blessed be the Lord"), (2) statements are made about God's person and what he has done on behalf of his people, which are introduced by a relative clause or substantival participle ("who" or "the One who"), (3) the verb in those statements is cast in the perfect tense ("has"), and (4) the content regarding God's activity is expressed either briefly or in extended fashion. The second may be called a "eulogy-type prayer," wherein a statement extolling God comes at the end of a long prayer, expresses itself not in the perfect tense but by an active verb or participle, and is mostly brief — usually no more than a few words of praise that reflect in summary fashion what has been prayed in the longer prayer.

Numerous instances of the *berakah*-formula prayer can be found in the Old Testament. For example, the words of Abraham's servant, after he had requested a sign from God and the request was granted, begin with "Blessed be the Lord (ברוך יהוה), the God of my master Abraham, who has not withheld his steadfast kindness from my master Abraham" (Gen. 24:27); and the words of Jethro on hearing from Moses "all that the Lord had done to Pharaoh and to Egypt" are similar: "Blessed be the Lord (יהוה ברוך), who has rescued you from the hand of the Egyptians and of Pharaoh, and who has rescued the people from the hand of the Egyptians" (Exod. 18:10). Other examples can be found in Gen. 14:20; Ruth 4:14; 1 Sam. 25:32, 39; 2 Sam. 18:28; 1 Kings 1:48; 5:7; 8:15, 56; 2 Chron. 2:12; 6:4; Ezra 7:27; Pss. 66:20; 124:6; and Dan. 3:28.

Eulogies at the end of prayers, however, have much less biblical precedent than *berakah*-formula prayers. Two clear examples are the conclusion of David's prayer to God, which was expressed "in the presence of the whole assembly" when gifts had been generously given by the people for the building of the temple — "Now, O God, we give you thanks, and praise your glorious name!" (1 Chron. 29:13) — and the praise expressed toward the conclusion of the second section of Psalm 119, that great teaching psalm — "Praise to you, O Lord; teach me your decrees" (Ps. 119:12). In most cases, eulogy-type praise at the conclusion of a longer prayer seems to have been derived in later Judaism from *berakah*-formula praise at the opening of prayers (cf. J. Heinemann, *Prayer in the Talmud*, 77-103).

Two rather explicit *berakah*-formula prayers of adoration in the Pauline letters are:

> Blessed be the God and Father of our Lord Jesus Christ *(eulogētos ho theos kai patēr tou kuriou Iēsou Christou),* the Father of compassion and the God of all comfort, who comforts us in all our troubles! (2 Cor. 1:3-4a);
> Blessed be the God and Father of our Lord Jesus Christ *(eulogētos ho theos kai patēr hēmōn Iēsou Christou),* who has blessed us in the heavenly realms with every spiritual blessing in Christ! (Eph. 1:3).

Statements about what God has done on behalf of his people are then given briefly in 2 Cor. 1:4b-7 (following the first) and quite extensively in Eph. 1:4-12 (following the second).

This type of adoration address is also reflected in Rom. 1:25 ("The Creator, who is to be praised/blessed [*eulogētos*] forever. Amen"); in Rom. 9:5 ("God over all, who is to be praised/blessed [*eulogētos*] forever. Amen"); in 2 Cor. 11:31 ("The God and Father of the Lord Jesus, who is to be praised/blessed [*eulogētos*] forever"), and, probably, in 1 Cor. 14:16 ("If you are praising/blessing God [*eulogēs*] with your spirit . . .") — as it is in such LXX passages as 1 Kings 1:48; 2 Chron. 2:12; 6:4; and Ps. 71 [72]:18 (cf. also Luke 1:68 and 1 Pet. 1:3).

Examples of closing eulogy-type prayers in the Pauline letters include the following:

To him [God] be the glory *(hē doxa)* for ever! Amen (Rom. 11:36);
To the only wise God be glory *(hē doxa)* forever through Jesus Christ! Amen (Rom. 16:27);
To whom [our God and Father] be glory *(hē doxa)* for ever and ever! Amen (Gal. 1:5);
To him [God] be glory *(hē doxa)* in the church and in Christ Jesus throughout all generations, for ever and ever! Amen (Eph. 1:21);
To our God and Father be glory *(hē doxa)* for ever and ever! Amen (Phil. 4:20).

Probably to be coupled with these eulogy-type prayers are expressions of praise that use (1) the verb *exomologeō* ("confess"), which came to mean "praise directed to God in prayer" (cf. LXX 2 Kings 22:50; 1 Chron. 29:13; Pss. 85 [86]:12; 117 [118]:28), in Paul's quotations of Rom. 14:11 (quoting Isa. 45:23), "every tongue will confess [give praise in prayer] to God," and Rom. 15:9 (quoting Ps. 17:50 [18:49]), "I will confess [give praise in prayer] to you [God] among the Gentiles"; and (2) the noun *epainos* ("praise"), which came to mean "praise given in prayer to God" (cf. LXX Ps. 21:26 [22:25]; 34 [35]:28; *Sirach* 39:10), as found in Eph. 1:6, 12, 14 and Phil. 1:11 and 2:11.

6. Paul's Prayers of Thanksgiving

The thanksgiving sections of Paul's letters have been the focus of a great amount of scholarly attention. In 1939 Paul Schubert noted that most of Paul's letters, after an epistolary greeting, have a thanksgiving section, and that these sections exhibit certain common structural and functional traits (cf. his *Form and Function of the Pauline Thanksgivings*). And Schubert's observations and analyses have been accepted and developed by many today.

Structurally, the Pauline thanksgivings are of two types. Type I*a* begins with the principal statement, "I thank God" *(eucharistō tō theō)* or its equivalent, and continues on with one or more participial constructions that modify the principal verb *eucharisteō* — with the fact that these participles are always in the nominative masculine (whether singular or plural) making it clear that it is the apostle himself (sometimes in conjunction with his associates) who has offered the prayer. Type I*b* also begins with the verb of thanksgiving *(eucharisteō)*, but instead of being followed by participles, it is succeeded by a causal *hoti*-clause that spells out the basis for the apostle's thanksgiving. The first type, in which both thanksgiving and intercessory prayer reports are featured, is the more elaborate and appears the greater number of times in the Pauline letters (i.e., Eph. 1:15ff.; Phil. 1:3ff.; Col. 1:3ff.; and Philem. 4ff., with 2 Cor. 1:11 being viewed as an inverted instance of this same type). The second is briefer and appears only two times in the Pauline corpus (i.e., 1 Cor. 1:4ff. and 2 Thess. 2:13f.). Three of the Pauline thanksgivings Schubert saw as being mixed forms of these two basic types (i.e., Rom. 1:8ff.; 1 Thess. 1:2ff.; and 2 Thess. 1:3ff.).

Functionally, Schubert argued that the purpose of the Pauline thanksgivings was "to indicate the occasion for and the contents of the letters which they introduce" *(ibid.,* 26). Thus they serve both epistolary and didactic purposes — that is, they establish contact with the readers, remind them of previously given instructions, set the tone and atmosphere for each of the writings, *and* indicate the main themes or topics to be presented in the respective letters.

While the Pauline thanksgivings are, indeed, to be understood as having epistolary and didactic functions, they should also be seen as expressing the apostle's deep pastoral and apostolic concerns for those he addresses. They do this by reporting, in summary fashion, on (1) his prayers of thanksgiving expressed to God for the addressees and (2) his prayers of petition offered on their behalf. So when speaking of his prayers, Paul tells his readers that they were directed "to God" (1 Cor. 1:4; 1 Thess. 1:2; 2:13; 3:9; 2 Thess. 1:3; 2:13) or "to my God" (Rom. 1:8; Phil. 1:3; Philem. 4), who is known to Paul as "the Father of Jesus Christ" (Col. 1:3), and that they have been offered "always" (1 Cor. 1:4; Phil. 1:4; Col. 1:3; 1 Thess. 1:2; 2 Thess. 1:3; 2:13; Philem. 4) or "unceasingly" (1 Thess. 1:2; 2:13) on their behalf — which does not mean that Paul was continuously in a state of prayer, but that he always included references to his addressees in his regular times of prayer (cf. G. Harder, *Paulus und das Gebet* [Gütersloh: Bertelsmann, 1936], 8-19).

Some of those for whom Paul gives thanks were well known to him (e.g., those at Corinth, at Philippi, and at Thessalonica). Others had been converted through the ministry of a colleague or colleagues (e.g., those at Colosse; perhaps also those referred to in some manuscripts as "at Ephesus"). Still others he considered to be within his Gentile mission, even though they were outside the scope of his previous ministry (e.g., those at Rome). The bases for Paul offering prayers of thanksgiving are: (1) God's redemptive actions on behalf of his readers, which stem from God's own eternal counsels, were manifest in the work and person of Jesus, and continue to be expressed in the ministry of the Holy Spirit (cf. 1 Cor. 1:4-9; Phil. 1:6; Col. 1:12-14; 1 Thess. 1:4; 2 Thess. 2:13-14); (2) the proclamation of the gospel and his readers' reception of it (cf. 1 Cor. 1:6; Phil. 1:5; Col. 1:6; 1 Thess. 1:3-10; 2:13-14; 2 Thess. 2:14); and (3) his readers' continued spiritual growth (cf. Rom. 1:8; Eph. 1:15; Col. 1:4-5; 1 Thess. 1:3; 2 Thess. 1:3-4; Philem. 5).

There are also eight instances of the expression *charis tō theō*, "thanks be to God," in the Pauline letters (Rom. 6:17; 7:25; 1 Cor. 15:57; 2 Cor. 2:14; 8:16; 9:15; 1 Tim. 1:12; 2 Tim. 1:3), sometimes appearing as a spontaneous outburst of praise. This shorter thanksgiving formula probably reflects, as Reinhard Deichgräber has argued, a mixture of Greek and Jewish features, since the expression is found also in Greek papyri and is comparable to the short eulogies of praise at the close of many Jewish prayers of adoration (*Gotteshymnus und Christushymnus*, 43). Furthermore, thirty-five times Paul uses the verb *kauchasthai*, "to boast," "glory," or "pride oneself in," in a manner that suggests the idea of thanksgiving before God (cf. Rom. 5:2, 3, 11; 15:17; 1 Cor. 1:29-31; 2 Cor. 1:12-14; chs. 10–12 *passim;* Phil. 2:16; 1 Thess. 2:19). And on six occasions the giving of thanks over food is referred to in the Pauline letters (*eucharisteō* in Rom. 14:6 [twice]; 1 Cor. 10:30; 11:24; *eucharistia* in 1 Tim. 4:3, 4).

7. Paul's Prayers of Petition

The twelve intercessory benedictions of the *Shemoneh Esreh* are framed by the first three prayers of adoration and the last three prayers of thanksgiving. The twelve prayers of petition, however, are not without praise or thanksgiving. Each of them includes expressions of praise and thanksgiving to God. And each of them ends (as do also the first three prayers of adoration and the last three prayers of thanksgiving) with the eulogistic formula, "Blessed art Thou, O Lord," which is then followed by a brief statement that summarizes the content of the respective prayer (e.g., "Blessed art Thou, O Lord, gracious Giver of knowledge" [benediction #4]; "Blessed art Thou, O Lord, who is pleased with repentance" [benediction #5]; "Blessed art Thou, O Lord, who heals the sick among your people Israel" [benediction #8]; etc.).

The first three prayers of adoration and the last three prayers of thanksgiving in the *Shemoneh Esreh* express timeless words of praise, and so have probably remained from very early times relatively fixed. The intermediate twelve prayers, which are intercessory in nature, have, however, evidently been revised from time to time in accordance with the nation's circumstances, the community's experiences, and the people's needs. Furthermore, while benedictions 1-3 (prayers of adoration) and benedictions 16-18 (prayers of thanksgiving) were always to be prayed in full, benedictions 4-15 (prayers of petition) could be reworded to fit particular situations or could be abbreviated — or even could be omitted, particularly where it was feared that their repetition might cause people worshiping in a synagogue to think more of themselves than God. In fact, when necessitated because of circumstances, all of the twelve intercessory benedictions could be condensed into a single prayer, such as "Save, O Lord, Thy people, the remnant of Israel. In every time of crisis let their needs be before Thee!" or "Do Thy will in heaven above, and grant equanimity to those who bear Thee before, and do that which is good in Thine eyes!" or "The needs of Thy people Israel are many, and their understanding is limited. May it be Thy will, O Lord our God, to give to each one his sustenance and to each body what it lacks!" — with every prayer, whether abbreviated or in full, to be concluded with the formulaic eulogy: "Blessed art Thou, O Lord, who hearest prayer" (*b. Berakoth* 29b).

Paul's intercessory prayers are often referred to in the Pauline corpus. They are mentioned most directly in the "prayer reports" found in the nine thanksgiving sections that use the *eucharistō* formula, "I give thanks" (i.e., Rom. 1:8-12; 1 Cor. 1:4-9; 2 Cor. 1:10b-11 [elliptically after the *berakah* of 1:3-4a]; Eph. 1:15-23 [after the *berakah* of 1:3-12]; Phil.

1:3-11; Col. 1:3-14; 1 Thess. 1:2-10; 2 Thess. 1:3-12; and Philem. 4-6), being omitted only in Galatians. And they are alluded to in the two thanksgiving sections of the Pastoral Epistles, which use the noun *charis* in expressing "thanks" to God (1 Tim. 1:12-14; 2 Tim. 1:3-7), being omitted only in Titus.

In the thanksgivings that use the *eucharistō* formula, the following prayer reports on behalf of the addressees appear:

> Constantly I remember you in my prayers at all times, and I pray that now at last by God's will the way may be opened for me to come to you (Rom. 1:9b-10);
>
> I always thank God for you (1 Cor. 1:4a);
>
> I remember you in my prayers. I keep asking that the God of our Lord Jesus Christ, the glorious Father, may give you a spirit [or, the Spirit] of wisdom and revelation, so that you may know him better. I pray also that the eyes of your heart may be enlightened in order that you may know the hope to which he has called you, the riches of his glorious inheritance in the saints, and his incomparably great power for us who believe (Eph. 1:16b-19a);
>
> In all my prayers for all of you, I always pray with joy because of your partnership in the gospel from the first day until now (Phil. 1:4-5);
>
> We always thank God, the Father of our Lord Jesus Christ, when we pray for you. . . . We have not stopped praying for you and asking God to fill you with the knowledge of his will through all spiritual wisdom and understanding (Col. 1:3, 9);
>
> We always thank God for all of you, mentioning you in our prayers. We continually remember before our God and Father your work produced by faith, your labor prompted by love, and your endurance inspired by hope in our Lord Jesus Christ (1 Thess. 1:2-3);
>
> We constantly pray for you, that our God may count you worthy of his calling, and that by his power he may fulfill every good purpose of yours and every act prompted by your faith (2 Thess. 1:11);
>
> I always thank my God as I remember you in my prayers (Philem. 4).

And in the thanksgiving sections where *charis* is used to express thanks to God, there are these prayer reports:

I thank Christ Jesus our Lord, who has given me strength, that he considered me faithful, appointing me to his service (1 Tim. 1:12); I thank God, whom I serve, as my forefathers did, with a clear conscience, as night and day I constantly remember you in my prayers (2 Tim. 1:3).

Elsewhere in the Pauline letters there are further reports as to what Paul prayed on behalf of his addressees and others:

Brothers, my heart's desire and prayer to God for them [the people of Israel] is for their salvation (Rom. 10:1);
We pray to God that you will not do anything wrong (2 Cor. 13:7);
Our prayer is for your perfection (2 Cor. 13:9b);
I pray that out of his glorious riches he [God] will strengthen you with power through his Spirit in your inner being, so that Christ dwells in your hearts through faith (Eph. 3:16-17a);
I pray that you, being rooted and established in love, will have power, together with all the saints, to grasp how wide and long and high and deep is the love of Christ, and to know this love that surpasses knowledge — so that you become filled to the measure of all the fullness of God (Eph. 3:17b-19).

Furthermore, Paul's concerns and prayers for his readers are reflected in the following "wish prayers," which use the optative "may":

May the God who gives endurance and encouragement give you a spirit of unity among yourselves as you follow Christ Jesus, so that with one heart and mouth you may glorify the God and Father of our Lord Jesus Christ (Rom. 15:5-6);
May the God of hope fill you with great joy and peace as you trust in him, so that you may overflow with hope by the power of the Holy Spirit (Rom. 15:13);
May the grace of the Lord Jesus Christ, and the love of God, and the fellowship of the Holy Spirit be with you all (2 Cor. 13:14);
May our God and Father himself and our Lord Jesus clear the way for us to come to you. May the Lord make your love increase and overflow for each other and for everyone else, just as ours does for you. May he give you inner strength that you may be blameless

and holy in the presence of our God and Father when our Lord Jesus comes with all his holy ones (1 Thess. 3:11-13);

May God himself, the God of peace, sanctify you through and through. May your whole spirit, soul and body be kept blameless at the coming of our Lord Jesus Christ (1 Thess. 5:23);

May our Lord Jesus Christ himself and God our Father, who loved us and by his grace gave us eternal encouragement and good hope, encourage and strengthen you in every good deed and word (2 Thess. 2:16-17);

May the Lord direct your hearts into God's love and Christ's perseverance (2 Thess. 3:5);

May the Lord of peace himself give you peace at all times and in every way (2 Thess. 3:16a);

May it not be held against them [those who did not come to Paul's aid at his "first defense" but "deserted" him] (2 Tim. 4:16).

There are also places in the Pauline letters where the readers are exhorted to pray (cf. Rom. 12:12c; Eph. 5:20; 6:18; Phil. 4:6; Col. 4:2; 1 Thess. 5:16-18; 1 Tim. 2:1-2) and where prayer is requested on behalf of Paul himself (cf. Rom. 15:30-32; 2 Cor. 1:11; Eph. 6:19-20; Phil. 1:19; Col. 4:3-4; 1 Thess. 5:25; 2 Thess. 3:1-2; Philem. 22).

8. Significant Features of Paul's Prayers

In concluding his discussion of early Christian hymns, Reinhard Deichgräber has aptly commented: "The praise of the church is the response to God's act of salvation . . . praise is never the first word, but always occurs in the second place . . . [it is] never *prima actio*, but always *reactio, reactio* to God's saving activity in creation and redemption, to his orderly working in nature and history" (*Gotteshymnus und Christushymnus*, 201; "Thanksgiving within the Structure of Pauline Theology," trans. P. T. O'Brien, 50). And this sense of response to God resonates throughout all the prayer materials of the Pauline letters as well. Prayer in the Pauline letters is never viewed as something initiated by humans in order to awaken a sleeping or reluctant deity. Nor is it understood as negotiating or bargaining with God. Rather, it is always an acknowledgment of dependence on God, a response to what God has done in both creation and redemption, and a declaration of God's goodness in inviting people to present their praise and petitions before him.

Paul's prayers of adoration evidently began with the acclamation: "Blessed be God" *(eulogētos ho theos)* — as do also the prayers of the Old Testament ("Blessed be the Lord") and the prayers of Judaism ("Blessed art Thou, O Lord"). This is a statement of praise that proclaims God to be the source of all human blessings. Yet while God is the Creator of all that exists and the Redeemer of all who turn to him for salvation — the One who alone is worthy to receive glory *(hē doxa)* — he has made himself known to his people as "Father." Thus they are to address him as "Father" *(abba, patēr)* — as also in the Old Testament (cf. Isa. 63:16: "But you are our Father; . . . you, O Lord, are our Father"), in Second Temple Judaism (cf. *Sirach* 51:10: "O Yahweh, my Father art Thou"), in Rabbinic Judaism (cf. *Shemoneh Esreh* benediction #6: "Forgive us, our Father"), and in Jesus' teaching (cf. Matt. 6:9: "Our Father in heaven"; Luke 11:2: "Father").

Distinctive to Paul's prayers (as well as Christian prayer generally), however, are the dual convictions (1) that prayer to God is through Jesus Christ, and (2) that because of being "in Christ" the Christian has a more intimate relationship with God the Father than was ever possible before (cf. esp. Rom. 8:15-17 and Gal. 4:6-7). Thus when Paul prays to God the Father, it is to "the Father of our Lord Jesus Christ" *(patēr tou kuriou Iēsou Christou;* cf. 2 Cor. 1:3-4a; 11:31; Eph. 1:3). And when Paul speaks to his addressees about their relationship to God, he urges them to recognize their more intimate relation as God's children, which has been brought about by God's Spirit, and so to pray to God more consciously in terms of "*Abba,* Father" (cf. Rom. 8:14-17; Gal. 4:6-7).

Paul's prayers of thanksgiving, as reported in his letters, have principally to do with (1) God's redemptive actions through the work of Christ and the ministry of the Holy Spirit on behalf of his readers, (2) the proclamation of the gospel and his readers' reception of it, and (3) his readers' continued spiritual growth. There is even something of a holy *chutzpah* ("brazenness" or "nerve") in Paul's thanksgiving prayers when he "boasts *(kauchaomai)* in the hope of the glory of God" (Rom. 5:2), "boasts in afflictions" (Rom. 5:3), "boasts in God through our Lord Jesus Christ" (Rom. 5:11), "boasts in the Lord" (1 Cor. 1:31), "boasts" in his ministry for God (2 Cor. 1:12-14, chs. 10–12 *passim*), and tells his converts that he expects to "boast" about them "in the day of the Lord Jesus" or "in the presence of our Lord Jesus Christ when he comes" (2 Cor. 1:14; Phil. 2:16; 1 Thess. 2:19).

Paul's prayers of petition, as deduced from his "prayer reports" and his "wish prayers," are focused primarily on the spiritual welfare of his readers. He also, of course, repeats in 1 Cor. 16:22 an eschatological petition — which was evidently drawn from the liturgy of the early church — that asks for the culmination of God's salvation: "O Lord, Come!" *(Marana tha)*. Furthermore, he prays in Rom. 10:1 for those who have spurned the gospel of Christ ("My heart's desire and prayer to God for them [the people of Israel] is that they may be saved") and requests prayer for himself and his missionary activities in Rom. 15:30-32; 2 Cor. 1:11; Eph. 6:19-20; Phil. 1:19; Col. 4:3-4; 1 Thess. 5:25; 2 Thess. 3:1-2; Philem. 22. But the main thrust of his intercessory praying was, it seems, for the welfare of his converts and those he considered within his Gentile mission. And while prayers for wisdom, revelation, knowledge, insight, and discernment (cf. Eph. 1:16b-19a; Phil. 1:9-11; Col. 1:9-10) might have been rather traditional, and so to be expected (cf. *Shemoneh Esreh* benediction #4, which is a prayer for "knowledge, understanding and insight"), most of the requests voiced in Paul's prayers of petition stem from his perceptions of his addressees' circumstances, seem to be suited to their particular spiritual needs, and are intertwined with his exhortations to them.

An Epilogue

To converts at Philippi and Thessalonica, whom Paul seemed to have viewed as some of his best friends, the apostle gave the following exhortations:

> Do not be anxious about anything, but in everything, by prayer and petition, with thanksgiving, present your requests to God (Phil. 4:6);
> Be joyful always; pray continually; give thanks in all circumstances, for this is God's will for you in Christ Jesus (1 Thess. 5:16-18).

Similar exhortations appear in the other Pauline letters as well — even in letters where Paul might not have personally known the addressees:

Be joyful in hope, patient in affliction, faithful in prayer (Rom. 12:12);

Be always giving thanks to God the Father for everything, in the name of our Lord Jesus Christ (Eph. 5:20);

Pray in the Spirit on all occasions with all kinds of prayers and requests; to that end, be alert and always keep on praying for all the saints (Eph. 6:18);

Devote yourselves to prayer, being watchful and thankful (Col. 4:2);

I urge, first of all, that requests, prayers, intercession and thanksgiving be made for everyone (1 Tim. 2:1);

I want people everywhere to lift up holy hands in prayer, without anger or disputing (1 Tim. 2:8).

Prayer, therefore, was not only significant in Paul's life and ministry — he also viewed it as of great importance for those to whom he wrote, whether well known to him or more distantly related. Prayer in the Pauline letters is not only the hallmark of true piety as one comes into God's presence, it is also the lifeblood of every Christian and the wellspring of all Christian ministry. And what was true for Paul and his readers in that day remains true for us, his readers, today.

Selected Bibliography

Charlesworth, James H. "A Prolegomenon to a New Study of the Jewish Background of the Hymns and Prayers in the New Testament." *Journal of Jewish Studies* 33 (1982): 265-85.

Cullmann, Oscar. "Basic Characteristics of the Early Christian Service of Worship." In *Early Christian Worship*, trans. A. S. Todd and J. B. Torrance. London: SCM, 1953, 7-36.

————. *Prayer in the New Testament*. London: SCM; Minneapolis: Fortress, 1995.

Deichgräber, Reinhard. *Gotteshymnus und Christushymnus in der frühen Christenheit. Untersuchungen zu Form, Sprache und Stil der frühchristlichen Hymnen*. Göttingen: Vandenhoeck & Ruprecht, 1967.

Gebaurer, Roland. *Das Gebet bei Paulus. Forschungsgeschichte und exegetische Studien*. Giessen-Basel: Brunnen, 1989.

Heinemann, Joseph. *Prayer in the Talmud. Forms and Patterns,* trans. R. S. Sarason. Berlin: de Gruyter, 1977.

Hunter, W. Bingham. "Prayer." In *Dictionary of Paul and His Letters,* ed. G. F. Hawthorne, R. P. Martin, and D. G. Reid. Downers Grove: InterVarsity, 1993, 725-34.

O'Brien, Peter T. "Thanksgiving and the Gospel in Paul." *New Testament Studies* 21 (1974): 144-55.

————. *Introductory Thanksgivings in the Letters of Paul.* Leiden: Brill, 1977, esp. 13-17.

————. "Ephesians 1: An Unusual Introduction to a New Testament Letter." *New Testament Studies* 25 (1979): 504-16.

————. "Thanksgiving within the Structure of Pauline Theology." In *Pauline Studies: Essays Presented to Professor F. F. Bruce on His 70th Birthday,* ed. D. A. Hagner and M. J. Harris. Grand Rapids: Eerdmans, 1980, 50-66.

Petuchowski, Jakob J., ed. *Contributions to the Scientific Study of Jewish Liturgy.* New York: KTAV, 1970.

————. *Understanding Jewish Prayer.* New York: KTAV, 1972.

Schubert, Paul. *Form and Function of the Pauline Thanksgivings.* Berlin: Töpelmann, 1939.

Stanley, David M. *Boasting in the Lord: The Phenomenon of Prayer in Saint Paul.* New York: Paulist, 1973.

Wiles, Gordon P. *Paul's Intercessory Prayers: The Significance of the Intercessory Prayer Passages in the Letters of St. Paul.* Cambridge: Cambridge University Press, 1974.

CHAPTER 11

Finding Yourself an Intercessor: New Testament Prayer from Hebrews to Jude

J. RAMSEY MICHAELS

CLEMENT OF ALEXANDRIA, who was head of the Christian cate-chetical school in that city during AD 190-202, once urged those who are rich:

> Appoint for yourself some man of God as trainer and pilot. . . . Fear him when he is angry, and be grieved when he groans; respect him when his anger ceases. . . . Let him spend many wakeful nights on your behalf, act-ing as your ambassador with God and moving the Father by the spell of constant supplications. . . . This is genuine repentance. (*Who Is the Rich Man Being Saved?* §41; for a similar exhortation, see *Shepherd of Hermas, Similitudes* 2.5-8)

Clement then provides a vivid example of such intercession in his story of the apostle John's rescue of a young convert who had wandered off to be-come the leader of a band of robbers:

> "Why do you flee from me, child?," John cried out; "You still have hopes of life. I will give account to Christ for you." When the young man wept and embraced him, John interceded for him with abundant prayers,

struggled along with him in continual fasts. . . . Nor did he depart, so they say, until he had set him over the congregation, setting a great example of true repentance and a great token of regeneration. (*Who Is the Rich Man Being Saved?* §42)

Concealed quite intentionally in my title for this article is a *double entendre.* "Finding yourself an intercessor" can mean either finding an intercessor *for* yourself, as Clement encouraged the rich to do, or finding *yourself* in the role of an intercessor for someone else, as the apostle John did in Clement's story. With both scenarios in mind, I will look at intercessory prayer in Hebrews and the so-called Catholic or General Epistles. For if there is a unifying theme in the rather diverse materials on prayer in these New Testament writings, it is that of intercession.

1. Hebrews

In one sense the whole of Hebrews is about the intercession of Jesus, "a great high priest who has passed through the heavens" (4:14). Yet for the most part, its language is that of worship and sacrifice, not explicitly prayer or intercession.

The Prayers of Jesus

The author of Hebrews mentions once that Jesus "offered up prayers and petitions in the days of his flesh, with strong crying and tears, to him who was able to save him from death, and was heard for his godly fear" (5:7). Those prayers, whether to be spared death or raised from the dead, were not for others but for himself. While they helped qualify him for his high priestly work, they did not in themselves constitute any part of that work.

In a strange way, Jesus' "prayers and petitions in the days of his flesh, with strong crying and tears," correspond to the principle that the Levitical priests under the old covenant offered sacrifices first for their own sins and then for the sins of the people (cf. 5:3; 7:27; 9:7). Jesus had no sins of his own (4:15), yet he shared, like the Levitical priests, in the weaknesses of the people he came to save. Consequently, he prayed first for himself out of his own weakness, and then for his people as their great high priest in heaven (cf. D. G. Peterson, "Prayer in the General Epistles," 103, who makes a similar point, but then backs away from it for fear of confusing "weakness" with "sin"). Jesus' tears stand in sharp contrast to the tears of Esau, an "immoral and godless" man who when he sold his birthright tried to be his own intercessor and failed (cf. 12:16-17). Jesus' prayers on earth, even in weakness, distinguish him as a godly man who, although he was God's Son, "learned obedience from what he suffered, and once perfected . . . was designated by God as high priest like Melchizedek" (5:8-10).

Only once in Hebrews is Jesus' ministry as high priest explicitly described as a work of prayer or intercession: "So then he is able to save for all time those who come to God through him, being alive always to intercede *(entunchanein)* for them" (7:25). The language echoes Paul in Rom. 8:34, where Christ is said to be "the One who died, but more than that was raised, who is also at the right hand of God and who intercedes for us." In Hebrews, as well, Jesus is presented as being "at the right hand of God" (cf. 1:1; 8:1; 10:12; 12:2). Furthermore, as our high priest he "entered heaven itself, now to appear in God's presence on our behalf" (9:24). So in this sense the topic of intercessory prayer encompasses the whole presentation of Jesus in the Book of Hebrews.

The Prayers of God's People

More directly relevant to our investigation is the matter of human prayer — that is, of God's people praying for themselves, for each other, or for their fellow human beings. The accent is on "boldness" or "confidence" *(parrēsia)*, with such boldness based and dependent on Christ's priestly work. In 4:16 the author urges us, because we have "a great high priest," to "come with *boldness* to the throne of grace, that we might receive mercy and grace as a help in time of need." In 10:19 he reminds us that we now have "*boldness* to enter the Most Holy Place by the blood of Jesus."

In the book's closing chapter, the conclusion to the whole matter of Christ's sacrifice and priesthood is that the sacrifices we must offer up to God are not the blood of animals, but "a sacrifice of continual praise to God, the fruit of lips confessing his name" — with a reminder to "not forget to do good and to share, for with such sacrifices God is pleased" (13:15-16). As in Judaism after the destruction of the temple, blood sacrifice is here reinterpreted as prayer and good deeds. The difference is that the reinterpretation of sacrifice in Judaism was made on the basis of the centrality of Torah, while in Hebrews it is made on the basis of the supremacy and priesthood of Jesus Christ. But as in Judaism, the two "bloodless sacrifices" to which Christians are called — that is, prayer and good deeds — are viewed as essentially the same thing.

In 13:18-19 the author asks his readers to pray for him, and particularly requests their prayers "so that I might be restored to you soon" (cf. v. 23) — which is a closing request in the manner of Paul (cf. Rom. 15:30-32; Eph. 6:18-20; 1 Thess. 5:25). But what is noteworthy is that in the material of 13:17, which immediately precedes this request and where he exhorts his readers to "obey your leaders and submit to their authority," the author of Hebrews writes: "They stay awake *(agrupnousin)* on behalf of *(huper)* your souls, as those who must give account *(hōs logon apodōsontes),* so that they may do this with joy and not groaning *(kai mē stenazontes).* For this would not be good for you."

Heb. 13:17 seems to have been the text that influenced Clement of Alexandria in speaking of one's intercessor — "Fear this man when he is angry and be grieved when he groans *(stenaxanta).* . . . Let him spend many wakeful nights *(agrupnēsato)* on your behalf" — and of John's promise to the robber that "I will give account *(logon dōsō)* to Christ for you." Clement seems to have read "staying awake" as a ministry of intercessory prayer for someone, and "giving account" as taking responsibility before God for the other person (cf. also *Shepherd of Hermas, Visions* 3.9.10, "that I too may stand before the Father joyfully and give account of you all to the Lord").

Clement's reading of Hebrews is one of the earliest readings we have of the letter. And his reading suggests a kind of reciprocity between the leaders of the community and the recipients of the letter, which seems, in fact, to be the case. In 13:17 the leaders are spoken of as taking responsibility for the members of the congregation and staying awake in prayer for them, and, in return, the congregation is urged to "obey" and "submit" to their authority. The writer of Hebrews could have added here an explicit command to pray for the community's leaders. Instead, he puts himself in the leaders' place: "Pray for us, for we are confident that we have a clear conscience, and we desire to behave properly in all things" (13:18). So as a teacher and something of a pastor to this community (cf. 5:11–6:12), he writes as if he too "must give account" — and, joining with the other leaders of the community, he wants to do so "with joy and not groaning" (13:17).

2. James

The Epistle of James, more explicitly than Hebrews, is about prayer and intercession. James seems to know certain prayers of Jesus, such as "Lead us not into temptation" (cf. Matt. 6:13//Luke 11:4). Likewise, he seems to know certain sayings of Jesus about prayer: "Ask and it will be given to you" (cf. Matt. 7:7//Luke 11:9) and "Ask and you will receive" (cf. John 16:24). Furthermore, James anticipates problems that his readers might have had in understanding or attempting to live by Jesus' words.

Prayer as Asking and Receiving

As for asking and receiving, the writer knows that matters are not always that simple. There are times when we ask and do not receive, and he looks for reasons why. "If anyone lacks wisdom," he writes, "let him ask from the God who gives to all generously and without grumbling, and it will be given him" (1:5). But, he quickly adds, "let him ask in faith, not doubting, for one who doubts is like a wave of the sea, blown and tossed by the wind. Such a person cannot expect to receive anything from the Lord; he is double-minded and unstable in all his ways" (1:6-8).

James insists that the promises of answered prayer are not unqualified. Conditions are attached, and when those conditions are not met the promises are not in effect. Using the same terminology, he writes: "You don't have because you don't ask. You ask and you don't receive because you ask wrongly, in order to satisfy your own pleasures" (4:2-3). Failure in prayer is symptomatic of a larger failure in one's life: "Go on now, you who say, 'Today or tomorrow we travel to this or that city, spend a year there and do business and make money.' . . . Instead, you should say, 'If the Lord wills it, then we will live, and do this or that'" (4:13-15).

At the same time, James insists that God is a generous God, more ready to answer than we are to ask. Thus he writes: "Every good and perfect gift is from above *(anōthen),* coming down from the Father of lights, with whom there are no changing or shifting shadows" (1:17). Preeminent among these gifts "from above" is God's wisdom, which is "first of all pure, then peace-loving, considerate, submissive, full of mercy and good fruit, impartial and sincere" (3:17-18; cf. 1:5).

Prayer and Integrity in Our Speech before God

James's teaching on prayer is firmly rooted in his teaching about human speech generally. There is no virtue in speech for its own sake: "Let everyone be quick to listen, slow to speak, and slow to get angry" (1:19). True piety is not a matter of speech but of action: "If anyone considers himself religious but does not control his tongue, he deceives himself; his religion is worthless" (1:26-27). James expands on his warning against careless speech in chapter three: "Anyone without fault in matters of speech is perfect, able to control the whole body" (3:2). The tongue, though small, "boasts of great things. See how small a fire ignites such a great forest! And the tongue is a fire, a world of evil placed among our bodily members, corrupting our whole body, setting the course of our life on fire, itself ablaze with the fire of hell" (3:5-6). The tongue is untamed, he concludes, "an unstable evil, full of deadly poison" (3:8).

The word "unstable" in 3:8 recalls the earlier reference in 1:6-8 to one who "asks" but not in faith — that is, the doubter who "cannot expect to receive anything from the Lord" because he is "double-minded and unstable in all his ways." James's harsh denunciation of the tongue in 3:1-8 sets the stage for a very simple point about "instability" — or, the inconsistency that exists between a person's prayer life on the one hand and the use of the tongue in normal everyday speech on the other: "With it we bless our Lord and Father, and with it we curse human beings, who are made in God's likeness. Out of the same mouth come blessing and cursing. My brothers and sisters, this is not the way it should be!" (3:9-10).

Prayer, therefore, according to James, is part of ordinary speech. His letter is not so much a call to prayer as it is a call to integrity in our speech generally. Our speech lacks integrity when we bless God while cursing our fellow humans — or when we tell someone in need to "go in peace; keep warm and well fed," but do nothing about that person's physical needs (2:16). In James's words, we are "double-minded and unstable in all our ways."

What is the remedy? James urges reconciliation with God and reconciliation with one another. In our sinful predicament, God "gives us more grace, which is why it says, 'God resists the proud, but gives grace to the humble'" (4:6). "Draw near to God, and he will draw near to you. Wash your hands, sinners, and purify your hearts, you double-minded. Grieve and mourn and weep. Let your laughter turn to mourning and your joy to gloom" (4:7-9).

This is James's call to prayer. It is a call to be like the tax collector in Jesus' story, who "beat his breast saying, 'O God, be merciful to me, the sinner'" (Luke 18:13). It is a matter of "drawing near to God" — not so much with the "boldness" urged in Hebrews, but with sorrow and tears, the signs of repentance. It is more like Jesus' own prayers in Hebrews, which were offered "in the days of his flesh, with strong crying and tears" (5:7), than like those of Christians who are exhorted by the writer of Hebrews to "come with boldness to the throne of grace" (4:16) and to have "boldness to enter the Most Holy Place by the blood of Jesus" (10:19).

What is missing in James is "the blood of Jesus." Neither the old sacrificial system nor Jesus' death on the cross plays any explicit role in James's theology. The only sacrifice he mentions is that of Abraham, who "was justified by his actions when he offered his son Isaac on the altar" (2:21). By analogy, we might infer that if James had chosen to speak of Jesus' death at all, his emphasis would not have been on the intrinsic value of the cross in securing our redemption, but rather on the obedience that brought Jesus there (cf. Phil. 2:8; Heb. 10:8-10). Echoing Jesus' words and Jesus' own practice, James exhorts his readers: "Humble yourselves before the Lord, and he will lift you up" (4:10; cf. Luke 14:11; 18:14; Matt. 23:12; 1 Pet. 5:6) — whether specifically in prayer or more generally in the ordering of their lives.

Prayer as Reconciliation with One Another

"Drawing near to God" has as its corollary reconciliation with one another. In 4:11-12 James exhorts: "Stop slandering each other, for whoever slanders or judges a brother or sister slanders and judges the law. . . . So who are you to be judging your neighbor?" And in 5:9, toward the close of the epistle, he makes a similar-sounding point: "Stop groaning against each other, brothers and sisters, lest you be judged. The Judge is standing at the doors!" Here in 5:9, in contrast to his words of 4:11-12, the warning is very abrupt and the context of 5:7-8 quite different: "Be patient, then, brothers and sisters, until the coming *(parousia)* of the Lord. See how the farmer waits for the precious harvest of the land, patiently watching over it until he receives the early and late rains. You too must be patient and strengthen your hearts, for the coming *(parousia)* of the Lord is near." Yet after the warning of 5:9, James resumes his conciliatory tone in 5:10-11: "Brothers and sisters, take as an example of suffering and of patience the prophets who spoke in the name of the Lord. You see, we call those blessed who have endured. You have heard of Job's endurance, and you have seen the Lord's purpose realized, for the Lord is full of compassion and kindness."

The warning not to "groan" or "complain" *(mē stenazete)* against one another is the only discordant note in an otherwise comforting and encouraging passage. The word recalls the warning in Heb. 13:17 to obey those who "stay awake on behalf of your souls . . . so that they may do this with joy and not groaning." "Groaning" elsewhere in the New Testament arises from unfulfilled longing (cf. Rom. 8:22-23; 2 Cor. 5:2, 4) or from difficulties encountered in pastoral care or intercession (cf. Mark 7:34; see also, perhaps, Rom. 8:26, which speaks of the Spirit's "unspoken groans" in interceding for us). In Hebrews, James, and various later writings, however, "groaning" begins to sound like the very opposite of intercessory prayer.

The rich in the *Shepherd of Hermas,* for example, are rebuked in a manner reminiscent of James: "See to it, then, you who rejoice in your wealth, that the destitute not groan *(stenazousin),* and their groaning go up to the Lord, and you with your goods be shut outside the door of the tower" (*Visions* 3.9.5-6). The passage recalls James's denunciation of the rich in this very chapter: "Now listen, you who are rich; weep and howl over the misery coming upon you" (5:1); "See how the wages you withheld from the workers who mowed your fields are calling out! The cries of the harvesters have reached the ears of the Almighty Lord!" (5:4).

The warning of 5:9 ("Don't groan against each other!"), however, is not quite interchangeable with that of 4:11 ("Stop slandering each other!"), because "groaning" is a natural and understandable response to oppression, while "slander" or "evil speaking" is not. James's concern is not simply that Christian believers should refrain from destroying or bringing each other down, but that they build each other up — specifically by intercessory prayer. I suggest, therefore, that the "groaning" here in 5:9 (as in Hebrews 13 and Clement of Alexandria) is intercessory prayer that becomes so burdensome to the one praying that it aborts or misfires, and thus does no good for those on whose behalf it is offered.

Prayer as Patience in the Face of Oppression

In 5:7-11 James turns his attention to his "brothers and sisters" in the Christian community whom he views as the wronged "workers" or "harvesters" spoken about earlier in 5:4. On them he urges "patience" *(makrothumia)* in the face of oppression as they await something as welcome to them as "the early and late rains" are to a farmer — that is, as they await the "coming" *(parousia)* of their Lord (see esp. vv. 7-8).

Yet as we have seen, a warning is embedded in verse 9 within the promise: "Don't groan against each other, brothers and sisters, or you will be judged." For if they "groan against each other," the Lord's coming is no longer a blessed promise but a threat; they need to be reminded that "the Judge is standing at the doors!" The danger, as James sees it, does not lie in "groaning" as such, but in groaning *against each other.* As Ralph Martin has observed: "It is only natural that afflicted people would express frustrations at the situation described in 5:1-6, but harmony is destroyed when the bitter spirit becomes personal and directed at criticism against fellow believers" *(James,* 192; cf. P. H. Davids, *James,* 185).

The Swearing of Oaths

James goes on to speak at some length about true intercessory prayer in 5:13-20. But first he takes time in 5:12 to highlight yet another misuse of the tongue, the swearing of oaths: "Above all, my brothers and sisters, do not swear — not by heaven or by earth or by anything else. Let your 'Yes' be yes, and your 'No,' no, so that you may not fall under judgment." The phrase "above all" *(pro pantōn)* is probably not intended to assign this warning more importance than what precedes it. More likely it governs the whole of verses 12-20, and so serves to place considerable emphasis on the theme of prayer and mutual responsibility within the letter as a whole.

The prohibition of oaths is linked to earlier warnings about the misuse of speech by the mention of "judgment." For if it is wrong to speak kind words and not mean them (cf. 2:16), or to teach what is false (cf. 3:1), or to speak evil of one another (cf. 4:11-12), or to vent our frustrations with those for whom we are praying (cf. 5:9), it is just as wrong to invoke God to serve our own ends (as here in 5:12). Following the Gospel tradition (cf. Matt. 5:33-37; 23:16-22), James insists that we speak with the simplicity and integrity of yes and no. He assumes that most of the time silence is better than speech (cf. 1:19; 3:1). But he insists that when speech is necessary, it should be simple and spontaneous — the honest expression of a heart right with God.

True Intercessory Prayer

James concludes his letter in chapter 5 with three examples of honest and spontaneous ways of responding to circumstances, each introduced by the pronoun "anyone" *(tis)* or the pronominal phrase "anyone among you" *(tis en humin)*. This can be shown as follows (with the relevant pronouns in bold print):

a. "Is **anyone among you** suffering? Let him pray *(proseuchesthō)*. Is **anyone** happy? Let him sing praise" (v. 13).

b. "Is **anyone among you** sick? Let him call for the elders of the congregation, and let them pray *(proseuxasthōsan)* over that person, anointing that one with oil in the name of the Lord, and the prayer *(hē euchē)* of faith will save the sick one, and the Lord will raise that person up, and if the one who was sick has committed sins, they will be forgiven. So confess your sins to each other and pray *(euchesthe)* for each other, that you may be healed. The prayer *(deēsis)* of a righteous person is effective and very powerful. Elijah was a man just like us, and he prayed a prayer *(proseuchēi proseuxato)* that it would not rain, and it did not rain on the land for three and a half years. And he prayed again, and the sky yielded rain and the earth produced her crop" (vv. 14-18).

c. "My brothers and sisters, if **anyone among you** wanders away from the truth, and **anyone** turns that person around, remember this: Whoever turns a sinner back from his or her wandering path will save a soul from death and cover many sins" (vv. 19-20).

The instruction divides naturally into three parts, as follows:

1. Prayer in Suffering and Happiness

In keeping with the context in 5:10-11, James introduces the subject of prayer against the background of suffering: "Is anyone among you suffering? Let him pray" (v. 13a). But then he immediately widens the application to cover all the circumstances of life: "Is anyone happy? Let him sing praise" (v. 13b). Because "singing praise" *(psalletō)* is also a kind of prayer, this is James's equivalent to Paul's advice to "rejoice always, pray without ceasing, in everything give thanks" (1 Thess. 5:16-18). Spontaneous prayer

— no matter what happens, good or bad — is James's positive alternative to all evil speaking, complaining, and swearing oaths. Prayer is not something appointed for certain fixed times of the day (in contrast to *Didache* 8:3), but an intuitive response to whatever the day holds in store.

2. Prayer for the Sick

James next addresses in verses 14-18 the question of what to do when someone is too weak or too sick *(asthenei)* to pray. His answer is: "Find yourself an intercessor" — that is, send for help to "the elders of the congregation." Whether he is reminding his readers of something already familiar, or sharing with them what went on in his own congregation, James is quite specific about the procedure. The elders are to "pray" over the sick person, "anointing that one with oil in the name of the Lord" (v. 14). Whether the oil is for ritual or medicinal purposes (cf. Mark 6:13), its use is fully in keeping with James's concern that speech and action go together (cf. 2:12, 15-16). Having described the procedure, James goes on to summarize its intended result: "The prayer of faith will save *(sōsei)* the sick one, and the Lord will raise that person up *(egerei)*, and if the one who was sick has committed sins, they will be forgiven" (v. 15).

"Prayer" — whether expressed by the nouns *euchē, proseuchē,* or *deēsis,* which are all used here for the first time in James — is a distinctly religious practice, and not precisely the same as "asking" *(aitein)* for something in particular, such as wisdom (cf. 1:5-6) or material possessions (cf. 4:2-3). It is probably best defined simply as speaking to God or worshiping God (cf. 3:9, "we bless the Lord and Father"). Nowhere is it said that the elders' prayer for the sick should consist of "asking" explicitly for healing, as one might ask for wisdom or material things. It is simply that James envisions healing and the forgiveness of sins as the *results* of the procedure he recommends.

The case study of 5:14-18 is not given as an absolute promise that God will heal the sick under any and all circumstances. James uses it, rather, with its indefinite subject (*"anyone* among you") and its third person imperatives ("let him call . . . let him pray"), to underscore the direct second person imperative that follows: "So confess *(homologeisthe)* your sins to each other, and pray *(euchesthe)* for each other, so that you may be healed *(iathēte).* The prayer *(deēsis)* of a righteous person *(dikaiou)* is effective and very powerful" (v. 16). This is where James's emphasis lies —

that is, on mutual confession and intercession within the community. The summoning of elders and prayer for physical healing constitute merely one possible scenario of how such mutuality might work out in practice. James could have just as easily, it seems, invoked a case in which the primary issue was the forgiveness of sins. The vocabulary in this passage is used in such a way as to suggest that healing and forgiveness are virtually interchangeable (cf. Mark 2:9) — with the verb "save" *(sōsei)* and the expression "the Lord will raise him up" *(egerei)* referring to physical healing (v. 15), whereas the verb "be healed" *(iathēte)* refers to salvation or the forgiveness of sins (v. 16).

James next appeals to Elijah as an example of a "righteous person" (cf. *dikaiou* in v. 16; see also "the righteous" in v. 6) who was subject to the same feelings of hurt and happiness that we are *(homoiopathēs, v.* 17; cf. v. 13), and yet was effective in prayer (vv. 17-18). The appeal to Elijah recalls the earlier appeal to Job and the biblical prophets as examples of "patience" or "endurance" in the face of "suffering" in verse 11. At the same time, it evokes the imagery in verses 7-11 of a farmer waiting patiently for "the early and late rains," which represents for James "the coming *(parousia)* of the Lord" (cf. vv. 7-8).

In effect, all prayer in the Epistle of James becomes eschatological prayer. James has hinted at this already by using the language of salvation and resurrection for the healing of the sick through prayer (cf. v. 15), and now he reinforces it by returning to the theme of "rain" as a metaphor for eschatological blessing. Neither the notion that Elijah prayed first that it would *not* rain, nor the precise time span of "three years and six months" as a time of drought is based on the Hebrew Bible (in 1 Kings 18:41-45 we are told only that Elijah's prayer ended the drought; see however, *Sirach* 48:1-3). An apocalyptic tradition is perhaps at work here in which "three years and six months" (or some equivalent thereof) represents a shortened period of divine judgment preceding the time of salvation (cf. Dan. 7:25; 12:7; Rev. 11:2-3; 12:6, 14; 13:5). Such traditions can easily become part of common lore, and thus help shape the language of writings that are not themselves apocalyptic (cf. Luke 4:25).

If all prayer is eschatological, then in an eschatological sense, at least, all prayer will be answered. "The Lord" *(ho kurios)*, who comes at the *parousia* (5:7-8), guarantees it. The elders anoint the sick "in the name of *the Lord*" (v. 14, italics mine), and "*the Lord* will raise him up" (v. 15). In appealing to biblical examples, James reminds his readers that "you have seen the Lord's purpose realized *(to telos kuriou)*, for *the Lord* is full of compassion and kindness" (5:10-11). Earlier he had warned, "Don't let that person think he will receive anything from *the Lord*" (1:7), and "You ought to say, 'If *the Lord* wills it'" (4:15; cf. also 1:1; 2:1; 3:9; 4:10; 5:4). Intercessory prayer for James, therefore, is simply a matter of placing things where they belong — that is, in the hands of "the Lord."

3. Pastoral Care and Intercession

In his final case study of 5:19-20, James looks beyond intercession in particular to pastoral care more generally, not as practiced just by "the elders of the congregation" (as in v. 14) but by "anyone" in the congregation. He speaks in very general terms about a case where someone "wanders away from the truth" (whether in belief or behavior) and someone else turns that person back from "his or her wandering path." Just as "the prayer of faith will save *(sōsei)* the sick one" in the previous case study of 5:14-18, so here the one who turns the sinner around "will save *(sōsei)* a soul from death and cover many sins" (v. 20).

Because the word "sins" *(hamartiōn)* at the end of verse 20 echoes the word "sinner" *(hamartōlon)* near the beginning of that same verse, it is likely that the one whose soul is saved and the one whose sins are covered are the same person — not the "shepherd" but the straying "sheep" (cf. P. H. Davids, *James*, 200-201; see also 1 Pet. 4:8). Thus pastoral care and intercession are not ways of covering one's own sins, but rather the normal and expected practices of a committed believer. They are as normal as praying when we suffer or singing God's praise when we are happy (cf. v. 13). And even though salvation is from beginning to end the work of "the Lord," James closes his letter with a reminder that the Lord both "saves" and "heals" through human instruments.

3. 1 Peter

Aside from the expression "grace and peace" at the beginning (1:2) and a brief doxology at the end (3:18), 2 Peter has nothing specifically on prayer (cf. M. J. Wilkins, "Prayer," 945-46). 1 Peter, however, shares with James a concern about the use and misuse of speech in general, and it places prayer within that framework. The calling of Christians is to "offer up spiritual sacrifices acceptable to God through Jesus Christ" (2:5), which Peter defines as "sounding the praises of him who called you out of darkness to his marvelous light" (2:9). Whether this involves worship and prayer to God or testimony to the world (cf. J. R. Michaels, *1 Peter*, 110), it obviously has to do with speech as well as action.

Jesus, the Model for Righteous Speech and Example for Christians

The model for righteous speech in 1 Peter is Jesus, who "committed no sin, nor was deceit ever found on his lips. He was insulted, but he would never insult in return; when he suffered, he never threatened, but left [his enemies] in the hands of the One who judges justly" (2:22-23). While here following Isaiah 53, Peter makes no use of Isaiah's statement in verse 7 that the Servant "did not open his mouth" and "like a lamb before its shearers was silent." Nor does he follow the Gospel tradition in stating that Jesus was silent before his accusers (cf. Mark 14:61; 15:5; Luke 23:9; John 19:9). This is because the response Peter wants to foster in his readers is not silence (3:1 is the only exception), but "blessing" (3:9) and a ready answer to charges made against them (3:15). His point is that, in contrast to the Maccabean martyrs who threatened their tormentors with divine judgment (cf. 2 Macc. 7:17, 19, 31, 34-36; 4 Macc. 9:5-9; 10:11), Jesus did not threaten those who insulted and tormented him but left them in God's hands.

Jesus' behavior is the supreme example for Christians. They, like Jesus, "invoke as Father the One who judges fairly according to each person's work" (1:17). Perhaps Peter shows an awareness here of the Christian use of *Abba*, "Father" in prayer (cf. Rom. 8:15; Gal. 4:6) — possibly even of the Lord's Prayer (cf. J. R. Michaels, *1 Peter*, 60-61). Christians who "suffer when God requires it" are told to "entrust their lives to the faithful Creator in doing good" (4:19), and "not return evil for evil, or insult for insult, but on the contrary, bless — for this is what you are called to do, so that you may inherit blessing" (3:9).

A Context of Verbal Opposition

Peter's accent on avoiding sins of speech (cf. 2:1) is probably traceable to the fact that much of the abuse that his addressees were facing was verbal in nature. He speaks of them being "accused" (2:12), "denounced" (3:16), and "ridiculed" (4:14) by their unbelieving fellow citizens in the Roman provinces, and he urges them to "put to silence the ignorance of the foolish" not by trading insults but by "doing good" (2:15; cf. 2:12; 3:16; 4:19). To "do good" to one's enemies, or to "bless" instead of curse (3:9), is an act of prayer. In words drawn from Psalm 34, Peter adds:

> Those who choose to love life and see good days must stop the tongue from evil and the lips from speaking deceit. They must turn from evil and do good *(poiēsatō agathon);* they must seek peace and pursue it. For the eyes of the Lord are on the righteous *(epi dikaious)* and his ears are open to their prayer *(eis deēsin autōn),* but the face of the Lord is against those who do evil. (3:10-12)

With this, Peter offers his own version of James's pronouncement that "the prayer of a righteous person *(deēsis dikaiou)* is effective and very powerful" (James 5:16).

Social and Eschatological Contexts

Like James, Peter also sees prayer both in the context of social relationships among Christians and in relation to the end of the age. The only two uses of the most common Greek word for "prayer" *(proseuchē)* in 1 Peter bear this out. In addressing families, Peter urges Christian husbands to "know how to live with a wife, showing her respect as somebody weaker — even as co-heirs of the grace of life. That way your prayers *(tas proseuchas humōn,* with the plural pronoun signaling the prayers of husband and wife together) will not be hindered" (3:7). Writing more generally to Christian congregations, he announces: "The end of all things is near. Prepare yourselves mentally, therefore, and attend to prayers" (4:7). In each instance "prayers" is plural, which suggests that Peter has in mind not the act of praying or "prayer" as a concept, but specific prayers uttered on specific and regular occasions in the home and in the congregation.

In the setting of the home (3:7), the phrase "co-heirs of the grace of life" reminds husbands that they are united to their wives by a common hope — that is, the gracious gift of eternal life at the last day (cf. 1:13, "the grace to be brought to you at the revelation of Jesus Christ"). Peter sees the believing husband and wife as a kind of church in miniature (cf. Clement of Alexandria on Matt. 18:20: "But who are the two or three gathered in the name of Christ in whose midst the Lord is? Does he not by the 'three' mean husband, wife, and child?" *Stromateis* 3.10). Peter assumes that husband and wife pray together, and that lack of attention to each other or to the hope they share will hinder their common life of prayer.

The same principle applies to actual congregations (4:7-11). Peter states first the basic conviction that "the end of all things is near" (4:7a), then spells out its implications. The believing community must "attend" (*nēpsate*, "sober up" or "pay attention") to prayers (v. 7b). The admonitions that follow in 4:8-11 suggest that he has in mind especially prayers for one another:

> Above all, remain constant in your love *for each other,* for love covers many sins [cf. James 5:20]. Show hospitality *toward one another* without complaining. Whatever spiritual gift each has received, use it in ministry *for each other* as good managers of *God's* diversified grace. If anyone speaks, do it as one bringing words from *God;* if anyone ministers, do it as out of the strength *God* provides, so that in all things *God* may be glorified through Jesus Christ, to whom belongs the glory and the might, forever and ever. Amen (italics mine).

The emphasis in these verses is simultaneously on (1) "one another" *(allēlous)* or "each other" *(heautous)* as the immediate beneficiaries of our words and actions, and (2) "God" as the One through whom and for whom all this is done. These acts of kindness to one another bring glory to God and give credibility to our prayers. In some sense they *are* our prayers.

Commands to Pray

The command to "prepare yourselves mentally . . . and attend *(nēpsate)* to prayers" (4:7) recalls Peter's earlier plea to "gird yourselves for action, therefore, in your mind, and with full attention *(nēphontes teleiōs)* set your hope on the grace to be brought to you in the revelation of Jesus Christ" (1:13). At the same time, it anticipates his later imperatives: "Pay attention *(nēpsate)!* Wake up *(grēgorēsate)!*" — because "your opponent, the devil, prowls around like a roaring lion ready to swallow you" (5:8).

The latter commands are framed by material similar to that found in James 4:7-10. In effect, Peter begins where James ends, with the words, "Humble yourselves under the mighty hand of God, and when it is time he will lift you up" (5:6; cf. James 4:10). And after describing the devil's movements (v. 8), he concludes with the counsel, "Stand against *(antistēte)* him firm in faith, knowing that the same kinds of suffering are being accomplished among your brothers and sisters throughout the world" (v. 9; cf. James 4:7, "Submit yourselves, therefore, to God. Stand against *(antistēte)* the devil and he will flee from you"). With his references to "paying attention" and "waking up," Peter takes up vocabulary from the Gospel traditions, which were known also to James, in order to highlight prayer as a weapon in spiritual warfare (cf. Mark 14:38, "Stay awake, and pray not to enter into temptation. The spirit is willing but the flesh is weak").

Prayer in 1 Peter, even more than in James, is eschatological prayer. Its goal is "the end of all things" (4:7) that will bring to us "the revelation of Jesus Christ" (1:7, 13), the "grace of life" (3:7), and the "marvelous light" (2:9) to which we are called. So Peter ends the letter with a prayerful benediction, which is at the same time a promise: "But the God of all grace, who called you in Christ to his eternal glory — after you have suffered a little — he will prepare, support, strengthen and establish you. To him belongs the might forever. Amen" (5:10-11).

4. 1 John

Except for a prayer-like request in 2 John 5 and a conventional health wish in 3 John 2, prayer is not mentioned in 2 or 3 John. In 1 John 3:21-22 and 5:14-17, however, the verb "to ask" *(aitein)* is used repeatedly of prayer, just as it was in James 1:5-6 and 4:2-3. And in these passages on prayer in 1 John, asking is coupled with our "receiving" *(lambanomen,* 3:22), God's "hearing" *(akouei hēmōn,* 5:14), our "having" *(echomen,* 5:15), and God through a human intercessor "giving" *(dōsei,* 5:16).

Boldness or Confidence in Prayer

What stands out in 1 John is "boldness" or "confidence" in prayer (cf. 3:21; 5:14; see also 2:28; 4:17), an emphasis that also appeared in Hebrews (cf. 4:16; 10:19; see also 3:6; 10:35). But if the basis for "boldness" in Hebrews was Jesus' intercessory work as high priest, the basis in 1 John is the role of "Jesus Christ the Righteous" as our "Advocate *(paraklēton)* with the Father" (2:2). The author leads up to this notion in the first main section of his work in 1:5–2:2, without even mentioning prayer explicitly. Building on the assertion that "God is light" (1:5), he creates a kind of chiasm (1:6-7):

    a. If we say we have communion *(koinōnia)* with him
      b. and *walk in darkness,* we lie, and do not do the truth (v. 6).
      b. But if we *walk in the light,* as he is in the light,
    a. we have communion *(koinōnia)* with one another, and the
       blood of Jesus his Son cleanses us from all sin (v. 7).

The chiasm begins and ends with "communion" *(koinōnia;* see also v. 3) — that is, communion with God in the first instance and with one another in the second.

The last clause of the chiasm in 1:6-7 introduces a series of assertions about "sin" that follow in 1:8-10, which the preceding emphasis on "communion" has placed in a distinctly social context. These three assertions, then, form a chiasm of their own, though a somewhat simpler one:

    a. If we say we do not have sin . . . (v. 8).
      b. If we confess our sins . . . (v. 9).
    a. If we say we have not sinned . . . (v. 10).

The two negative assertions frame the middle term, which is where the accent falls: "If we confess *(ean homologōmen)* our sins, he is faithful and righteous to forgive us our sins and to cleanse us from all unrighteousness" (v. 9).

But confess to whom? To God only or to each other (as in James 5:16)? The pronouncements preceding and following — "If we say we do not have sin"; "If we say we have not sinned" — have to do with claims made "publicly" within the community, and so it is fair to conclude that the same is true of the confession of sins. "Confession" to each other, or at least the acknowledgment of sins to the community, is necessary in order to receive forgiveness and cleansing from God. Such confession is a kind of prayer. And its answer is assured on four grounds: that God is "faithful and righteous *(pistos kai dikaios)* to forgive" (1:9); that Jesus is our "Advocate" *(paraklēton,* 2:1); that Jesus, too, is "righteous" *(dikaion,* 2:1); and that Jesus is our atoning sacrifice *(hilasmos,* 2:2; cf. 4:10).

In the same vein, the author argues that by putting our love into action we "reassure our heart" (3:18-19), because "if our heart does not condemn us, we have boldness *(parrēsian)* toward God, and whatever we ask *(aitōmen)* we receive from him, because we obey his commands and do what pleases him" (3:21-22). Once our sins are forgiven through the intercession of Jesus our Advocate (2:1), we can pray with "boldness," knowing that our prayers will be answered. The author repeats this assurance two chapters later in 5:14-15: "And this is the boldness *(parrēsia)* we have toward him, that if we ask *(aitōmetha)* anything according to his will he hears us. And if we know that he hears us, whatever we ask, we know that we have *(echomen)* the requests *(ta aitēmata)* we have asked *(ēitēkamen)* from him" (the difference between *aitōmetha,* middle voice, in 5:14 and *aitōmen,* active voice, in 3:22 is probably not significant).

The key phrase in this assurance of 5:14-15 is "according to his will" *(kata to thelēma autou,* v. 14), just as the key clause in 3:22 was "because we obey his commands and do what pleases him" (cf. "in my name" in John's Gospel: 14:13-14; 15:16; 16:23-24, 26-27). Answers to prayer are conditional on doing what God wants. And doing what God wants is the same as obeying Jesus' commands — above all, the command to love one another (cf. 3:18-22; 4:17; see also John 15:17). The more we do what God wants, the more we know what God wants (cf. John 7:17) and, consequently, the more we know what to ask for in our prayers.

Praying for Sins "Not Unto Death"

1 John 5:16-17, which are the next two verses, provide a concrete example: "If anyone *(tis;* cf. James 5:13, 14, 19) sees a brother or sister *(ton adelphon autou)* sinning a sin that does not lead to death, that person should ask *(aitēsei)* and will give *(dōsei)* life to such a one — to those whose sinning does not lead to death. There is sin that leads to death. My point is not that one should raise a question *(hina erōtēsēi)* about that. All unrighteousness is sin, and there is sin that does not lead to death." The situation is one that invites communal love, just as surely as the one described earlier in 3:17-18: "But if someone has the world's goods and sees a brother or sister *(ton*

adelphon autou) having need, and yet withholds compassion from them, how can the love of God be in that person? Children, let us not love in word or speech, but in action and truth." Whether the problem is material (being "in need") or spiritual ("sinning"), love requires of us immediate and unquestioning help — in the first instance, sharing "the world's goods"; in the second, intercessory prayer.

The "sin" is unspecified. All we know is that it is a specific act, something "seen," and something that "does not lead to death" (*mē pros thanaton,* 5:16). The question of whether or not the sin "leads to death" is, in any case, not a matter to be determined by observation. Perhaps the author put it this way because a sin committed by a "brother or sister" is *by definition* not a sin that leads to death, or a mortal sin. If it were, the person committing it would not be a "brother or sister" — that is, a believer (cf. D. M. Scholer, "Sins Within and Sins Without," 232; D. G. Peterson, "Prayer in the General Epistles," 118). For this reason the believer who sees a sin being committed does not have to make a judgment about whether or not it is a "sin leading to death." By definition, it is not!

This is probably the meaning of the much-discussed last clause in 5:16, where the verb for "ask" is not the verb *aitein,* which is used everywhere else for prayer in 1 John, but the verb *erōtan.* This verb can mean either "request" in prayer (as in John 14:16; 17:9, 15, 20) or "ask a question" (as in John 16:5, 23, 30). The latter, more common meaning makes better sense here. Believers should go ahead and pray for a sinning brother or sister without raising the question of whether or not the sin is "mortal" or "leads to death" (cf. P. Trudinger, "Concerning Sins, Mortal and Otherwise," 542). Alternatively, if *erōtan* is read as "making request" (as in Jesus' prayers in John's Gospel, or 2 John 5, "I beg you"), then the author is *not* urging intercession for some kinds of sin — or, at least, not promising a positive answer (cf. John 17:9, "I do not pray for the world").

While commentators have been preoccupied with the mysterious "sin leading to death," the author's attention in 1 John 5:16-17 is focused rather on "the sin that does not lead to death" (v. 17). If "all unrighteousness is sin" — and if, by definition, believers do not commit mortal sin — there is plenty of scope for intercession. The command to "pray for each other" (James 5:16) is in no way blunted or compromised in 1 John.

Where we would have expected "ask and it will be given" (*dothēsetai,* as in Matt. 7:7//Luke 11:9), we find instead a promise that "that person should ask *(aitēsei)* and will give *(dōsei)* life to such a one" (1 John 5:16).

Surprisingly, it is not God who "will give," but the intercessor — just as in James it is not said to be God but the responsible fellow believer who "will save" *(sōsei)* the sinner's "soul from death and cover many sins" (James 5:20).

Intercession, of course, assumes the sovereignty of God. God is the effective Author of all healing, all forgiveness, and all salvation. Intercession presupposes not only that God is able to save, but also that he is more willing to give than we are to receive. Yet texts such as 1 John 5:16-17 and James 5:20 assign to the intercessor a kind of derivative sovereignty over life and death that is almost breathtaking in its expression.

5. Jude

Jude identifies himself as "a brother of James" (v. 1), and his letter ends, like the Epistle of James, on a note of prayer and pastoral responsibility (vv. 20-23). After a series of descriptions of false teachers and blasphemers who were threatening the community (cf. "these" in vv. 10, 12, 14, 16, 19), Jude turns his attention to the addressees of his small tract and urges them: "Build up yourselves in your most holy faith. Pray in the Holy Spirit. Keep yourselves in the love of God, as you wait for the mercy of our Lord Jesus Christ, bringing eternal life" (vv. 20-21). "Praying *(proseuchomenoi)* in the Holy Spirit" (v. 20b) certainly includes mutual intercession — just as "building up yourselves *(heautous)* in your most holy faith" (v. 20a) is equivalent to "building up one another" and "keeping yourselves *(heautous)* in the love of God" (v. 21a) is equivalent to taking responsibility for each other in the community of faith.

In verses 22 and 23 we learn that the community of faith embraced some whose Christian walk was far from perfect, whose garments were defiled by sin, and who seemed to be teetering on the very brink of hellfire. While there is general agreement on the last clause of verse 23 ("hating even the garment stained by the flesh"), verses 22-23a are notoriously confused — and confusing — in the textual tradition. Some manuscripts have two clauses, and so seem to point to two distinct groups: "Snatch some from the fire, but on those who dispute have mercy with fear" (so R. Bauckham, *Jude, 2 Peter,* 108, based on the third to fourth-century papyrus manuscript P[72]). Other manuscripts have three clauses, and so may be read: "Be merciful to those who doubt; snatch others from the fire and save them; to others show mercy mixed with fear" (so NIV, based on the fourth-century codex ℵ; such a threefold reading is also found in the NRSV).

Whether the text is read as having two clauses or three, it is doubtful that any sharp distinction was intended among the groups of sinners listed. For while Jude, unlike 1 John, is not quite certain whether their sins "lead to death" or not, all of them in a general way sound rather like the one who "wanders away from the truth," as referred to in James 5:19. Jude's text can even be read as a continuous description of a single group: "Have mercy on those who are doubting; save them, seizing them from the fire; have mercy on them with fear, hating even the garment stained by the flesh" (so J. S. Allen, "New Possibility," 133, based on the three-clause format). Or, one can adapt slightly Bauckham's two-clause format: "Snatch some from the fire, and when they dispute have mercy on them with fear, hating even the garment stained by the flesh." However one resolves the textual problem, Jude's main point is clear: there are certain risks involved when we undertake to "rescue the perishing" within the community of faith. There are good reasons why any intercessor or shepherd of souls might be tempted to "groan" (cf. Heb. 13:17; James 5:9) in the face of possible dangers to one's own salvation or spiritual life.

Taken by themselves, the active verbs "have mercy" (*eleate*, vv. 22-23) and "save" (*sōzete*, v. 23) imply that the fate of those who are wavering rests in the hands of their would-be rescuers. They seem to have the power to save by "snatching from the fire," just as the rescuer in James was said to "save a soul from death" (5:19) or the intercessor in 1 John to "give life" (5:16). But the context here in Jude suggests otherwise. Verses 22-23 must be read in the light of verses 20-21, where Jude tells his readers to "pray in the Holy Spirit" and "wait for the mercy of our Lord Jesus Christ, bringing eternal life." Even the sound of the Greek word "waiting for" (*prosdechomenoi*) echoes the sound of "praying" (*proseuchomenoi*).

What the community prays for and waits for is "mercy" (*to eleos*) — that is, "the mercy of our Lord Jesus Christ, bringing eternal life." This, presumably, is mercy extended in advance to the doubters. Sovereignty here, as elsewhere, rests with God, who alone has the power to snatch souls from the fire. We "have mercy" and we "save" only by intercession, invoking the One to whom salvation and mercy belong. As Richard Bauckham says: "Jude does not say how this mercy is to be expressed in action. . . . Perhaps the most likely form of action is prayer" (*Jude, 2 Peter*, 116).

The last clause, "hating even the garment stained by the flesh," suggests that in extreme cases intercessory prayer must be from a distance, without pastoral or personal contact between the intercessor and the sinner. Ignatius speaks of "beasts in human form, whom you must not only not receive, but if possible not even meet, but only pray for them, if perhaps they might repent, difficult as that may be — but Jesus Christ, our true life, has authority over this" (*To the Smyrneans* 4.1). In short, intercessory prayer is hard work!

6. Conclusions

From a collection as diverse as Hebrews and the General Epistles, it is difficult to draw conclusions about prayer — and, in particular, intercessory prayer — that fit each individual writing. But there are some conspicuous features that are common to two or more of the group.

In Hebrews and 1 John, Jesus is set forth as our unique and supreme Intercessor. These two writings, consequently, are the two works that emphasize "boldness" in prayer. Hebrews and James make clear, as well, our need for human intercessors — whether they be the leaders who "watch over our souls," as in Hebrews, or the "elders of the congregation" who pray for us, as in James. Eschatological prayer is conspicuous in James, 1 Peter, and Jude, whether for "the coming of the Lord" (James), the "end of all things" (1 Peter), or "the mercy of our Lord Jesus Christ" (Jude). James, 1 Peter, and 1 John emphasize mutuality in prayer, laying stress on the importance of confessing our sins to each other and praying for one another for healing, salvation, or spiritual growth. 1 Peter applies this principle to husbands and wives as well. Most significantly, James, 1 John, and Jude all draw to a close with strong reminders of our personal responsibility for those "wandering from the truth" (James), or "sinning" (1 John), or "wavering" on the brink of destruction (Jude).

The last, or almost last, words in each of these writings focus on the fact that we are all pastors and shepherds to one another, whether through action or prayer. Hebrews, James, and especially Jude add the cautionary note that intercession costs something. It is arduous, even dangerous business. And though Jesus has accomplished our redemption once and for all, the hard work of intercession still goes on — and must constantly go on — within the household of faith.

Selected Bibliography

Abbot, Ezra. "The Distinction between *aiteō* and *erōtaō.*" In *The Author-ship of the Fourth Gospel and Other Critical Essays.* Boston: Ellis, 1888, 113-36.

Achtemeier, Paul. *1 Peter* (Hermeneia). Minneapolis: Fortress, 1996.

Allen, Joel S. "A New Possibility for the Three-Clause Format of Jude 22-3." *New Testament Studies* 44 (1998): 133-43.

Attridge, Harold W. *The Epistle to the Hebrews.* Philadelphia: Fortress, 1989.

Bauckham, Richard. *Jude, 2 Peter* (Word Biblical Commentary). Waco: Word, 1983.

Brown, Raymond E. *The Epistles of John* (Anchor Bible). Garden City: Doubleday, 1982.

Davids, Peter H. *The Epistle of James: A Commentary on the Greek Text* (New International Greek New Testament Commentary). Grand Rapids: Eerdmans, 1982.

Francis, Fred O. "The Form and Function of the Opening and Closing Paragraphs of James and 1 John." *Zeitschrift für die neutestamentliche Wissenschaft* 61 (1970): 110-26.

Kelly, J. N. D. *A Commentary on the Epistles of Peter and of Jude* (Harper New Testament Commentaries). New York: Harper & Row, 1969.

Lane, William L. *Hebrews* (Word Biblical Commentary), 2 vols. Dallas: Word, 1991.

Martin, Ralph P. *James* (Word Biblical Commentary). Waco: Word, 1988.

Michaels, J. Ramsey. *1 Peter* (Word Biblical Commentary). Waco: Word, 1988.

Peterson, David G. "Prayer in the General Epistles." In *Teach Us to Pray: Prayer in the Bible and the World,* ed. D. A. Carson. Exeter: Paternoster; Grand Rapids: Baker, 1990, 102-18.

Scholer, David M. "Sins Within and Sins Without: An Interpretation of 1 John 5:16-17." In *Current Issues in Biblical and Patristic Interpretation: Studies in Honor of Merrill C. Tenney Presented by His Former Students,* ed. G. F. Hawthorne. Grand Rapids: Eerdmans, 1975, 230-46.

Trudinger, Paul. "Concerning Sins, Mortal and Otherwise: A Note on 1 John 5,16-17." *Biblica* 52 (1971): 541-42.

Wilkins, Michael J. "Prayer." In *Dictionary of the Later New Testament and Its Development,* ed. R. P. Martin and P. H. Davids. Downers Grove: InterVarsity, 1997, 941-48.

CHAPTER 12

Prayer in the Book of Revelation

RICHARD BAUCKHAM

THE BOOK OF REVELATION is full of worship — praise and thanks-giving — offered to God. Praise and thanksgiving, for the most part, appear in visions of the worship of God in heaven. In this article, however, I want to take the word "prayer" in its more restricted sense as referring to petitionary prayer — that is, to prayers of asking, rather than to worship, praise, or thanksgiving. This reduces our subject matter considerably.

There are three references in the main body of the Book of Revelation to the prayers of God's people: 5:8; 6:9-10; and 8:3-4. Three references are not many. But these three references suffice to attribute to the prayers of God's people a key place in the coming of God's kingdom in the world, which is the content of the revelation given to the prophet John in his visions and to us in his accounts of those visions. They therefore merit close attention — not simply in themselves, but with a view to their role in John's visionary narrative.

None of these three references in the main body of Revelation contains the words of prayers offered by God's people on earth, though 6:10 reports the cry of the souls of the martyrs. The epilogue to the book, however, contains three prayers — or, rather, a threefold repetition of one prayer: the prayer to Jesus to come (22:17 [twice], 20). This is the sole prayer in which the Book of Revelation invites its hearers or readers to join (22:17). And it is the sole prayer which John himself prays (22:20), using it to conclude his book.

All of the prayers of the Book of Revelation are fully eschatological

— that is, they are prayers for the coming of God's kingdom, for the completion of God's purposes for his creation, for the fulfillment of all that God has promised, for everything that is finally to come, and, in the end, for God himself to come to his creation to perfect it by his own presence throughout eternity. Revelation is unique among all of the books of the Bible in that it refers only to this kind of fully eschatological prayer. Especially in its closing verses — which in its canonical position are the closing verses of Scripture — it draws its hearers or readers into (1) desiring what God desires and intends for his whole creation finally and forever, and (2) expressing this in the simple but all-encompassing prayer for the *parousia* or "coming" of Jesus. Revelation teaches us the importance, as well as the possibility, of eschatological prayer, which is the prayer for everything.

1. The Prayers of the Saints in 5:8

In Revelation 4–5 the prophet John is taken up into the heavenly sanctuary or throne room of God. This is both the throne room from which God rules his whole creation and the temple where God is unceasingly worshiped by those who attend on him in his presence. As a temple, it is depicted, in part, by analogy with the earthly temple in Jerusalem, since the latter was commonly thought to be modeled on the heavenly sanctuary. This temple imagery is fundamental to all three of the references to the prayers of God's people in the main body of the Book of Revelation.

The Portrayal of Their Prayers

In the first of these prayer references in 5:8 we are told that the twenty-four elders, who represent heavenly beings who compose God's council of ministers, hold "golden bowls full of incense, which are the prayers of the saints" (5:8). In the earthly temple incense was burned on the golden altar of incense, which was situated within the sanctuary building, close to the presence of God in the Holy of Holies. Such an incense offering occurred every morning and evening at the times of the regular daily burnt offerings (cf. Exod. 30:7-9; Luke 1:9-10). These were the times when the people gathered in the temple courts to pray. The incense, ascending in smoke from the altar, was understood to symbolize the prayers of the people or symbolically to carry these prayers into God's presence.

This is why even Jews who lived far from Jerusalem prayed at the times when the burnt offering and incense offering were being offered by the priests in the temple (cf. Dan. 9:21; Judith 9:1). It is also why the psalmist is able to ask that his prayers be accepted as though they were the evening incense offering and burnt offering:

> Let my prayer be counted as incense before you
> and the lifting up of my hands as an evening sacrifice. (Ps. 141:2)

This passage should perhaps be recalled when we read in Revelation that the incense in the heavenly temple actually is the prayers of the saints (5:8) — though later, of course, we are told that incense is offered along with the prayers of the saints (8:3). Probably we should not be too concerned about this difference. In either case, the heavenly incense indicates the way in which the prayers of the saints reach God in heaven.

In the earthly sanctuary incense was kept in golden bowls on the table of "the bread of the Presence" (cf. Exod. 25:29; Lev. 24:7). These are apparently the bowls whose heavenly archetypes the twenty-four elders hold. Commentators often seem to assume that the prayers of the saints in 5:8 are being offered to God by the elders, but this is not the case. To be offered, the incense had to be burned on the golden altar. At this point in chapter 5, however, the prayers of the saints are simply being held in readiness for the time when they will be offered to God in 8:3-4.

The Rationale for Their Prayers

The question may then legitimately be asked: Why are the prayers of the saints mentioned at all in 5:8? As petitionary prayers (not praise or thanksgiving) made by the people of God on earth, they seem out of place in this scene of heavenly worship — especially as it is difficult to see how the elders can play harps, which they hold in one hand, while also holding the bowls of incense in the other! Part of the reason may be that the prayers of God's people are mentioned immediately prior to what would otherwise be the first reference to the earthly people of God in this vision — that is, in the hymn of praise in 5:9-10, which the living creatures and the elders sing to the Lamb. This may account for the specific point at which reference is made to these prayers. But more fundamentally, the reason why the prayers are mentioned at all in chapter 5 is to prepare the way for their role in the coming of God's kingdom on earth, as this is seen to happen in the visions which follow.

In Revelation 5 the Lamb is seen enthroned on God's heavenly throne, having achieved in his earthly witness — even to the point of sacrificial death — the decisive victory, which must now be carried through in the events that lead to the complete and uncontested realization of God's kingdom (11:15). Revelation 4 portrays God's sovereign rule in heaven. Revelation 5 onwards, however, presents God's sovereign rule as implemented on earth through the victory of the Lamb and those who follow him. The Lamb's people must be introduced, for they are indispensable to the visionary story that follows. But the prayers of the Lamb's people must also be introduced, for they, too, play an important part in the coming of God's kingdom.

Set in the context of chapter 5, it is natural to suppose that "the prayers of the saints" of verse 8 are for the coming of God's kingdom — indeed, prayers which could be summed up in the words of the Lord's Prayer: "Your kingdom come, your will be done, on earth as it is in heaven" (Matt. 6:10). This supposition is correct; though, as we will see later, these prayers of the saints also envisage the coming of the kingdom in a specific way.

2. The Prayers of the Saints in 8:3

Revelation is a highly complex literary work, with much of its meaning dependent on intertextual allusions to the Hebrew Bible and intratextual connections within the Book of Revelation itself, whereby passages are constantly related to other passages by verbal and thematic links. From a key passage such as that of 5:8, it is possible to follow a chain of links to other passages. And this is what we need to do in order to elucidate the full significance of the reference in that verse to the prayers of the saints. (The links we will trace out are diagrammatically presented in an appendix to this article entitled "The Prayers of the Saints Answered.")

The most obvious connection from 5:8 is to 8:3, where again there are references to incense and the prayers of the saints. Here at 8:3 we are at the end of the first of the Book of Revelation's three septenary (i.e., set or group of seven) series of judgments, each of which culminates with its seventh item in a provisional vision of the end of history: the coming of God's kingdom in all creation. The first of these three series is the series of openings of the seven seals with which the scroll of revelation is sealed.

The Portrayal of Their Prayers

At the beginning of chapter 8 the Lamb opens the seventh and last seal and there is "silence in heaven for about half an hour." The account of the events accompanying the opening of this seventh seal continues in verses 3-5. Interrupting this account in verse 2, however, is a reference to the seven angels with trumpets — a reference that is then taken up in verse 6 and continued on in the series of the seven trumpet blasts, which form the second septenary of judgments in 8:6–9:21 and 11:15-19. This is an example of the interlocking device that Revelation uses to link one visionary narrative closely into another. For we are to understand that the seven trumpet blasts are a kind of further development of the opening of the seventh seal, which spiral in again on the same goal — that is, the coming of God's kingdom at the end. Verse 2 of chapter 8, therefore, is a kind of parenthesis, preparing for verses 6 and onwards. And so we should not be inhibited by the reference to seven angels with trumpets in verse 2 from reading verses 3-5 in close connection with verse 1.

The reference to "silence in heaven" in 8:1 reflects a Jewish tradition that at the time of the incense offering in the Jerusalem temple there was silence in heaven so that the prayers of God's people on earth could be heard by God in heaven. The explanation of the puzzling period of "about half an hour" may be simply that this was how long the offering of incense in the Jerusalem temple took. Revelation was written when there were no longer incense offerings in the Jerusalem temple, but it has adapted the tradition.

The incense offering, which symbolizes and accompanies the prayers of the saints, is made on the incense altar in the heavenly temple by an angelic priest. This is the point at which the prayers, held in readiness by the elders in chapter 5, are finally offered to God. They can now be heard because, as we will see, they can now be answered. So important is it for them to be heard that heaven is hushed while the incense is burned and wafts the prayers to the throne of God.

Moreover, these prayers are described as the prayers of *all* the saints.

For what all the people of God have for so long asked in their prayers is now at last to be done. The prayer for the coming of the kingdom will now, at the opening of the seventh seal, be answered. Here, in fact, we can see the key significance that the prayers of the saints are given in Revelation's portrayal of the outworking of God's purpose for the world.

The answering of the saints' prayers is then graphically depicted in verse 5. From the altar on which the prayers are offered the angel takes fire and casts it onto the earth. There follow "peals of thunders, voices, flashes of lightning, and an earthquake." This is the second occurrence in Revelation of a formula that appears four times in all. It is found first in the description of the throne of God in 4:5; then at the climax of each of the three septenaries of judgments in 8:5, 11:19, and 16:18-21. In each instance the formula is expanded, so that the series makes a kind of crescendo. The phenomena it describes are descriptive both of a theophany — in particular, the appearance of God in the thunderstorm on Mount Sinai — and of divine judgment. It is the manifestation of God's numinous holiness that effects the final judgment of the world.

The Significance of Their Prayers

So the offering of the prayers of the saints in 8:3-5 results in the eschatological theophany-and-judgment of the world. From the very altar on which the prayers are offered the fire of divine judgment descends on the world. The saints' prayers for the coming of the kingdom are answered. God's kingdom comes when God manifests his holiness in such a way that all evil must perish before him. The prayers, we now see, are prayers for the final judgment of the enemies of God and his people.

We should not be surprised that it is in this that the prayers of the saints for the coming of God's kingdom consist. The Old Testament and Jewish tradition generally, as we will see in more detail shortly, regularly thought of the coming of God's kingdom as the deliverance of his oppressed and suffering people from the forces and people who oppose God and his people. Prayers for the coming of the kingdom are prayed by those who see and suffer the injustice of the world as it is — and who long for God to display his righteousness in putting all wrongs to rights. The evil of this world is such that to pray for the coming of God's kingdom is to pray also for God's judgment.

3. Further Intratextual Connections

As we have noticed, the second septenary of judgments — that is, the seven trumpet blasts — is closely linked to the conclusion of the first septenary of judgments. That second set of seven judgments, therefore, must also be related to the prayers of the saints. We are reminded of this when, at the sixth trumpet blast, John hears "a voice from the horns of the golden altar before God" commanding the implementation of the fearsome form of judgment that follows (9:13-14). This explicit reference to the heavenly "golden altar" of incense, which is described very similarly to its initial description in 8:3, recalls the prayers of the saints which have been offered on it. Judgment now issues from it — that is, as answer to the prayers — just as it did in 8:5.

Intratextual Connections with 14:18

There is, in my view, one and only one further reference to the altar of incense in the Book of Revelation, and that is in 14:18. Here the angel who is in charge of fire — perhaps the same angel as the one who took fire from the altar and cast it on the earth in 8:5 — comes out from the altar. Assuming that the model of the earthly temple is still being followed, this must be the altar of incense, since the altar of burnt offering was outside the sanctuary building, while the altar of incense was within it.

In 14:18-20 the angel comes from the altar of incense to command that the vintage of the earth begin. This image of the end is one of a pair of images in 14:14-20: the first being that of the grain harvest (vv. 14-16); the second, that of the grape harvest (vv. 17-20). These are, I believe, contrasting images. The grain harvest is the positive image of the gathering into God's kingdom of the full harvest of those who have come to accept and to welcome God's rule, whereas the vintage — with its gory picture of the vast river of blood that flows from the wine press of God's wrath (vv. 19-20; cf. 19:15) — is the negative image of the judgment of those who have opposed God's rule.

It is striking and important to note that, of the two images of the eschatological grain harvest and the eschatological grape harvest, only the second is connected with the prayers of the saints by the reference to the altar of incense. And if we further observe that the unfinished image of the vintage is completed in 19:15, where the identity of the one who will tread the wine press is revealed (cf. 19:11-16), then we can conclude that the

258

prayers of the saints are for the coming of the Lord Jesus to judge his enemies and to deliver his people.

Intratextual Connections with 15:7

We have followed one trail of connections as far as it can take us, but we
must now return to its starting-point in 5:8 in order to observe the beginning of another trail. For in 5:8 the elders are holding "*golden bowls full* of
the prayers of the saints," while in 15:7 the angels, who are to administer
the seven last plagues with which the wrath of God is ended (15:1), are
given seven "*golden bowls full* of the wrath of God." The phrase "golden
bowls full" is identical in both occurrences in the Greek. Such verbal coin-
cidences are not fortuitous in Revelation, but part of the book's intricately
designed network of internal cross-references.

We need not, however, suppose the bowls to be the same. Nonetheless, the verbal correspondence indicates a connection, which it is now not
difficult for us to spell out: the prayers of the saints are answered by the final judgments, which the series of seven bowl pourings produce. The initial reference to the prayers of the saints in 5:8 is thus linked not only to the
first two of Revelation's three septenaries of eschatological judgments —
that is, the opening of the seven seals and the blasts of the seven trumpets
— but also to the book's third septenary of final judgments — that is, the
pouring out of the contents of the seven bowls. Thus the connection between the prayers and the negative aspect of the coming of God's kingdom
is confirmed and reinforced.

4. The Cry of the Souls under the Altar in 6:9-10

As we noted at the beginning of this article, there are three references in
the main body of the Book of Revelation to the prayers of the people of
God. We have so far discussed two: the closely connected materials of 5:8
and 8:3-4. In addition, we have traced out intratextual connections in
9:13-14, 14:18, and 15:7. The third reference that also needs to be treated is
6:9-10, which is a passage from which we can trace out another trail
through Revelation's visions of judgment (see again the diagram, "The
Prayers of the Saints Answered").

The Portrayal of Their Cry

Revelation 6:9-10 occurs within the sequence of the opening of the seven seals, at the fifth seal opening. The plagues let loose on humanity at the first four openings are evils that are characteristic of human history in general, not special eschatological judgments. And so it is understandable that, at the fifth seal opening, the souls of the martyrs — "those who had been slaughtered for the word of God and for the testimony they had given" — should ask how long it is to be until the eschatological judgment on those who oppress the saints.

The souls of the martyrs are said to be "under the altar" (v. 9). This is a phrase that raises two related questions: Which altar is this? and, Why are these souls under it? Many commentators hold that Revelation knows only one heavenly altar, which is either the altar of incense (here as elsewhere) or an altar that combines the characteristics of both the altars in the Jerusalem temple — that is, the altar of incense and the altar of burnt offering. Both possibilities, however, are unlikely. A Jew as familiar with the Hebrew Bible as the author of Revelation is not likely to have conflated the two altars, which in the earthly temple fulfilled quite different functions. If the altar in 6:9 is the altar of incense, why are the souls of the martyrs under it? One explanation sometimes offered — that, in line with a later rabbinic tradition which places the souls of the righteous under the heavenly throne of God, the souls are in a place of protection — is implausible. The incense altar is not the throne of God.

The generally very precise use of imagery in Revelation means that a specific reason related to the altar itself is required. And if the altar is that of burnt offering — that is, the altar that in the earthly temple stood outside the temple building in the court of the priests and on which animal sacrifices were burned — then there is a very plausible explanation. Two considerations need here to be taken into account and correlated: (1) that the blood of the slaughtered animal was poured out at the base of the altar of burnt offering (cf. Lev. 4:18, 30, 34), and this blood was also said to contain the life or the soul of the animal (cf. Lev. 17:11), and (2) that the martyrs are depicted as having been sacrificed, so that their blood, containing their life, has been poured out at the base of the altar.

This coheres with the facts that the word "slaughtered," which is used here of the martyrs (6:9), has previously been used of the sacrificial death of the Lamb (5:6, 9), and that Revelation portrays the deaths of the martyrs as a kind of participation in the shed blood of the Lamb (7:14; 12:11). It also means that we should not take our passage as a literal description of the prayers made by the dead martyrs. Rather, it is their life poured out in sacrifice that cries out to God for vengeance — just as Abel's blood cried out to God from the ground (cf. Gen. 4:10; see also 1 Enoch 22:5-7) and the blood of the murdered righteous cries out to God for justice in other Jewish literature (cf., e.g., 1 Enoch 9:1-3; 47:1).

The references to a heavenly altar in 8:3-5, 9:13, and 14:18, as we have seen, are unequivocally to the altar of incense. A Jewish reader would have no difficulty in recognizing that the altar in 6:9, as well as the altar in 16:7, is not the altar of incense but the altar of burnt offering. The association with blood in both 6:10 and 16:6 would make this clear, since it was only the altar of burnt offering that was connected with bloody sacrifices. We must not, therefore, confuse the two different images used with reference to the prayers of the saints in 8:3-4 and 6:9-10 respectively.

The Significance of Their Cry

The martyrs' complaint "how long?" of 6:10 echoes throughout the Psalms of the Hebrew Bible (cf. Pss. 6:3; 13:1-2; 74:9-10; 79:5; 80:4; 89:46; 94:3; see also Hab. 1:2), where it voices the individual complaint of a suffering, righteous person who cries out to God for justice. It is the question of practical theodicy in which the righteousness of God itself is at stake. How long will the righteous God delay in delivering his faithful people? And, furthermore, which is the necessary and unquestioned corollary, how long will God delay in judging their enemies and oppressors?

Especially relevant to our passage is Psalm 79, where the psalmist complains that the nations have destroyed Jerusalem and poured out the blood of God's servants like water (vv. 1, 3) — and then prays for "the avenging of the outpoured blood of your servants" (v. 10). The complaint "how long?" was also taken up by the apocalyptic writers, for whom it was the question of God's justice in the face of the continued oppression of God's people by the nations and in situations that demanded the judgment of God on an eschatological scale (cf. Dan. 8:13 [which is echoed in Rev. 11:2]; 12:6; 4 Ezra 4:33; 6:59; 2 Baruch 21:19; 81:3). In such a Jewish context, the cry of the outpoured lives of the martyrs in Rev. 6:10 is a prayer not for personal revenge, but for God's righteousness. God's holiness and truth — that is, his faithfulness — are at stake, with the verbs "judge" and "avenge" belonging to the language of legal justice.

1. Connection with the Third Bowl Pouring in 16:4-7

The trail of connections from the martyrs' cry "how long?" of 6:10 bypasses the merely preliminary judgments of the trumpet blasts in the Book of Revelation and takes us first to the third bowl pouring in 16:4-7, where the words "judge," "blood," "altar," and "true" provide a much closer link with 6:9-10 than with 8:3-5. The judgment of the third poured-out bowl turns all fresh water to blood and provokes the angel in charge of the waters to acclaim God's justice, which has given blood to drink to those who shed the blood of the saints and prophets. This is an example of *lex talionis* ('law of retaliation'), which was popular in both Jewish and early Christian literature — that is, where the punishment is made to fit the crime by some form of correspondence between them. (Other examples in Revelation are in 11:18; 22:18-19, while for examples elsewhere in the New Testament see 1 Cor. 3:17; Jude 6; Mark 8:38; James 2:13.)

The correspondence between shedding blood and drinking blood emphasizes that the strict requirements of absolute justice are operative. Likewise, the angel's final comment highlights the justice of the act: "They are worthy" — that is, they deserve such a punishment. The altar responds in agreement and praise of God's justice: "Yes, Lord God Almighty, true and just are your judgments" (16:7). For this altar, which is the altar of burnt offering, is that at which the blood of the saints and the prophets was poured out in sacrifice.

2. Connection with the Oracle of Judgment in Revelation 18–19

Another connection from the opening of the fifth seal in 6:9-10 leads us to the great oracle of judgment against Babylon in chapters 18 and 19, which expands on the reference to the destruction of "Babylon" at the climax of the septenary of the poured-out bowls in 16:19. Here in the verbal correspondences of 18:20, 24 and 19:2 with 6:9-10 it is even clearer that the cry of the martyrs for vengeance is answered by God's judgment on the city and culture that have been portrayed in 17:6 as "drunk with the blood of the saints, the blood of those who bore testimony to Jesus."

Two features of this judgment are for our purposes worth noticing.

The first is that what is judged is primarily the religious, social, and economic system that the city of Rome represented and Babylon here symbolizes. This system had shown its utter incompatibility with God's rule by putting his witnesses to death, and so it must be destroyed. Judgment falls primarily on the system. People are judged for their adherence to and participation in that system.

Second, it needs to be noted that it is not only the blood of the Christian martyrs that is avenged in Babylon's destruction, but also the blood of "all who have been slaughtered on earth" (18:24). The martyrs are seen as representatives of, or in solidarity with, all the victims of Babylon's oppression. (The same point may be made in chapter 6 by the use of the same verb "to slaughter" [*sphazō*] in verse 4, where it refers to victims of war, and in verse 9, where it refers to Christian martyrs.) Because it is for their witness to God's rule that the martyrs die, their deaths make especially evident the fundamental opposition to God's kingdom that Babylon enacts in every murder of an innocent person.

From the above connections, we can now see more clearly that the vengeance for which the outpoured life of the martyrs cries out in 6:10 is not personal revenge, but the justice that is owed to all the victims of injustice. God's kingdom — which, unlike every earthly kingdom, is truly for the benefit of all its subjects, but especially for the victimized who need redress — cannot come without the judgment of all those who persist in opposing it.

5. God's Answer to the Prayers Is Delayed

We should note, however, that Revelation does not command or encourage the saints to pray for judgment. It simply takes it for granted that they pray such prayers — that is, that all the saints who long for God's righteousness pray for his judgment on evil and injustice. Such prayer for judgment runs throughout the prayer literature of the Hebrew Bible. It even makes at least one appearance in the Gospels, in Jesus' words of Luke 18:7-8: "Will not God bring about justice for his chosen ones, who cry out to him day and night? Will he keep putting them off? I tell you, he will see that they get justice, and quickly." And its legitimacy is endorsed in the Book of Revelation by the assurance that the prayers of the righteous for justice will be answered, eventually and finally.

263

But it is also notable that the answer to the prayer of the saints for justice is delayed. This is a feature of the visions to which we have not yet attended. Nonetheless, it is a feature of considerable importance for an understanding of the place of the prayer for vengeance in the wider picture of God's purposes that Revelation gives us.

The immediate response to the agonized and urgent "how long?" of 6:9 is that the martyrs must "rest a little while longer, until the number should be completed of their fellow servants and of their brothers and sisters who were going to be killed just as they themselves had been killed" (v. 10). This delay in the coming of divine judgment, for which the martyrs pray, is very effectively embodied in the literary structure of the visions that come after. For following their prayer at the opening of the fifth seal, the events at the opening of the sixth seal in 6:12-17 seem to bring us to the very brink of the final judgment. The cosmic signs of the end in verses 12-14 suggest its imminent occurrence, while the cry of all the people of the earth in verse 17 ends with the lament: "The great day of his wrath has come, and who is able to stand before it?"

Readers may rightly expect the opening of the seventh seal to bring about this great day — that is, the end of history. But reading on in 7:1-3 they find that the opening of the seventh seal is delayed and that other things happen instead. In fact, the whole of chapter 7, which consists of a narrative as long as that of the opening of the first six seals, intervenes. Its content — the numbering of the innumerable company of triumphant martyrs from all nations — corresponds to what the martyrs had been told in 6:10 they must await: the completion of the number of their fellow martyrs, who must be killed as they had been.

This same pattern of delay before the end is incorporated into the next septenary, the seven trumpet blasts, which, as we have seen, are represented in 8:1-6 as the effect of the prayers of all the saints offered on the altar of incense. The judgments of the first four trumpet blasts seem remarkably restrained, affecting, as they do, only a third part of each sector of creation. But the announcement in 8:13 that the last three blasts of the angelic trumpeters have to do with three great eschatological woes raises expectations that this sequence will now lead directly to the final judgment. At the sixth trumpet blast the reference in 9:13 to the altar of incense reminds us of the prayers of the saints and suggests that their prayers are now at last about to be answered. But before the seventh and last trumpet blast, once again there intervenes a long section in 10:1–11:14 — which, although it contains the message "There will be no more delay!" (10:6), itself constitutes a major delay in the narrative movement toward the end.

This interlude between the sixth and the seventh trumpet blasts, as I have argued elsewhere in detail (cf. R. Bauckham, *Climax of Prophecy*, ch. 9), serves to explain in a preliminary fashion — which is then developed at length in chapters 12–15 — the purpose of God in delaying the end, with that delay resulting in many more Christians dying for their witness to the truth at the hands of those powers that contest God's kingdom. That purpose, in brief, is the conversion of the nations to God. Or stated more fully: the witness of those who suffer to the extent of death leads to repentance and faith on the part of many of those who have hitherto worshiped the beast (11:7-14); the firstfruits of the harvest of redemption, the army of martyrs (14:1-4), leads to the full harvest of the earth, which will be gathered into God's kingdom at the end (14:14-16).

In another expression of God's purpose in delaying judgment, the martyrs' song of triumph in 15:3-4 proclaims in its closing words: "All nations will come and worship before you" (v. 4). This song — like those praising God for avenging the blood of the martyrs by the destruction of their enemies in 16:7, 18:20, and 19:2 — refers to God's righteousness and faithfulness. But these words here refer not to the punishment of enemies, but to the victory that God won through the deaths of the Lamb and his followers, the martyrs — a victory over the powers of evil that gains for God the allegiance of the nations, who have previously submitted to the rule of his opponents. This is also how God's kingdom comes. And this constitutes, as I have argued elsewhere (cf. R. Bauckham, *Climax of Prophecy*, ch. 9; *Theology of the Book of Revelation*, ch. 4), the heart of the "revelation" given to John in his visions.

6. Praying for the Coming of God's Kingdom — Vengeance or Conversion?

Insofar as the prayers of the saints are for the coming of God's kingdom, they are answered by the conversion of the nations as well as by judgment on the finally unrepentant. And insofar as the prayers of the saints are specifically for judgment, their answer must be delayed so that their witness may be borne before the nations.

The message of Revelation is not only that God will answer the prayers of the saints for vengeance, as he must if his righteousness is finally to prevail absolutely. The message of Revelation is also that God will do better than that: that through the very suffering of his witnesses at the hands of the unrighteous, God will win the unrighteous to righteousness. Thus, important as prayers for vengeance are in the structure and the theology of Revelation, the distinctive message of Revelation requires that the prayer for the coming of the kingdom not be limited to them. It must be prayer not only for vengeance on the inhabitants of the earth, as in 6:10, but also prayer for the conversion of the inhabitants of the earth. Even though Revelation does not portray the latter form of prayer within its visionary narrative, the impact of its message encourages such prayer.

It is significant that the first reference to the prayers of the saints in 5:8 does not specify their content. While in context it can be assumed that they are for the coming of God's kingdom, there is no reason at this point in the visionary narrative to focus on the negative aspect of God's kingdom. Following out the intratextual connections, however, as we have, references to the prayers of the saints in 8:3 and 15:7 strongly suggest that they are prayers for vengeance, like those of the martyrs in 6:10.

But if we observe the connection in 5:8 to the "new song" of 5:9-10, which is sung by the elders as they hold the prayers of the saints and play their harps, another trail of connections also seems possible. That new song about the slaughtered Lamb and his ransomed people reappears in 14:3, where it is sung to the sound of harps by the Lamb's army of martyrs, who are redeemed from humankind as firstfruits (14:4) and who have followed him in faithful witness as far as death. Then in 15:2 we see these martyrs, now triumphant in heaven, standing like the twenty-four elders before the throne of God and playing harps as the twenty-four elders did in 5:8 — and then in 15:3-4 singing the song of Moses and of the Lamb, which declares: "All nations will come and worship before you" (v. 4).

Thus the saints have followed their own prayers to heaven. The faithfulness with which they lived and died in hope of the kingdom for which they prayed, has made them part of the answer to their prayers.

7. The Prayer for the Parousia in 22:17, 20

The Book of Revelation ends with prayer. If we leave aside the epistolary conclusion of 22:21, which is John's prayer for grace for all, then the final words of the book are those of 22:20: "Come, Lord Jesus!" These words are a Greek version of the prayer that Paul quotes in Aramaic in 1 Cor. 16:22: *Maranatha* ("Our Lord, come!").

For Paul to be able to assume that his Corinthian Christian readers — most of whom were Gentiles — would know this Aramaic formula, it must have had a very special significance in early Christian prayer. Originating in the Aramaic-speaking circles of the earliest Jewish Christians in Jerusalem, it must have been so centrally and frequently used in Christian worship that, like *Abba* and *Amen,* it was adopted, still in its Aramaic form, into the worship of Greek-speaking Christians. (In Christian literature outside of the New Testament, the Aramaic form is also preserved in *Didache* 10:6.) Revelation, therefore, concludes with a prayer expressing the urgent expectation of the Lord's coming in the way that it had been expressed in Christian communities from the beginning.

The prayer of 22:20 occurs not simply as a prayer but as a response to Jesus' promise to come. This is why the prayer is prefaced by "Amen," which is a solemn expression of assent. Jesus has been quoted in the first part of the verse as saying, "Surely, I am coming soon," to which John replies, in effect, "Yes, Lord Jesus, do as you promise — come!" This promise "I am coming," which is attributed to Jesus, has occurred six times previously in the Book of Revelation (2:5, 16; 3:11; 16:15; 22:7, 12), so that this occurrence at the end of the book (22:20) is the climactic seventh. The seven promises are thus:

	I am coming to you		(2:5)
	I am coming to you	soon	(2:16)
	I am coming	soon	(3:11)
Behold,	I am coming		(16:15)
Behold,	I am coming	soon	(22:7)
Behold,	I am coming	soon	(22:12)
Surely,	I am coming	soon	(22:20)

Only in the concluding instance is there the additional assurance "Surely," to which John's "Amen" (which is virtually synonymous with "surely") responds. It is the way that John had also responded in the prologue to a scriptural assurance that the Lord is coming. For in 1:7, to the words "Behold, he is coming with the clouds . . ." (which is a conflated quotation from Dan. 7:13 and Zech. 12:10), John added, "Surely, Amen." This is one of the respects in which the epilogue to Revelation corresponds with the book's prologue.

Three of the occurrences of Jesus' promise "I am coming soon" are in the epilogue, in 22:7, 12, and 20; and it is probably no accident that the epilogue in 22:17 (twice) and 22:20 also contains three prayers asking Jesus to "Come!" Thus, just as John's concluding prayer "Come, Lord Jesus!" in 22:20b responds to Jesus' promise in 22:20a, so the repeated "Come!" in 22:17 responds to Jesus' repeated promise in 22:7 and 12.

Whereas in 22:20 the prayer is John's own, in 22:17a it is attributed to other speakers:

The Spirit and the bride say, "Come!"
And let the one who hears say, "Come!"

"The Spirit" should probably be understood as the Spirit speaking through Christian prophets (cf. 2:7, 11, 17, 29; 3:6, 13, 22; 14:13) — though in this case the Spirit-inspired words are not those of the exalted Christ to his churches (as in 2:7, 11, 17, 29; 3:6, 13, 22), but those of a prayer addressed to Christ: "Come!" "The bride," who joins with the Spirit in this prayer, is not simply the church, but the church in her eschatological purity — that is, the church ready and prepared for the coming of her husband the Lamb (cf. 19:7-8; 21:2). The Christian prophets — or, perhaps, simply John himself — pray in the Spirit, expressing what the church, insofar as she is ready to welcome her returning Lord, should pray. This prayer gives a lead to the prayers of the whole church, whose members are therefore invited to repeat the prayer: "Let everyone who hears say, 'Come!'"

"The one who hears," who is referred to also in 22:17, is each person who is present in a worship service in which the book is to be read aloud (cf. 1:3). As in many cases in Revelation, an individual response by each hearer is required (cf., e.g., 2:7, 11, 17, 28-29; 3:5-6, 12-13, 21-22; 16:15; 22:7). Each hearer must individually join in the eager entreaty to the Lord to come. In so doing, each proves to be a member of the church in her state of eschatological readiness for the Lord's coming. And as they do so, the Spirit is making ready the bride for her husband.

The way that 22:17 continues has led some to doubt whether the repeated "Come!" of the first half of the verse is addressed to Christ, since the second half is clearly an invitation to believers to come:

Let the one who is thirsty come.
Let the one who wishes take the water of life as a gift.

The use of the same verb "come" in the first half of the verse and again here in the second half could be simply a kind of catchword connection with no semantic significance. But the transition from an invitation to join in prayer to Jesus to come, to an invitation to come and receive the gift of the water of life is, in fact, a quite intelligible transition of thought. Believers who make the prayer for the *parousia* (i.e., the "coming" of Jesus) their own are orienting their lives toward the eschatological future from which their Lord is coming. Also from that future comes the water of life, which belongs to the new creation (21:6) and flows through the new Jerusalem (22:1). The invitation to receive the water of life, therefore, is an invitation into the new Jerusalem (as depicted in 21:1–22:5) — or, to vary the image, an invitation to "the marriage supper of the Lamb" (cf. 19:9).

The invitations of the latter half of 22:17 do not mean that those who are "thirsty" and "wish" for the water of life must wait for the *parousia* in order to drink that water of life. But if the life of the new creation is available to people in the present, this is to be understood as a present participation in the eschatological future. There is no taking "the free gift of the water of life" without a turning toward the future from which the Lord promises to come. Thus to trust his promise and to pray for his coming is also to begin to live out of the new possibilities of the future that the Lord's coming will bring.

The *parousia* is the object of eager expectation and patient waiting throughout the New Testament (cf., e.g., 1 Thess. 1:10; James 5:7-11; 2 Pet. 3:12; Jude 21). But apart from Paul's one citation of the Aramaic prayer *Maranatha* (1 Cor. 16:22), it is only in the last few verses of Revelation — in the last few verses of the Bible! — that the "coming" of Jesus is explicitly the object of prayer. It could also be observed, however, that it is only in the two versions of the Lord's Prayer that prayer for the coming of God's kingdom is explicit in the New Testament (cf. Matt. 6:10; Luke 11:2). This petition in the Lord's Prayer and the church's prayer *Maranatha*, of course, are equivalent (cf. Rev. 11:15). It is to complete God's purposes for the world — that is, to bring God's rule to its ultimate perfection — that Jesus is coming. Indeed, it is in the *parousia* of Jesus that God himself is coming to his creation (cf. Revelation's other most significant uses of the verb "to come" in 1:8 and 4:8, where God himself is the subject).

The prayer for the *parousia* in 22:20b, therefore, encompasses and completes all other prayers. It is, as it were, the most that can be prayed. It asks for everything — for all that God purposes for and promises to his whole creation in the end. In the understanding that this everything is to be expected of *Jesus*, who declares himself "the Alpha and the Omega, the first and the last, the beginning and the end" (22:13), it takes the form of the simple entreaty to the Lord Jesus to come.

Selected Bibliography

Aune, David E. *Revelation*, 3 vols. (Word Biblical Commentary). Nashville: Nelson, 1997-1998.

Bauckham, Richard. *The Climax of Prophecy: Studies on the Book of Revelation*. Edinburgh: T. & T. Clark, 1993.

―――. *The Theology of the Book of Revelation*. Cambridge: Cambridge University Press, 1993.

Beale, Gregory K. *The Book of Revelation* (New International Greek Testament Commentary). Grand Rapids: Eerdmans; Carlisle: Paternoster, 1999.

Boring, M. Eugene. *Revelation* (Interpretation). Louisville: John Knox, 1989.

Caird, George B. *A Commentary on the Revelation of St John the Divine* (Black's New Testament Commentary). London: Black, 1966.

Heil, John P. "The Fifth Seal (Rev 6.9-11) as a Key to Revelation." *Biblica* 74 (1993): 220-43.

Klassen, William. "Vengeance in the Apocalypse of John." *Catholic Biblical Quarterly* 28 (1966): 300-311.

Michaels, J. Ramsey. *Interpreting the Book of Revelation*. Grand Rapids: Baker, 1992.

Schüssler Fiorenza, Elizabeth. *The Book of Revelation: Justice and Judgment*. Philadelphia: Fortress, 1985.

Sweet, John P. M. *Revelation* (Pelican Commentaries). London: SCM, 1979.

Vanni, Ugo. "Liturgical Dialogue as a Literary Form in the Book of Revelation." *New Testament Studies* 37 (1991): 348-72.

Yarbro Collins, A. *Crisis and Catharsis: The Power of the Apocalypse*. Philadelphia: Westminster, 1984.

Appendix: The Prayers of the Saints Answered

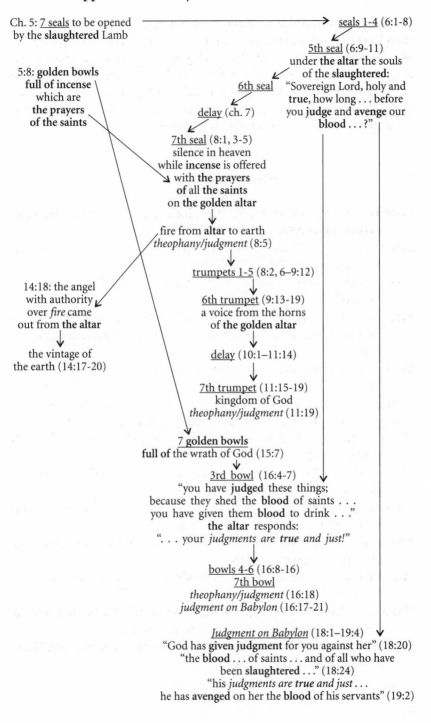

Ch. 5: <u>7 seals</u> to be opened ⟶ <u>seals 1-4</u> (6:1-8)
by the **slaughtered** Lamb

<u>5th seal</u> (6:9-11)
under **the altar** the souls

5:8: **golden bowls** of the **slaughtered:**
full of incense <u>6th seal</u> "Sovereign Lord, holy and
which are true, how long . . . before
the prayers <u>delay</u> (ch. 7) you **judge** and **avenge** our
of the saints **blood** . . . ?"

<u>7th seal</u> (8:1, 3-5)
silence in heaven
while **incense** is offered
with **the prayers**
of all **the saints**
on the **golden altar**

fire from **altar** to earth
theophany/judgment (8:5)

<u>trumpets 1-5</u> (8:2, 6–9:12)

14:18: the angel <u>6th trumpet</u> (9:13-19)
with authority a voice from the horns
over *fire* came of the **golden altar**
out from **the altar**

the vintage of <u>delay</u> (10:1–11:14)
the earth (14:17-20)

<u>7th trumpet</u> (11:15-19)
kingdom of God
theophany/judgment (11:19)

<u>7 **golden bowls**</u>
full of the wrath of God (15:7)

<u>3rd bowl</u> (16:4-7)
"you have **judged** these things;
because they shed the **blood** of saints . . .
you have given them **blood** to drink . . ."
the altar responds:
". . . your *judgments* are *true and just!*"

<u>bowls 4-6</u> (16:8-16)
<u>7th bowl</u>
theophany/judgment (16:18)
judgment on Babylon (16:17-21)

<u>*Judgment on Babylon*</u> (18:1–19:4)
"God has **given judgment** for you against her" (18:20)
"the **blood** . . . of saints . . . and of all who have
been **slaughtered** . . ." (18:24)
"his *judgments* are *true and just* . . .
he has **avenged** on her the **blood** of his servants" (19:2)

Index of Subjects and Modern Authors

Index of Scripture and
Other Ancient Literature

INDEX OF SCRIPTURE AND OTHER ANCIENT LITERATURE

11:13-21	59-60, 209	8:25	28	**Psalms**	
16:16	47, 53	8:35-53	17	2:12	51
18:6	19	8:41-43	178	6:3	261
29:12	59	8:44	178	9:11-12	93-94
29:22-29	16	8:48	178	9:13	94
30:1-5	16-17	8:56	216	13:1-2	261
31:10-13	53	18:41-45	239	22	18
32:39	52	19:26-29	122	22:1	117, 128
33	162			25:11	158
33:7	162	**2 Kings**		29	210
33:8	162	6:17	30	31:3	158
33:11	162	6:20	30	31:5	117
		19:19	28	34	242
Joshua		22:50	217	34:28	217
7–9	141			35:9	106
		1 Chronicles		41:9	166
Judges		16:36	208	48:12-15	55
5:1-31	109	29:13	216-17	50:21	56
13:8	30			55:17	209
		2 Chronicles		66:20	216
Ruth		2:12	216-17	71:18	217
4:14	216	6:4	216-17	74:8	46
				74:9-10	261
1 Samuel		**Ezra**		78:18	145
1:11	106	7:27	216	78:41	145
2:1-10	106, 109			78:56	145
25:32	216	**Nehemiah**		79:1	261
25:39	216	8:1-12	46	79:3	261
		8:6	208	79:5	261
2 Samuel		8:13-18	47	79:9	158
7:25	28	10:1-39	44	79:10	261
15:31	30			80:4	261
18:28	216	**Job**		85:12	217
		1:6–2:6	14	89:46	261
1 Kings		1:9	14	90–106	19
1:48	100, 216-17	1:21	14	94:3	261
5:7	216	3–26	14	95:9	145
8:11	178	31	14	103–4	81
8:15	216	38–41	14	105:8-9	107
8:16	178	38:1	14	106:10	107
8:17	178	40:6	14	106:14	145
8:19	178	42:1-9	14	106:45	107
8:20	178	42:5	14-15	107:22	83
8:22-53	17	42:8-9	15	109:21	158
		42:10	14		

278